REASSEMBLING THE FRAGMENTS

Reassembling the
FRAGMENTS

Voice and Identity in Caribbean Discourse

Edited by

PAULA MORGAN AND VALERIE YOUSSEF

UNIVERSITY OF THE WEST INDIES PRESS
Jamaica • Barbados • Trinidad and Tobago

University of the West Indies Press
7A Gibraltar Hall Road, Mona
Kingston 7, Jamaica
www.uwipress.com

A catalogue record of this book is available from
the National Library of Jamaica.

ISBN: 978-976-640-410-9

Book and cover design by Robert Harris.
Set in Scala 10/14 x 27
Printed in the United States of America.

CONTENTS

Introduction

REASSEMBLING THE FRAGMENTS
The Burden of the Antilles

[PAULA MORGAN]

THIS BOOK ON THE THEME "reassembling the fragments" was inspired by the 2011 commemoration conference held at the University of the West Indies, St Augustine, Trinidad and Tobago, in honour of professors Bridget Brereton, Barbara Lalla and Ian Robertson, all of whom retired from the University of the West Indies in 2010. For over thirty years, these scholars have spearheaded the highest quality of research in their respective areas of history, literature and linguistics. Within their respective fields, they are internationally recognized for their contributions to theoretical constructs, original data collection and analysis, and the realization of a Caribbean-based ethos. Their intellectual breadth and curiosity, which have challenged generations of students to become independent thinkers, make them worthy of acknowledgement. "Reassembling the Fragments", the theme of the event held in their honour, was drawn from the Caribbean writer and scholar Derek Walcott's 1992 Nobel Prize speech: "Break a vase, and the love that reassembles the fragments is stronger than that love which took its symmetry for granted when it was whole. . . . This gathering of broken pieces is the care and pain of the Antilles."[1] The theme was deemed a fitting acknowledgement of their intellectual passion, their lifelong engagement and their substantial output.

Volume 1 is based on literary and linguistic papers initially presented at that conference which have since been considerably expanded and peer reviewed. Part 2 comprises papers in history in honour of Professor Brereton. These chapters provide a forum for scholars and practitioners to interrogate the body of work compiled by these intellectual giants, examine the sociocultural con-texts that framed and informed their endeavours and evaluate the tangible working out of their enquiries. This book's theoretical objective is also to high-light broader interdisciplinary research and pedagogical formulation during the period of Brereton's, Lalla's and Robertson's tenure, which coincides roughly with four decades of the university's sixty years of existence. The vol-ume also contains some of the tributes and appraisals of a number of interna-tional scholars who were long-term colleagues of the honourees. These contributions were pivotal in defining both the individual contribution to their fields of endeavour, to the institutions and to the nation in transition.

Part 1, "Tributes and Critical Appraisals", opens with Ohio State University's Donald Winford's tribute to Ian Robertson "Challenging the Old and Exploring the New". As a former University of the West Indies colleague, Winford focuses on Robertson's sterling contribution to Caribbean Creole linguistics and particularly his concern with theorizing, which is informed by objective data and applicability to practical problems of Creole-speaking communities. According to Winford, Robertson's landmark discovery of the Dutch-lexicon Creole, which developed in the colony of Berbice, provided an oppositional model for a range of contentious interventions that were being debated in the field of Creole linguistics in the 1970s and 1980s. Robertson's discovery also constituted a challenge to the Bickertonian notion of Creole language creation as attributed to an innate language bioprogramme. Robertson's discovery and stance proved highly instrumental in a measured reorientation that occurred in Creole Linguistics in the 1990s, with implications for rethinking second-language-acquisition processes as a whole. Robertson's research has also been instrumental in reaffirming the status of Creoles as true manifestations of "the human capacity to create and reshape language according to cognitive princi-ples common to all human beings". This, Winford argues, laid the groundwork for recognizing Creoles as worthy of the respect accorded to all other contact languages, hence lifting the pejorative view on these languages and affirming the importance of preserving a balanced and positive linguistic self-concept.

Lalla's love of language took her along different pathways. Velma Pollard, in her tribute to Lalla, lays claim to a borrowed phrase, "transdisciplinary intellectual giant" to describe the work of one who straddles the disciplines of literary critique, literary linguistics and creative writing. Pollard, faced with this array of foci, identifies an overarching concern with history. In chapter 2, Pollard indicates that "[i]t is a long look at the history of Caribbean language that has engaged her linguistic eye, and it is a long look at the history of Caribbean literary expression that has engaged her literary eye. How these two eyes interlock/interact is Lalla's preoccupation." The interplay of these concerns has not only produced a substantial body of scholarly work, it has also produced generations of transdisciplinary scholars who engage the literature and language of the regions in the way in which Lalla does.

In chapter 3, "Towards a 'Wholeness of Vision': Criticism Lalla's Way", Jennifer Rahim acknowledges a legacy: "We are the inheritors of an invaluable resource that is as much a testament to the extraordinary exercise of mind as of spirit." Rahim engages the synthesis of Lalla's critical sensibility, which has led her to conceive of medieval literature as postcolonial. Rahim identifies an underlying collision of unevenly weighted cultures, spatiotemporal and ideological relations, and the emergence of a characteristic literary discourse. In the process, Lalla valorizes indigenous approaches, not only to the substantial body of Caribbean literature, but to the entire corpus of British literature. Rahim points to Lalla's mapping of the interface between literature and collective self-understanding and how this interacts with human attitudes and behaviours and interactions within and between nations. Yet this global focus never occludes the specificity of the local. Lalla undertakes to define the specificity of Jamaican national literature and the development of an indigenous aesthetic of marronage with a specific native critical language and interpretative perspectives as pivotal to the emergence of the postcolonial social order.

What, then, is criticism Lalla's way? It is the rupture of neat classifications such as imperial, colonial, margin, centre and dialectic. It is recognition of the multiple affiliations that inform Caribbean writing: recognition of intertextuality and subtle and nuanced possibilities of locating consciousness and perspectival shifts. The approach, according to Rahim, displaces a discourse of victimization with a vision of shared responsibility for and proliferating potential of the new society. Lalla's way is to balance ethnic and other differences in the interest of humanizing of relations. It is also to seek modalities for reading fictional formulations regarded as long settled, to discern and inscribe an excess of meaning that goes beyond received perspectives and brings a new critical sensibility to canonical works.

Postcolonial nation creation is the focus of my chapter, "Restoring the Shattered Nation Family", which reads Lalla's 1988 *Arch of Fire*[2] against concepts of nationhood and the problematic of constructing the modern New World nations given the ignominies of their beginnings, the ethnic diversity of their populations and the macro- and micro-cracks and fissures along which they threaten to fall apart. Citing Walcott's 1992 evocation of the Caribbean social order as a cracked heirloom, I point to the ways in which Lalla's construction of the Jamaican nation in crisis incorporates and ultimately transcends "the domestic image of marring, fragility, lack of resilience and impaired functionality intended to convey the jarring impact of historical collisions". Chapter 5 identifies Lalla's epic family saga as an act of reassembling the fragments in relation to the island of Jamaica when the island was hurtling into the social chaos that fuelled its middle class's mass migration. This ambitious historical novel inscribes a female-oriented narration of the nation, incorporating alternative storytelling paradigms of domestic lore, myth, legend, recipes and intimate social practices. As its central motif, it also reflects a reworking of the patriarchal narrative of the Jewish diaspora. The chapter argues that the tenacity and transcendence of the nation-state is evoked most powerfully in the nation as family trope and the evocation of landscape as palimpsest that carries traces of belonging etched by its diverse people, groups and ethnicities.

Ian Robertson's quest for a new sensibility regarding the indigenous languages of the region has produced generations of students whose enduring perception of linguistic study has been hammered out in the field in distant localities of the sprawling Guyanese hinterland. The cultural assertiveness and linguistic range of indigenous Creole speakers have shaped Robertson's approach to the thorny issue of language education in the Caribbean. In chapter 6, in her incisive assessment of Ian Robertson's contribution to language education in the Caribbean, Valerie Youssef focuses on the specificity of Robertson's perspective on the validity of Creole and its place in education. This perspective, which originated in extensive study of language usage and teaching in the classroom, ripened in Robertson's contribution to language policy in Trinidad.³ Youssef summarizes its key elements as the requirements to recognize and respect primary school students' Creole language production as a way of affirming positive language identity and facilitating their eventual acquisition of Standard English. The premise is respect for native language identity as a significant contributor to positive second-language acquisition. Pointing to the challenges of taking Robertson's conceptualization to the stage of implementation, Youssef advocates transitional bilingualism as expounded in the 2001 Jamaican language-education policy,⁴ including acceptance and use of children's first language to facilitate comprehension, and the use of role play and contrastive analysis to facilitate mastery of English. She posits that full acceptance of both Creole and Standard English is the property of each individual who commands them as pivotal if we are to truly become postcolonial.

Youssef's chapter on Lalla's contribution to linguistics, notes that in her analyses of historical texts and fiction, Lalla demonstrates the significance of code-switching so often lost in Creole linguistics's necessary search for the pure Creole. Youssef also demonstrates the importance of Lalla's work in appropriately setting up parameters for assessment of the validity of the Caribbean voice in ostensible Caribbean writing and its progressive development down through the twentieth century. While Lalla challenges the notion of a text's capacity for realism, Youssef argues that Lalla's focus on code-switching is not only insightful but contributes to the current explorations in sociolinguistics for truly authentic spoken data. Youssef suggests that the fictional voice is not so far from that of the real speaker in a twenty-first century, postmodern world in which identities are fluid, ever-changing performances.

Youssef's chapter is in dialogue with chapter 7, Barbara Lalla's "Possible Caribbeans: Assembling the Fictional Voice", which explores the diverse ways in which the Caribbean voice is delicately fabricated as a textual construct. Identifying the sense of mimesis as emanating from the interplay between the invented world and actual prototypes, Lalla argues that the fictional reality thus produced constitutes possible Caribbeans or, in the case of speculative fictions, credibly (im)possible Caribbeans. Given the complex and diverse political and ideological investments in the construction of Caribbeanness, the representation of "authentic" voice in narrative and characterization demands extensive contrivance on the part of the creative writer. Central to this process is the deployment of multiple possibilities of meaning and multidimensional Caribbeans. Since Caribbean reality is culturally composite, the fictional Caribbean must of necessity be polyphonic.

In support of this contention, Lalla offers astute readings of meta-discursive strategies, slippage between narrative levels and Creole/Standard English multilingual competence, code-shifting and code ambiguity, skilfully used in fictions. Moreover, Lalla argues that the fictional voice is deployed to effectively construct the interface between home and away, between here and elsewhere. In the process, the fictional voice revisions for its own ideological purposes traditional representations of the West Indies in the British canon as the symbolic other – the marginal, unknowable, uncivilized and unrepresentable. Speculative fiction, such as the work of Nalo Hopkinson, builds on that British convention of associating the West Indies with estrangement to generate a contemporary Caribbean reality where the Other is the alien.

Part 2 of the text picks up the broad conference subtopic "Trajectories of Creolization". In chapter 8, "Fragments, Centres and Margins", Lise Winer traces Creole language studies from their inception, when scholars undertook to stem the deleterious impact of persistent denigration of immigrant Creole speakers within metropolitan educational systems. The pioneering, ground-breaking discipline of Creole linguistics gave rise to the linear concept of the *Creole continuum* and subsequently more fluid metaphors of "Creole space";[5] she references the artistic technique of pointillism, in which multiple patterns emerge when the work is viewed from diverse vantage points. In an odd twist, as new processes of centring and marginalization evolve, Winer identifies sub-sequent dialogues turning on the conceptualization of real as opposed to unreal Creoles based on the extent to which language production veers proximate to Standard English as reflective of ossifying assumptions of Creole norms. Turn-ing attention to applying the metaphor of reassembling of fragments to Creole language and ontology, Winer queries whether this can conceivably be the reassemblage of fossil reconstruction, in which, with the help of liberal doses of inference and imagination, the part can be held to encode and bears the like-ness of the whole. Or is it Walcott's archeological metaphor of reassemblage that we undertake as a work of love, honour and duty while recognizing the limitations of the absence of a representation of the original. Drawing infer-ences from the trajectories of the creolization debate, Winer concludes by iden-tifying the University of the West Indies as an institution that has successfully centred the margins.

Chapter 9, by María Landa Buil, offers a close analysis of a practical example of the creolization process. Buil compares developmental features of Palen-quero's noun phrase with the data of the Spanish Interlanguage (IL) of four Swahili speakers. Palenquero is a Creole language with Spanish as its lexifier and a Bantu language as its substrate. The originality of this work derived from comparing a Creole and an IL that share lexifier/target language (Spanish) and substrate/first language (a Bantu language). This chapter questions whether, in a situation of similar languages in contact, adult second-language learners will put to work similar mental processes and create a grammar similar to that of Palenquero. Buil observes the development of the noun phrase, trying to find in the IL the absence of grammatical gender, and the presence of post-nominal determiners and pre-nominal plural markers.

Turning attention to the fluid processes of embracing Creole as an identity marker, Nivedita Misra, in chapter 10, "Postcolonial Historiography: Brereton and Naipaul Documenting Ethnic Histories over and against National Paradigms", identifies the Caribbean dilemma not as the emergence of subaltern histories, as is the case in India, but as competing multi-voiced and dialogic ethnic histories. Misra's chapter poses a bold juxtaposition of Naipaul's and Brereton's attempts to negotiate contestation between ancestral ethnic identities and a national Creole identity. Identifying a common impulse towards social documentation, Misra located these writers' stances in relation to primary sources and the challenge of writing histories that vie for inclusion in the national narrative. While Misra credits both with affirming the significance of subaltern histories, she argues that, in this process, Brereton relies heavily on what the data does or does not tell, while Naipaul uses his creative imagination generously to fill and embody the fissures and interstices of history. The chapter points to disjunctures between official narratives and historical narratives shaped to support diverse ideological leanings and divergent ancestral traditions. Misra also alludes to the process by which exploratory formulations of history solidify into new hegemonies, which then invite ongoing challenge.

Ian Robertson's paper in chapter 11 of this volume typifies his brand of scholarship. It is a painstaking re-creation of the historical circumstances in the Guyanese interior in the period of the establishment of colonies primarily by the Dutch. It argues from the historical facts that it is highly unlikely that pidginization occurred during the contact between Amerindian tribes and the colonists since the Amerindians were too large a group and too secure in their value to the invaders, to seek to make any kind of linguistic accommodation towards them. He argues further that too little is known generally of the socio-historical circumstances in which so-called pidgins and Creoles were established to allow linguists to theorizing too securely about them. They may be potential sub-types of larger group of contact languages whose precise evolutionary circumstances need far more insight than we presently have.

The book concludes with chapter 12, an annotated bibliography of the work of Barbara Lalla and Ian Robertson. It is a practical work of gathering up the fragments, so that, in the end, nothing will be lost.

NOTES

1.   Derek Walcott, "The Antilles: Fragments of Epic Memory" (Nobel lecture, 7 December 1992), http://www.nobelprize.org/nobel_prizes/literature/laureates/ 1992/walcott-lecture.html.

2.   Barbara Lalla, *Arch of Fire: A Jamaican Family Saga* (Kingston: Kingston Publishers, 1998).

3.   Ian Robertson, "Language and Language Education Policy" (report to the Seamless Education Project Unit, Ministry of Education, Trinidad and Tobago, 2010).

4.   "Language Education and Policy" (report prepared for the Jamaican Ministry of Education, Youth and Culture, Government Printery, 2001).

5.   Lawrence Carrington, "Images of Creole Space", *Journal of Pidgin and Creole Languages* 7, no. 1 (1992): 93–99.

PART 1

TRIBUTES AND CRITICAL APPRAISALS

1.

CHALLENGING THE OLD AND
EXPLORING THE NEW

A Tribute to Ian Robertson

[DONALD WINFORD]

I FIRST CAME TO KNOW Ian Robertson during the 1970s, when he was doing his PhD at the University of the West Indies, St Augustine, Trindad. He was the first person ever to be awarded a PhD in linguistics at that campus. I got to know him better when he joined the School of Education at St Augustine as a temporary research fellow from 1983 to 1984. Fortunately for us, the temporary appointment became a permanent one in 1985, when he was appointed lecturer in the Faculty of Education. From that point on, Robertson never looked back, first assuming the duties of head of the Department of Educational Foundations and Teacher Education from 1989 to 1994.

Then, in a move that was somewhat of a surprise to many, he accepted an appointment as lecturer in what was then the Department of Language and Linguistics in 1989, one year after I left my own position there. As we all know, Robertson continued his rise through the ranks, becoming a senior lecturer in 1996, deputy dean from 1999 to 2000 and dean of the newly created Faculty of Humanities and Education in 2000. I think his administrative record speaks for itself. Anyone who survived eight years as dean must have been doing something right.

I am concerned here more with the academic side of Robertson's career, a career spent with a foot in two fields of Creole study – the descriptive and the applied, which have become more and more integrated in the current Department of Liberal Arts here at St Augustine. The two-faceted nature of Robertson's research interests and accomplishments goes a long way towards explaining his important legacy to Creole studies in the Caribbean in particular and to the field of Creole linguistics in general. Having a foot in both camps, I think, explains the subtle tensions we find in his work between a concern with theory informed by realistic and objective data and a concern for the application of that theory to practical problems of Creole-speaking communities. In both these dimensions of research, Robertson's work has become an important contribution to the development of thinking in Caribbean Creole linguistics. Throughout, he challenged the old (and not-so-old) conventional wisdom, while at the same time exploring new avenues of research. He will no doubt go down in history primarily as the person who discovered the existence of Berbice Dutch, an event that shook up the Creole world in more ways than one. For those who may not know, Berbice Dutch was probably the first instance of a Dutch-lexicon Creole that developed in a Dutch colony: the colony of Berbice, in Guyana. Robertson's work on this Creole was central to his exploration of a number of issues which were being debated in the field of Creole linguistics in the 1980s and 1990s.

CREOLE AND UNCREOLE: CHALLENGING THE STEREOTYPE

A recurring theme of Robertson's work is his scepticism towards theoretical models and assumptions that fail to meet the tests of solid empirical verification. His 2006 paper, "Challenging the Definition of Creole",[1] questions a number of claims about the definitive characteristics of Creoles and the nature of their genesis. This paper was originally titled "Creole and UnCreole: Challenging the Stereotype", a title that I personally prefer. It was first presented in 1988 at the Society for Caribbean Linguistics conference in the Bahamas. This is significant, because this was the heyday of Bickertonian thought on the nature of Creoles and their origins, which dominated the field for most of that decade. Robertson, however, was not impressed.

In his paper, he decried the fact that some of the criteria by which Creole languages have been defined have "attained a false level of assuredness". He explained this as follows: "Perhaps the most significant reasons for this are the tendency to be preoccupied with theory, the tendency to have the theory drive the analyses rather than to adapt to them, and the tendency to use one tiny subsection of the language (usually the TMA [tense/mood/aspect] system) to make far-reaching decisions about the language."[2]

The dig at Bickertonian models of Creole formation and the Creole "proto-type" is patently evident in these remarks. Again, for those who may not know, Bickerton ascribed Creole creation to the workings of an innate language bio-programme to which children appealed in acquiring a deficient pidgin as their first language.[3] According to this view, Creole formation was a special type of first-language acquisition, in which the putative bioprogramme provided the major input to the creation of Creole grammar. This view essentially ruled out the possibility of any genetic continuity between Creoles and their lexifiers.

Bickerton's hypothesis has been rejected by most creolists, based on over-whelming counter-evidence, both linguistic and sociohistorical.[4] The general consensus among creolists today is that Creoles arose via processes of language shift or "naturalistic" second-language acquisition (SLA). In challenging the Bickertonian model, Robertson was challenging the dominant theory of Creole origins and all the assumptions that went with it. He was led to this especially by his experience with Berbice Dutch.

For a Creole, it was an unusual language. For one thing, it seemed to have been created primarily by speakers of a single set of closely related dialects of Eastern Ijo. The evidence could be found in the retention of many lexical items of Eastern Ijo origin, including core vocabulary. More interestingly, Berbice Dutch had retained a number of grammatical morphemes, including bound inflectional morphemes, expressing notions like plurality as well as tense/aspect, from its Ijo substrate. There were no parallels to this in any other known Creole. Robertson was quick to point out the consequences. First, he noted: "The retention of [Ijo] suffixes, for instance, clearly points to a process of trans-fer. . . . Clearly they could not have been reinserted by some child relying on his bioprogramme in the process of 'nativising' the pidgin inputs of its parents. A much more reasonable explanation appears to be that the adults were an essen-tial part of the creolising population."[5] This was a bold statement in a context in which Bickerton's and not Robertson's views of Creole formation dominated most of the field. In some ways, the preoccupation with this model had an adverse effect on the development of the field, as Robertson pointed out: The "complex nature of theory, or the complexity of its consequent explanations, has caused creolists to believe that Creole linguistics has advanced considerably more than it actually has".[6] It was only when the field threw off the shackles of the bioprogramme hypothesis that its horizons began to expand in many direc-tions. One of these directions was the growing awareness of the connections between Creole formation and natural SLA, discussed later in this chapter.

Berbice Dutch challenged orthodox thinking about Creoles in other ways. It prompted John Holm to ask whether Berbice Dutch "is even the same kind of language as the other Atlantic Creoles or whether it belongs to a category of mixed language for which we do not yet have a name".[7] Robertson, scarcely masking his impatience with what he always referred to as "damn chupidness", dismissed this as another instance of the kind of "false level of assuredness" that was dogging the field.[8] Faced with exceptions to its predictions, orthodoxy can either yield or maintain its position. In the latter case, instead of adapting the facts to the theory, as Robertson advocated, it denies any connection between the two. Hence Berbice Dutch must be relegated to some as-yet-undetermined category of mixed language, since it clearly does not conform to fixed assumptions about what a Creole is. The question is, of course, inextricably related to the origins of Creoles as second-language creations.

CREOLE FORMATION AS SECOND-LANGUAGE ACQUISITION

Most creolists today would accept the view that Creole formation was a type of SLA, although it is clear that there are some significant differences between the two due to disparities in the nature of the two types of learning situation. We can describe the creation of Creole grammar as involving a process of restructuring, that is, the process by which interlanguage (IL) grammars are created and elaborated in the course of acquisition. This process of restructuring involves three major components: input (intake) from the target language, native language (L1) influence and internally motivated innovations. These factors operate in varying degrees in different cases of Creole formation, yielding differences in the outcomes. It seems clear that such differences result in part from the nature of the superstrate input and the degree of access that learners had to it. Degree of access, in turn, depends on such aspects of the contact situation as demographics and degree of social interaction among superstrate and substrate speakers. Greater degrees of access to superstrate models lead to more input from the latter, while reduced access leads to greater degrees of substrate influence. The types of substrate influence, of course, depend on the demographics of the groups involved. As Robertson pointed out,[9] the conventional wisdom was that "Creoles arose in a population where no more than 20% of the population were speakers of the dominant language, and where the remaining 80% was composed of diverse language groups".[10]

Again, Berbice Dutch was a clear exception since its substrate was relatively homogeneous, leading to the use of overt Ijo grammatical machinery in the resulting Creole. Such a development, while unusual, is by no means unattested even in cases of tutored SLA. For instance, Nemser's study of the second language (L2) English of German-speaking Austrian students revealed many instances of the use of German grammatical morphemes in their interlanguage.[11] So we do not need to treat the "transfer" of Ijo-bound morphology into Berbice Dutch as unique in any way.

EXPANDING THE HORIZONS OF CREOLE LINGUISTICS

The reorientation that occurred in Creole linguistics in the 1990s opened the way for relationships to be established not only with the field of SLA, but also the broader field of contact linguistics. With regard to SLA, creolists such as Claire Lefebvre[12] and Jeff Siegel[13] have attempted to reinterpret processes of substrate influence in terms of the theories of relexification and transfer, respectively. As a result, we now have a much better understanding of the ways in which Creole formation relates to other outcomes of "natural" SLA in terms of the processes of restructuring that are involved.

ON UNIVERSALS AND CREOLE FORMATION

The role of universals in Creole formation has begun to receive more attention of late. Bickerton's language bioprogramme hypothesis (LBH) proposed that there were a number of universal properties shared by Creoles because they were shaped by the workings of the bioprogramme.[14] Among the properties he cited as evidence were the tense/mood/aspect (TMA) systems of Creoles. According to Bickerton, these TMA systems displayed the famous "tripartite" organization into an "irrealis" mood, a "non-punctual aspect" and an "anterior" tense. However, various recent studies and comparisons of tense/aspect systems in Creoles in general[15] and Caribbean-English-lexicon Creoles in particular[16] have shown that there are no tense/aspect universals shared by Creoles. The term "universal" must be understood to refer to a generalization about cross-linguistic structures, or what Smolensky and Dupoux refer to as "a superficial descriptive property true of the expression of all languages – a descriptive universal".[17]

Robertson's own description of the TMA system of Berbice Dutch showed that it resembled that of other Caribbean English Creoles in various ways. But at the same time, he demonstrated that Berbice Dutch departed from the so-called prototypical system in significant ways. However, the similarities among the TMA systems of Caribbean-English-lexicon Creoles are striking and invite further explanation. They do in fact show evidence of the workings of universal processes but of a very different kind from those proposed by Bickerton.

We are concerned here with the notion of a cognitive universal, that is, "a property true of all human minds".[18] Bickerton's concept of such universals was rooted in the tradition of Chomskyan generative grammar, which proposes a set of universal principles that are specific to language, enshrined in an innate human language faculty that guides language acquisition and places limits on possible grammars. A quite different view is taken by functionalist linguists. Rather than viewing language structure and acquisition as guided by universal principles specific to the language domain, they seek to explain universals of language design in terms of human cognitive skills and the influence of individual cognitive abilities on language development.[19]

Creole tense/aspect systems provide evidence for functional perspectives on the relationship between universal principles and paths of change. Certain tense/aspect categories, such as future and past, result from internally motivated patterns of grammaticalization found universally in language change. Other tense/aspect categories, such as perfects and progressives, are more idiosyncratic since they are shaped by substrate influence in a process of contact-induced grammaticalization. Winford (to appear) has argued that the mechanism of change underlying this process is imposition, which can itself be regarded as a universal mechanism.[20] It involves assigning semantic and structural properties of an L1 category to an L2 lexeme via analogy. The creation of all tense/aspect categories, whether internally or externally motivated, follows universal cognitive tendencies that come into play in language production and processing. Ultimately, it is possible that such tendencies derive from innate principles that are not restricted to language alone, but are part of more general cognitive capacities peculiar to human beings. This possibility simply reaffirms the status of Creoles as true manifestations of the human capacity to create and reshape language according to cognitive principles common to all human beings.

ON THE STATUS OF CREOLES

The discussion of Creole origins leads naturally to the question of whether Creoles should be considered continuations of their lexifier languages or entirely new creations. This issue has led to a great deal of acrimonious debate among creolists, who remain divided. Robertson would consider this particularly unfortunate, since he has charged creolists with the task of educating the public on the legitimacy of Creoles as forms of communication. The Caribbean public is still unconvinced that Creoles are really true languages as distinct from corruptions of their lexifiers.

The controversy is not restricted to Creoles, however. It also involves the status of all of the New Englishes, the contact varieties of English that emerged in British colonies from the seventeenth century on. These are the varieties found in the so-called outer circle of English, consisting of "indigenized" varieties such as Indian English and Singapore English, as well as the Creoles of Africa, the Pacific, and the Caribbean. Some have proposed a division between "native" (meaning British, American, Australian and the like) and "non-native" (meaning "colonial") varieties of English. As Gupta[21] points out, this is a misnomer at best, since most contact varieties used in the former colonies are native languages in the true sense of that term. Gupta herself suggests a classification based on a distinction between normal and discontinuous transmission in the emergence of colonial Englishes.[22] In this classification, "native/old varieties spoken by descendants of the British" would be cases of normal transmission, whereby children acquire their parents' language as a native language. On the other hand, Creoles and indigenized varieties would have originated through "discontinuous transmission", involving informal learning by adults in the case of Creoles, and scholastic learning in the case of indigenized varieties. The issue of transmission is especially problematic, since it is not clear where to draw the lines between "normal" and "discontinuous" types of transmission. This question is germane to the contentious debate concerning the origins of Creoles and their affiliation to their lexifiers.

Thomason and Kaufman propose that so-called abrupt Creoles like basilectal Caribbean-English Creole should be treated as "a special case of language shift", to be distinguished from "ordinary language shift", in which "the target language as a whole is available and is, for the most part, acquired by the shifting group".[23] This approach treats "indigenized" varieties such as Irish English and Indian English as cases of "normal transmission", while certain Creoles are seen as results of "abnormal transmission", that is, not in direct genetic descent from their lexifier language. The more "radical" Creoles, they argue, derive most of their grammar from their substrate languages and cannot therefore be considered as continuations of their lexifiers. This view has been roundly rejected by scholars like Chaudenson, DeGraff and Mufwene,[24] who consider it to be based on the myth of "Creole exceptionalism", the idea that Creoles are in some sense "special" creations. Mufwene argues that "there is no clear measure of what extent of mixedness would make a language variety genetically not derivable from another".[25] For scholars like Mufwene, the differences between Creoles and indigenized varieties are only matters of degree, not kind. Indeed, Mufwene extends his argument to include the so-called ancestral or native Englishes of places like Australia, North America and so on, and even the varieties of English that evolved in the British Isles. All of these forms of English were influenced to varying degrees by contact with other languages, leading to externally motivated change in one form or another.

Herein lies the heart of the controversy concerning the relationship between Creoles and other contact varieties of English. Are the processes of change that gave rise to Creoles similar in kind to those that have operated, not just in the history of other contact varieties, but even in the history and evolution of British English itself? Most scholars today see creolization as involving types of change that have occurred in the history of most languages, including the lexifiers of Creoles. Creoles therefore should be afforded the same recognition as continuations of their lexifiers, as other languages that have evolved through processes of SLA, such as Spanish, Italian, French and Portuguese, the daughters of Latin. All of these involved significant influence from substrate languages. Recognizing that Creoles have more than one line of descent would allow us to preserve the notion that they are cases of normal transmission, while at the same time recognizing that they are autonomous creations in their own right. Such an approach is in keeping with Robertson's concern that creolists should "help to contribute to the development of a well balanced, positive linguistic self-concept" among Creole speakers.[26] This is only one element in his vision for a well-balanced and rational approach to language-education policy in the Caribbean, which he has outlined in several recent papers.

QUESTIONS OF SOCIOLINGUISTIC STATUS AND FUNCTION

The adoption of the New Englishes as primary vernaculars or as lingua francas vital to intergroup communication in former English colonies has brought with it a range of problems that are typically associated with low-prestige varieties that compete with standard varieties. On the one hand, the New Englishes serve as reflections of the social identities of their users, many of whom in fact acquire them as native languages. On the other hand, socioeconomic and political reality dictates that they are relegated to the status of unwelcome and disadvantaged deviations, even corruptions, of the standard language, which is the avenue to educational and social advancement. This means that a command of Standard English is a prerequisite for socioeconomic success, political participation, economic and technological advancement, and modernization. On the one hand, since those who have a command of Standard English have a clear advantage over those who do not, this state of affairs reinforces existing inequalities in the social hierarchy. On the other hand, the vernacular varieties serve as primary media for everyday informal interaction and have become markers of local community identity for large sections of the population. Inevitably, there is continuing conflict between the public or overt image of standard varieties as symbols of prestige and power and the private or covert perception of the vernaculars as symbols of shared community membership and identity.

The solution advocated by Robertson and other Caribbean scholars is to reaffirm the separate status of the vernaculars and promote their recognition as legitimate instruments of public communication. Such scholars emphasize the autonomy of Creole and argue that its alleged heteronomy (dialectal status) vis-à-vis English is a fiction, a construct of sociolinguists committed to a particular view of Creole continua. Despite this view, acceptance of the autonomy of vernaculars has been slow to come in most Caribbean communities, though the tide may be turning in some cases.

LANGUAGE-EDUCATION POLICY FOR CARIBBEAN STATES

Crucially, Robertson has long been concerned that the area of applied linguistics in the Caribbean has been restricted to issues of language teaching alone. Language teaching is of course a vital component of the kind of applications he envisaged for Creole linguistics. But his vision was much broader, since he saw the critical objective of an applied creolistics as being "the improvement of the lot of Creole language speakers".[27] Simple and to the point, as Robertson always was. The steps he proposed included:[28]

1. development of an awareness among Creole speakers of the potential of the languages they speak. This would involve, in part, standardization, instrumentalization, and legitimization of Creole languages.
2. development of appropriate interpretations of the literature that exploits and validates the Creoles and their social-class dialects. This reflects Robertson's concern with the need for Creole societies to fully appreciate the range of serious creative work that has been done through the medium of Creole languages.
3. development of the oral traditions of Creole societies. Robertson saw these as presenting "a uniquely rewarding opportunity for applying Creole linguistics, and for contributing to a positive self-concept" among Creole speakers.[29] He lamented that much of the stored wisdom enshrined in these oral traditions has been lost to us.

EDUCATION AS SOCIAL RECONSTRUCTION

For Robertson, the broader vision of an applied creolistics meant that Creole studies had to move "beyond the realm of academic rationalism into that of social reconstruction".[30] He saw this programme of reform as extending into the development of political, economic and environmental literacy. Robertson even saw Creole studies as having the potential to solve political disputes such as that between Guyana and Venezuela over their border. His own research had discovered that linguistic items of Dutch Creole origin were still being used by indigenous groups inhabiting the area that was being claimed by Venezuela. For him, this supplied important evidence in support of Guyana's claim to the territory under dispute.[31] In scope, his vision is very much the same as that of current generations of reform-minded scholars who wish to revolutionize educational policy in places like Curaçao, Jamaica, Haiti and so on.

EDUCATIONAL POLICY IN HAITI AND CURAÇAO

The disastrous consequences of a language-education policy that totally ignores the linguistic reality of a society are well demonstrated in the case of Haiti. According to Hebblethwaite, in Haiti, Creole is natively spoken by all ten million Haitians, while French is spoken by less than five hundred thousand members of the elite.[32] French-language dominance in Haitian schools adversely impacts millions of children and is the source of broad societal inefficiency. As Hebblethwaite points out, "The Francophilic elite hold to 'creole exceptionalism' which claims that Creole languages suffer from some deficiency and possess some quality that makes them lesser than the related European lexifier languages."[33]

The effects of the current educational policy are devastating: According to recent records from the Haitian government's statistics bureau, 61 per cent of the population over the age of ten is illiterate, the rural rate is 80.5 per cent and the urban rate is 47.1 per cent.[34] Of the population over the age of five, 37.4 per cent has no level of schooling, 35.2 per cent has enrolled in primary school, 21.5 per cent has enrolled in secondary school and 1.1 per cent has enrolled in university-level education. The net secondary-school attendance ratio from 2005 to 2009 was 18 per cent for males and 21 per cent for females.[35] In 2003, only 21.99 per cent of all those enrolled in school passed the *rhétorique* exams, and 17.75 per cent passed the *philosophie* exam.[36]

EDUCATIONAL REFORM

Reformists like Yves Dejean, Michel DeGraff, Benjamin Hebblethwaite and others have long been advocating a complete transformation, in which Creole would be used as the sole language of instruction, with French taught as a second language. Much of their vision seems to be in accord with Robertson's view of what a relevant and rational language-education policy should be for Creole societies. As Hebblethwaite points out, "A common language is an economic asset because all members of society can be drawn into the economic process and goods and services can be related together. Linguistic equality promotes social cohesion, facilitates social mobility, and fosters broad political participation."[37]

The policy also promotes the use of the considerable literature that exists in

Haitian Creole, ranging from literary works to treatises on the environment. This would fit well with Robertson's emphasis on the use of Creole-medium education to promote development of political, economic and environmental literacy.

Contrasting strongly with Haiti is the situation in Curaçao.[38] The private Papiamentu primary and secondary school, Kolegio Erasmo, has operated successfully since 1987 and has proven itself to be a worthy model for the expansion of first-language education on that island.[39] The use of the students' native language has positive psychological effects.[40] Many students who had been abandoned by other schools were able to integrate and succeed in Kolegio Erasmo. The school's enrolment has increased to 440 students. Between 2001 and 2008, 84.1 per cent of the students completed elementary school. Since the secondary school was added, 82 per cent of students passed in 2001, 95.3 per cent in 2002 and 90.3 per cent in 2003, compared to the national average of between 60 per cent and 70 per cent.[41] In 2003, the government of the Netherlands Antilles announced plans to include Papiamentu through the university level and used the Kolegio Erasmo as a pilot school.

Creolists can look to Kolegio Erasmo as a shining example of the benefits of employing Creole languages in education. It is perhaps the kind of model that Robertson has long been advocating for the Creole-speaking Caribbean as whole. Throughout his career, he has shown an abiding concern for what Creole studies could contribute towards improving the lot of Creole speakers. In "Applying Creole Linguistics",[42] Robertson quotes Derek Bickerton's confession that creolists have profited greatly from their work on Creole languages but have given little back in return. Bickerton notes, "For many years now I and other people like me have lived well off Creole languages. . . . We enjoy salaries that are probably. . . at least twenty times what the average speaker of these languages earns. Moreover, we have a voice and they do not. . . . Do we not owe them something?"[43] For Robertson, "[t]he comparison to King Lear on the heath is too striking to ignore": "Poor naked wretches, wheresoever you are. . . . How shall your houseless heads and unfed sides . . . defend you from seasons such as these? O, I have taken too little care of this."[44] I suppose that only Robertson could perceive the plight of the uneducated poor of Caribbean communities in terms of a Shakespearean tragedy.

Those who conduct linguistic research and gather data from particular speech communities have become increasingly concerned of late with the ways in which they can use their findings to benefit those communities. Morgan views this as one of the persistent challenges to creolists and sociolinguists, but of course it applies equally well to those who document any language, particularly the languages of minority and disadvantaged groups.[45] As Labov pointed out, the two questions that the public most frequently ask linguists are what linguistics is all about, and what it is good for.[46] And, as Morgan reminds us, the response of linguists to these questions is of far more import to the speech community under investigation than the theoretical frameworks and analyses that are of prime concern to linguists. Robertson would no doubt heartily agree with this.

Rickford also laments the fact that sociolinguistic research on African American speech communities has contributed immensely to the advancement of the field but has given relatively little in return.[47] The same might be said of research in many other speech communities, among them the Creole communities of the Caribbean. Recent developments in the practical applications of sociolinguistic research to social problems in such communities suggest that some progress is being made towards redressing the imbalance between what we take from the community and what we give back. Robertson's work is at the forefront of such efforts.

Such progress can be observed in most of the areas identified by Rickford as key targets of socially responsible sociolinguistics. These include

1. increasing the representation of minorities in the field of sociolinguistics and linguistics more generally,
2. contributing to educational policy and practice, and
3. promoting equality in the courts and the workplace.

Above all, perhaps, Creole studies has most to offer in the area of education, particularly in the teaching of language arts in the schools. This has been one of the major ways in which Robertson has paid back his debt to the communities that he serves.

CONCLUSION

Robertson's research, teaching and practical wisdom will continue to influence the future directions of both descriptive and applied work on Creole languages. There are several aspects of his scholastic record that I have not discussed here. His work on indigenous languages of the Caribbean, and on the endangered enclave varieties of French Creole in Guyana and Trinidad are two noteworthy examples of his broad interest in Caribbean languages. He has made invaluable contributions to the field in his capacity as secretary-treasurer and president of the Society for Caribbean Linguistics. He has also left his mark on the new generations of scholars who are doing vital research on Caribbean languages. His contribution to Creole studies also includes a substantial body of data, consisting of both audio- and videotaped materials, which should be given a permanent home in the university library. But he will perhaps be remembered most of all for his concern for an approach to Caribbean languages that, in his words: "would ensure the establishment of the bona fides of Creole studies in the eyes of the speakers of Creoles, and which would at the same time facilitate their development".[48]

For Robertson, the speakers of the languages always come first.

NOTES

1. Ian Robertson, "Challenging the Definition of Creole", in *Exploring the Boundaries of Caribbean Creole Languages*, ed. Hazel Simmons-McDonald and Ian Robertson (Kingston: University of the West Indies Press, 2006), 3–19.

2. Ibid., 9.

3. Derek Bickerton, "The Language Bioprogram Hypothesis", *Behavioral and Brain Sciences* 7 (1984): 173–88.

4. T. Veenstra, "Creole Genesis: The Impact of the Language Bioprogram Hypothesis", in *The Handbook of Pidgin and Creole Studies*, ed. S. Kouwenberg and J. Singler (Oxford: Wiley-Blackwell, 2008), 219–41.

5. Ian Robertson, "Creole and UnCreole: Challenging the Stereotype" (paper presented at the Seventh Biennial Conference of the Society for Caribbean Linguistics, Nassau, Bahamas, 1988), 13

6. Robertson, "Challenging the Definition", 9.

7. John Holm, "Social Factors in Pidginization and Creolization" (mimeo, n.d.), quoted in Robertson, "Challenging the Definition of Creole", 9–10.

8. Robertson, "Challenging the Definition", 9.

9. Ibid., 10.

10. Derek Bickerton, *Roots of Language* (Ann Arbor, MI: Karoma, 1981).

11. William Nemser, "Language Contact and Foreign Language Acquisition", in *Languages in Contact and Contrast: Essays in Contact Linguistics*, ed. Vladimir Ivir and Damir Kalagjera (Berlin: Mouton de Gruyter, 1991), 345–64.

12. Claire Lefebvre, *Creole Genesis and the Acquisition of Grammar: The Case of Haitian Creole* (Cambridge: Cambridge University Press, 1998).

13. Jeff Siegel, "Transfer Constrainsts and Substrate Influence in Melanesian Pidgin", *Journal of Pidgin and Creole Languages* 14, no. 1 (1999): 1–44.

14. Bickerton, "Language Bioprogram Hypothesis", 173–88.

15. John Singler, ed., *Pidgin and Creole Tense-Mood-Aspect Systems* (Amsterdam: John Benjamins, 1990).

16. Donald Winford, "A Comparison of Tense-Aspect Systems in Caribbean English Creoles", in *Due Respect: Papers on English and English-Related Creoles in the Caribbean in Honour of Professor Robert Le Page*, ed. Pauline Christie (Kingston: University of the West Indies Press, 2001), 155–83.

17. Paul Smolensky and Emmanuel Dupoux, "Universals in Cognitive Theories of Language", *Behavioral and Brain Sciences* 32, no. 5 (2009): 468.

18. Ibid.

19. Edith L. Bavin, "Widening the Field: The Process of Language Acquisition", *Behavioral and Brain Sciences* 32, no. 5 (2009): 450.

20. Donald Winford, "Substrate Influence and Universals in the Emergence of Contact Englishes: Re-Evaluating the Evidence", in *English as a Contact Language*, ed. Daniel Schreier and Marianne Hundt (Cambridge: Cambridge University Press, 2013).

21. Anthea F. Gupta, "Colonisation, Migration, and Functions of English", in *Englishes around the World: General Studies, British Isles, North America* (Amsterdam: John Benjamins, 1997), 1:53.

22. Ibid., 52.

23. Sarah G. Thomason and Terrence Kaufman, *Language Contact, Creolization and Genetic Linguistics* (Berkeley: University of California Press, 1988), 166.

24. Robert Chaudenson, in collaboration with Salikoko Mufwene, *Creolization of Language and Culture*, rev. ed. (1992; repr., London: Routledge, 2001); Michel DeGraff, "Linguists' Most Dangerous Myth: The Fallacy of Creole Exceptionalism", *Language in Society* 34, no. 4 (2005): 533–91; Salikoko Mufwene, *The Ecology of Language Evolution* (Cambridge: Cambridge University Press, 2001).

25. Mufwene, *Ecology*, 19.

26. Ian Robertson, "Applying Creole Linguistics" (paper presented at the Ninth Biennial Conference of the Society for Caribbean Linguistics, University of the West Indies, Cave Hill, Barbados, 1992), 5.

27. Ibid., 3.

28. Ibid., 4–6.

29. Ibid., 6.

30. Ibid., 2.

31. Ibid., 9.

32. Benjamin Hebblethwaite, "French and Underdevelopment, Haitian Creole and Development: Educational Language Policy Problems and Solutions in Haiti", *Journal of Pidgin and Creole Languages* 27, no. 2 (2012): 255–302.

33. Ibid.

34. Institut Haïtien de Statistique et d'Informatique, http://www.ihsi.html.

35. http://www.unicef.org.

36. Yves Dejean, *Yon lekòl tèt anba nan yon peyi tèt anba* (Port-au-Prince: FOKAL, 2006), 152.

37. Florian Coulmas, *Language and Economy* (Oxford: Blackwell, 1992), 36.

38. Hebblethwaite, "French and Underdevelopment".

39. Marta Dijkhoff and Joyce Pereira, "Language and Education in Aruba, Bonaire and Curaçao", in *Creoles in Education: An Appraisal of Current Programs and Projects*, ed. Bettina Migge, Isabelle Léglise and Angela Bartens (Amsterdam: John Benjamins, 2010), 252.

40. Ibid.

41. Ibid, 253.

42. Robertson, "Applying Creole Linguistics".

43. Ibid.

44. Ibid.

45. Marcyliena Morgan, "The African-American Speech Community: Reality and Sociolinguistics",in *The Social Construction of Identity in Creole Situations*, ed. Marcyliena Morgan (Los Angeles: Centre for Afro-American Studies, 1994), 121.

46. William Labov, "Objectivity and Commitment in Linguistic Science: The Case of the Black English Trial in Ann Arbor", *Language in Society* (1982): 11.

47. John Rickford, "Unequal Partnership: Sociolinguistics and the African American Speech Community", *Language in Society* 26, no. 2 (1997): 161–97.

48. Robertson, "Applying Creole Linguistics", 2.

2.

BARBARA LALLA

A Transdiciplinary Intellectual

[VELMA POLLARD]

WHEN I HEARD BARBARA LALLA introduced at a meeting some years ago as a "transdisciplinary intellectual giant", I had no idea I would need to borrow the phrase, but I do so now because I think it describes so accurately what Barbara Lalla has become in the academic arena. It is less, however, as a giant straddling different disciplines than as one allowing the different disciplines to inform each other and work transformations on each other that her contribution has been significant. In this enterprise, she has facilitated the entrance of other scholars into an understanding of and an appreciation for the disciplines she has merged. But if I had to mention a primary discipline, an overarching one in considering this work, I would have to say "history", whether or not history might be listed in a curriculum vitae as one of the areas Lalla has pursued in a formal academic way. It is a long look at the history of Caribbean language that has engaged her linguistic eye, and it is a long look at the history of Caribbean literary expression that has engaged her literary eye. How these two eyes interlock/interact is Lalla's preoccupation.

This chapter is an introduction to the academic contribution of Barbara Lalla to the field of studies in Caribbean language. For those who know the work, I hope that this will serve as a confirmation of its breadth and depth; for those who do not, I hope it will serve as an invitation, a taste to whet your appetite, so you will go with enthusiasm to a body of work to which I cannot possibly do justice. I have selected a few texts for my attention, all in the area of language. First, I lean briefly towards linguistics, then towards literature and then I comment very briefly on creative writing. Do not expect neat lines of demarcation. There can be no real division in what is essentially a set of currents flowing together.

LANGUAGE/LINGUISTICS

Barbara Lalla with Jean D'Costa wrote *Voices in Exile*[1] and *Language in Exile*,[2] sister volumes published by University of Alabama Press in the years 1989 and 1990, respectively. These books have become institutions in Caribbean literary studies, reference books forever used by people writing today on matters of the sixteenth century onward and will continue to serve generations of scholars to come in the same way. Studies as far removed from each other as Carolyn Cooper's *Noises in the Blood*[3] and my own "The Scots in Jamaica",[4] have had to go to *Voices in Exile* for texts made easily accessible by these scholars. Another I am aware of is Allison Irvine on *Defining Good English in Jamaica.*[5]

In the preface to *Language in Exile*, one reads that the book "discusses the external and internal language history of Jamaican Creole. Working against the background of Jamaican social history it considers the nature and consequences of language contact, examines the sound system and related orthographical problems, comments on the difficulties of reconstruction and interpretation implicit in the data and connects the varieties of the past to the known structure of Jamaican Creole."[6]

The sister volumes are a reflection of one of the most obvious features of Lalla's character. She is a scholar for the long haul. A term that comes to me in relation to her way of operating is "gestation". It is perhaps not a precise descriptor of the process I am thinking about, but it will do, and I will return to it again and again. The preface of *Language in Exile* actually begins "Ten years ago the writers of this book embarked on a search for the beginnings of Jamaican Creole".[7] Lalla's academic papers in the years preceding this publication reflect that, beginning with 1979, ten years from the 1989 date of publication, there are titles like the following:

- 1979: "Sources for a History of Jamaican Creole"[8]
- 1981: "Quaco Sam: A Relic of Archaic Jamaican Speech"[9]
- 1983: "The Consonant System of Early Jamaican Creole"[10]
- 1986: "Tracing Elusive Phonological Elements in Early Jamaican Creole"[11]

These articles form a kind of progression moving towards the 1989 to 1990 publications.

LANGUAGE/LITERATURE

In 1996, Lalla published *Defining Jamaican Fiction: Marronage and the Discourse of Survival*, also for the University of Alabama Press.[12] But first a brief comment on the field in general. Over the last fifty years, creative writers in the Caribbean have increasingly sought to accurately portray characters from all strata of the societies they describe in the different genres in which they write. Just as the physical environment, the landscape, is the backdrop to the story, so language has become the vehicle for underlining the identity of the different individuals who occupy the landscape. The territories all have a popular language (a Creole) and an official language (a European language to which it is lexically related), which allows the writers to exploit a situation that includes the sociology of the interaction between the languages.

Critics of this writing have welcomed the increasing sophistication of the portrayal of the Caribbean individual through his or her speech as reproduced on the page. The analysis of the language, however, and how it functions in the poem or story or novel, has had to await the arrival on the scene of the literary critic who is also a student of linguistics. A few names come to mind, beginning with Jean D'Costa, who writes about language choice from the production side in "The West Indian Novelist and Language: A Search for a Literary Medium", presented at a conference on Caribbean Linguistics in 1980 but published later.[13] Then comes Maureen Warner-Lewis,[14] myself[15] and Merle Hodge,[16] among others writing from the reception side. Taking that to its highest level has been Barbara Lalla,[17] who analyses the language in the writing of some of the finest architects of Caribbean prose and poetry.

This is a self-conscious contribution to the study of Caribbean literature and a highly appreciated one. Here is Lalla on the role of that contribution: "In widening the applications of Caribbean Linguistics, scholars in this area have much to contribute to the understanding of literary texts in their own region, and much to gain from accepting as a valid concern of their discipline the nature of literary discourse in the region."[18]

Defining Jamaican Fiction takes a leap in the direction indicated in that quotation. The subtitle, *Marronage and the Discourse of Survival*, guides the selection of texts on which the study focuses "not on the Maroon as a sociohistorical phenomenon but on the developing persona of the maroon as a character type in creative literature". The analysis, Lalla says, "supplements traditional tools of critical analysis by some recourse to linguistics and discourse analysis",[19] and, looking at the larger picture, the kind of enhancement I like to call "transformation", adds, "Although this study does not pursue linguistics and discourse analysis for their own sake it presupposes the view that exploring literary discourse in the Anglophone Caribbean extends the scope of Caribbean language study and the application of Creole linguistics."[20] *Defining Jamaican Fiction* may be concerned with themes and character types in a wide selection of Jamaican fiction, but what sets it apart from any similar attempt is the way it elucidates for the attentive reader, for the ardent scholar, the linguistic and discourse moves that form the backbone of these narratives, the grammatical, lexical and discourse manoeuvres behind the texts.

Now while the data may be Jamaican, the analyses the study presents have application to all anglophone Caribbean Creoles and therefore can inform studies about Creoles in the Caribbean in general. Indeed the earlier studies to which it alludes are by no means exclusively about Jamaican Creole. What emerges is a kind of anglophone Caribbean prototype of landscape and language. So, for example, the critic asks with regard to the character Antoinette in Jean Rhys's *Wide Sargasso Sea*,[21] "What is Antoinette's mother tongue?", the response is, "Antoinette's mother tongue is presumably composite. She has grown up understanding the language of Annette, Christophine and Tia but also that of her father whose people . . . have been slave-owners for generations . . . in Jamaica."[22] This response speaks to a condition that has increasingly been receiving attention in Caribbean linguistic research. I think, for example, of Carrington's work on language acquisition in a Creole-speaking environment in which Trinidad is the location.

A few examples of the manoeuvres to which I referred will suffice. In terms of word and meaning, here is an example from a short story by Olive Senior, "Country of the One Eye God".[23] The story is a two-hander played out over no more than a day. It is a tragedy in which a grandson is prepared to murder his grandmother to have access to the money she is saving for her funeral. Among other things, Lalla underlines the differing perceptions of the same lexical item to Ma Bell, the grandmother, and Jacko, the grandson. Among the examples she gives is *dead*: "*Dead* for Jacko is final. In his view Ma Bell will soon 'dead and lef' the money. The concept of burial money is not one he can readily grasp. For MaBell, *dead* is not a terminal concept. Apart from her vision of attending her own glorious funeral, MaBell's convictions certainly include certainty of an afterlife."[24]

In terms of time expression, here is an example of the manipulation of tense and voice: in John Hearne's *Sure Salvation*,[25] the critic quotes the authorial comment that, on the ship, stuck on the ocean, "time itself must have been tricked, frozen by violence",[26] and comments that that message is as much encoded in narrative structuring and in tense manipulation as in actual wording. She goes on to illustrate this point:

> Time, both in sequence and in the duration of events, is repeatedly stressed. The opening of the novel marks the eternity of the crew's stagnation over days and then over weeks ("the ship was the still centre of a huge stillness" [p. 7]). Existential verbs hold action in abeyance and convey situation rather than process. Passive voice undermines the agency of the ship by shifting it, with its crew, to the role of patient of the action ("The barque was ringed. . . . Labour was invented. . . . Bursts of activity were succeeded. . . . They were tantalized" [p. 7]).[27]

Lalla comments on the language of a very different kind of text as an example of linguistic deviance, partly because of how unusual it is. She cites Winkler's *The Lunatic*,[28] where much of the language is downright crude: "*The Lunatic* is conspicuous in its open disregard for taboos. Deviance in language is here more than a support for the theme. Linguistic deviance, which is often a message that there is something to discover in the content, in this novel constitutes part of the message itself. Rule breaking is not only a strategy but also an important point of the utterance."[29] *The Lunatic* also illustrates the multi-codal language environment of the Caribbean and how it serves the artist's intention. A butcher has killed a goat. There are two reactions to the act and to the perpetrator, one expressed in English and the other in Jamaican Creole. I give you both as well as the critic's interpretation of the emotion behind each comment: " 'He is an artist,' Inga breathed. 'Him a butcher,' Aloysius muttered."[30] – "Inga romanticizes death, but she does so with the interest of a predator, 'stalking around it like a hunter'. Aloysius shrinks from it 'and would not meet the piercing stare of the decapitated head mounted on the ruins of bone and flesh'."[31]

I want to return to the matter of time expression and Lalla's take on how the Caribbean writer manipulates it. In the example from Hearne, the environment is English. In this example, we look at the "multidimensional time reference" at a point at which English and Creole meet. I am taking the opportunity to extend our view to Lalla, commenting not on prose but on poetry, a paper on Martin Carter's famous poem "The University of Hunger". She comments on an important Creole feature, the Creole verb, which is unchanging. It is the feature that most facilitates the convenient ambiguity the Caribbean artist exploits so well, for example in Olive Senior's short story "Ballad": "Creole may convey reference to past time without marking past tense." Lalla states this fact and points to "They come" repeated in the lines "They come treading in the hoofmarks of the mule / . . . They come from the distant village of the flood" where "the time may be present or past depending on whether the voice is English or Creole".[32]

In *Defining Jamaican Fiction*, the necessity for this special brand of critical analysis is validated again and again. The notion of "legibility" is given special attention. Insider and outsider to Caribbean language both need to understand the language in which Caribbean artists write. Lalla states:

> lexical items that are deceptively identical in form to those of an English base but conveying other meaning in Creole especially where the Creole speaker mentally pronounces the word so differently from its international counterpart as to render it unintelligible to the uninitiated. Thus the literary discourse subverts the imperial code to convey not only the written Standard but oral Creole. All this summed up formally as "secret encoding of Creole epistemes under guise of conformity (and with all the advantages of international 'legibility' ".[33]

I think of a chunk of dialogue from Olive Senior's title story in the *Discerner of Hearts* (1995) when the child of the house has a conversation with the helper concerning the Balmer in a balmyard in the village:

> "What is a balmyard Cissy?"
> "Where people go for healing."
> "What is healing?"
> "What people need when they have sickness."
> "Why they don't go to Dr. Carter?"
> "There is sick and then again there is sick."
> "But Mr. Burnham isn't a doctor?"
> "There is doctor and then there is doctor."[34]

Before I leave the book *Defining Jamaican Fiction*, I want to underline a statement of position articulated in it because I consider it important enough to be highlighted: "Departing from a position in which linguistic units are viewed as endowed with intrinsic meaning this book argues that 'Meaning without context is meaningless'."[35] This sentence suggests permanent movement beyond the sentence-based analysis on which so much early linguistic description has been built.

I realize that not every reader wants to understand the linguistic and discourse structures that inform the writer's craft or to appreciate the linguistic environment in which he or she creates, but for those who so wish, this kind of study is invaluable especially now when the creative writing of the region more and more includes the speech of the local people and their language as a mark of identification. Lalla looks at the history of the inclusion of Creole in Caribbean texts in a paper presented in Hawaii and sees that expansion as a phased progression beginning with the ventriloquist phase, "in which the colonizer textualizes (distorted) Creole in inscribing the 'invented' voice of the Other", on through censorship, "under which local verbal artists operate torn between strong oral traditions on the one hand and alien scribal conventions on the other", to an alternation phase in which "Code-shifting contributes to a hybrid discourse comprising plural and often dissonant voices. Privileging of the Creole in turn contributes to perspectival shift that relocates the speaker to the centre (rather than margin) of a valorized discourse which becomes an instrument of identity construction."[36]

The current phase is expansion, in which "[t]he indigenous voice occupies more if not all of the literary text and is drawn on to assert Caribbean perspective in rewriting imperial texts . . . Thus the sheer quantum of indigenous literature is enlarged. The Creole voice being privileged boundaries between official and vernacular discourses become permeable and (permitted) characteristics of their codes diffuse across the boundaries".[37] Put another way, in a later paper, Lalla describes the situation like this: "As Creole use expands over domains spreading more into public use rather than being restricted to private domestic use, Creole also spreads into written use rather than remaining exclusively in oral use or even in written representation of oral use. In other words, Creole in scribal discourse is no longer restricted to representation of dialogue. . . . This multidimensional change in the context of Caribbean literary discourse has definable linguistic implications".[38]

I am not comfortable with terms like "earlier" and "later". We have no idea when things are written; we only know when they come to our attention in a talk or a published paper, and with somebody like Lalla, in whose mind things are always in gestation, ideas are constantly being refined, such that those are terms begging to be inaccurate.

Twenty-two years after the publication of *Defining Jamaican Fiction* comes *Postcolonialisms: Caribbean Rereadings of Medieval English Discourse*,[39] which is Lalla's largest achievement to date, not merely in terms of size (439 pages), but in terms of what it attempts and achieves. This product gives a new meaning to the term "gestation", to which I said I would return. As Jean D'Costa (personal communication) tells it, the ideas that form the core of this study have been part of Lalla's interest since the days of undergraduate class discussions, when D'Costa lectured to her. Of course the work is all the better for these decades of delay/of gestation. The young scholar could not have dealt as efficiently with the theme as the mature scholar who has authored several articles and books in the area. Both her own craft and the development of discourse on literature have become more sophisticated in the thirty years or so.

Postcolonialisms makes a comparison between the postcolonial society that produced Middle English literature and the postcolonial society that produced Caribbean literature. The text admits that the situations are by no means identical: "Although the circumstances differ under which the plural societies were assembled and through which hybridization proceeded, although ethnicity and race are differently conceived, although the languages that interface in the context of multiculturality and power differentials demonstrate different linguistic structures, the resonances persist and are inescapably haunting."[40] And forestalling specific criticism, Lalla underlines one aspect by adding that "the absence of comparable racial difference in those contacts that contributed to Middle English discourse need not preclude an argument for postcoloniality in Middle English".[41]

Boldly claiming her right to pursue the study, Lalla writes: "Having lived in what hegemonic cultures regard as exotic spaces fraught with marvelous reality, the Caribbean critic is especially equipped to demystify a medieval space stereotyped as at once backward and exotic and laden with superstition. Such colonial inscription of a misunderstood space is familiar territory, as is a hybrid culture encoded in vernacular literature that is characterized by a dialogic discourse."[42] Parallels, if not similarities, exist within the bodies of writing, within the cultures within which they are set: a pilgrimage, for example, has features of Carnival, offering a "performative dimension of hybridity".[43]

The Canterbury Tales, Chaucer's famous pilgrimage with all its shenanigans, is the major text of Lalla's consideration from the early/foreign side of the comparisons. The Pardoner's self-conferred mandate to "rant, rave and misbehave" is indeed she says "a Caribbean carnivalesque directive".[44] She relates the calypsonian's confession to the Pardoner's directive in this way: "In Trinidad, the calypsonian relates his encounter with ghoulish dancers in a 'Jumbie Jamboree' 'Back to back, belly to belly / I don't give a damn, I done dead already.' "[45]

The commentary runs: "Attitudes towards Pilgrimage were ambivalent in the later Middle Ages, pilgrimage having come to be associated with outrageous behaviour. The setting of the tale thus bears resemblance to festivals such as ole mas', a pre-carnival celebration in Trinidad and Jonkanoo, a hybrid tradition in Jamaica, centering around a masquerade band."[46] This kind of relationship seems obvious after Lalla has made the point.

Earlier in the book, she mentions "dislocated consciousness" in "The Wife's Lament", "the first poem of feminine dispossession extant in the literature of England"[47] and notes the extraordinary resonance with *Wide Sargasso Sea*, "in which the location of Antoinette as narrator remains uncertain even as she relates the circumstances . . . that led to her death". There she writes: "Little comparison has been made between this early Caribbean discourse of feminine marronage and very early texts of feminine marronage in British literature . . . Comparison of *Wide Sargasso Sea* and the Old English 'Wife's Lament' throws a curious light on all these works."[48]

There are echoes here as well of the concept of marronage, which forms the basis of text selection in the earlier *Defining Jamaican Fiction*. In the later book, *Postcolonialisms*, Lalla speaks of the "growth of the vernacular literature in the developing society of England and the implications of this discourse for resistance".[49] Marronage hangs in the air as I pronounce that word.

Postcolonialisms is by no means the first work to connect the old (empire) with the new (colony) in what seemed at first an unlikely link. Lamming, in *The Pleasures of Exile*,[50] uses a much later text, Shakespeare's *Tempest*, in which is established the Prospero/Caliban (master/slave) relationship. This has become such a commonplace theme in Caribbean critical writing that a quotation from Nettleford, which heads the concluding chapter of *Postcolonialisms*, can run in part "if the new masters choose to become Prosperos, they will discover that they too will soon have their Calibans and Ariels who will be no less eager to become free of a debilitating dependency".[51] Nettleford writes this, confident that there is no need for explanation.

Postcolonialisms is, however, the work that has gone farthest into the past in terms of history and is the most comprehensive in depth and breadth of coverage. Lalla is conscious of the point on which she stands; her advantageous location in relation to the material with which she is working. I see her atop a maypole looking out and around as the ribbons interweave at the impulse of the child dancers' movements:

> We are justified in applying experience from the discourse of developing societies to societies that were new so long ago as to have been thought of for so many centuries as "old". . . . Similarly, ways of knowing that we generally treat as "new" because they are relevant to recent developments in our own time may well have constituted a dimension of ideology in an earlier culture of what was then a developing society.[52]

Throughout the book there are reminders, however, of the limitations of the study, including in terms of the texts it is able to work on, and while there is confidence that she is capable of doing what she set out to do, there is no arrogance as Lalla moves through selected texts and makes the connections under her unflinching gaze. Finally in considering this academic work, I am reminded of priests in the Anglican community, introducing the Gospel reading as a "continuation of the holy gospel", even when the selections are taken from different apostles. In my mind I hear "to be continued, to be continued, to be continued", for I am sure she has much more to say.

CREATIVE WRITING

You would think that what I have described, together with a full portfolio of university duties such as head of department and a member of various committees, was work enough for Lalla. But always, in gestation just beneath the surface of her life, have been products of Lalla's creative imagination. One might also be tempted to think that the activity of looking closely at other people's imaginative output might be a disincentive for creativity or might lead the writer to a kind of pedantic delivery because of excessive consciousness of the reader's need. But no, every ten years or so, Lalla, the fiction writer, produces an excellent novel. Here, as if to exploit freedom from the strictures of academic writing, she moves easily within the world of the creative imagination.

As in the academic enterprise, there is the preoccupation with history, so there is in the creative writing. *Arch of Fire,* published in 1998, is a historical novel set in Jamaica.[53] On the dust cover, it is stated that Barbara Lalla "traces

Taino, Maroon and other paths to reveal the intertwining of Jamaican roots and transports the reader through five hundred years of incendiary Jamaican history". It is a "gripping family saga and Jamaica's epic novel". It *is* gripping. I finished it as I reached the airport one summer when I had had surgery and had to use a wheelchair. I had the same attendant going as coming. She asked, "You finish the book?" She was surprised that I had. It is a fat book but interesting and well written.

Bear in mind Professor Lalla's daunting academic output, her service to the university and to students: thirty or more postgraduate degrees achieved and in progress; eight books, some co-edited, several academic articles. Marvel that within another twelve years she produces another fat novel, presumably gestating all that time.

In 2010, Lalla's *Cascade* was published, initiating the University of the West Indies Press's foray into publishing fiction.[54] In this book, Lalla looks at ageing, portraying in honest, sympathetic ways the passage of time as it affects people who must make moves they could hardly have predicted. Given all that has been said about Lalla's engagement with language and with history, it is hardly surprising that, on the dust cover, Nicholas Laughlin observes that the author "delineates the separate characters through the nuances of their speech and memories and draws a poignant portrait of educated middle-class Jamaicans from Independence to the present".

I want to quote a comment from a foreign (outsider) reader on the Internet. She says the novel is beautifully written, which we know. But I am interested in the language and the reaction of the foreign reader. After all, we have been talking about this. Consider the following comment online: "In the beginning the challenge to understand the accented speech of some Jamaican characters especially the underprivileged and uneducated slowed my reading pace. But Barbara Lalla knew when to pull back, using these characters primarily to illustrate important developments, or to illuminate backstory, or show the personalities of major characters."[55] This is the "legibility" that Lalla talks about, and she has succeeded.

NOTES

1.   Jean D'Costa and Barbara Lalla, *Voices in Exile: Jamaican Texts of the Eighteenth and Nineteenth Centuries* (Tuscaloosa: University of Alabama Press, 1989).

2.   Barbara Lalla and Jean D'Costa, *Language in Exile: Three Hundred Years of Jamaican Creole* (Tucaloosa: University of Alabama Press, 1990).

3.   Carolyn Cooper, *Noises in the Blood: Orality, Gender and the "Vulgar" Body of Jamaican Culture* (Durham, NC: Duke University Press, 1995).

4.   In Giovanni Covi, Joan Anim-Addo, Velma Pollard, and Carla Sassi, *Caribbean-Scottish Relations: Colonial and Contemporary Inscriptions in History, Language and Literature* (London: Mango, 2007).

5.   Alison G. Irvine, "Defining Good English in Jamaica: Language Variation and Language Ideology in an Agency of the Jamaican State" (PhD diss., University of the West Indies, 2005).

6.   Lalla and D'Costa, "Languages in Exile", xiv.

7.   Ibid., xiii.

8.   Barbara Lalla, "Sources for a History of Jamaican Creole", *Carib* 3 (1979): 37–51.

9.   Barbara Lalla, "Quaco Sam: A Relic of Archaic Jamaican Speech", *Jamaica Journal* 45 (1981): 20–29.

10. Barbara Lalla, "The Consonant System of Early Jamaican Creole", *Carib* 3 (1983): 37–51.

11. Barbara Lalla, "Tracing Elusive Phonological Elements in Early Jamaican Creole", in *Varieties of English around the World: Focus on the Caribbean*, ed. Manfred Görlach and John Holm (Amsterdam: John Benjamins, 1986), 117–32.

12. Barbara Lalla, *Defining Jamaican Fiction: Marronage and the Discourse of Survival* (Tuscaloosa: University of Alabama Press, 1996).

13. Jean D'Costa, "The West Indian Novelist and Language: A Search for a Literary Medium", in *Studies in Caribbean Language*, ed. Lawrence Carrington, Dennis Craig and Ramon Todd Dandare (St Augustine, Trinidad and Tobago: Society for Caribbean Linguistics, 1983), 252–65.

14. Maureen Warner-Lewis, "Samuel Selvon's Linguistic Extravaganza: Mose Ascending", in *Critical Issues in West Indian Literature*, ed. E. Smilowitz and R. Knowles (Parkersburgh, IA: Caribbean Books, 1984), 101–11.

15. Velma Pollard, "Mother Tongue: Voices in the Writing of Olive Senior and Lorna Goodison", in *Motherlands: An Anthology of Critical Writing on Black Women Writers from Africa, the Caribbean, South Asia, Great Britain*, ed. S. Nasta (London: Women's Press, 1991): 239–45.

16. Merle Hodge, "A Study of Language in Trinidad and Tobago Prose Fiction of the

Twentieth Century with Special Reference to the Works of Earl Lovelace" (PhD diss., University of the West Indies, 2007).

17. Lalla, *Defining*.

18. Barbara Lalla, " A Sociolinguistic Approach to Critical Analysis in the Caribbean" In *Studies in Caribbean Language II*, edited by Pauline Christie et al. (St Augustine, Trinidad and Tobago: Multimedia Production Centre, School of Education, 1998), 112–27.

19. Lalla, *Defining*, 3.

20. Ibid.

21. Jean Rhys, *Wide Sargasso Sea* (Harmondsworth, UK: Penguin, 1966).

22. Lalla, *Defining*, 70–71.

23. Olive Senior, "Country of the One Eye God", in *Summer Lightning and Other Stories* (Kingston: Longman, 1986).

24. Lalla, *Defining*, 110.

25. John Hearne, *The Sure Salvation* (New York: St Martin's Press, 1982).

26. Lalla, *Defining*, 159.

27. Ibid.

28. Anthony Winkler, *The Lunatic* (Secaucus, NJ: Lyle Stuart, 1987).

29. Lalla, *Defining*, 139.

30. Winkler, *Lunatic*, 111.

31. Lalla, *Defining*, 144.

32. Barbara Lalla, "Conceptual Perspectives on Time and Timelessness in Martin Carter's "University of Hunger", in *All Are Involved: The Art of Martin Carter*, ed. Stewart Brown (Leeds: Peepal Tree Press, 2000), 106.

33. Lalla, *Defining*, 198.

34. Olive Senior, *Discerner of Hearts* (New York: Twayne Publishers, 1994), 3–4.

35. Lalla, *Defining*, 128.

36. Barbara Lalla, Abstracts from Plenaries, Society for Pidgin and Creole Linguistics Summer Conference (University of Hawai'I, Honolulu, 2003), 2.

37. Ibid.

38. Hazel Simmons-McDonald and Ian Robertson, eds., *Exploring the Boundaries of Caribbean Languages* (Kingston: University of the West Indies Press).

39. Barbara Lalla, *Postcolonialisms: Caribbean Readings of Medieval English Discourse* (Kingston: University of the West Indies Press, 2010).

40. Ibid., 28.

41. Ibid.

42. Ibid., 27.

43. Ibid., 29.

44. Ibid., 318.

45. Ibid., 295.

46. Ibid., 294.

47. Ibid., 70–73.

48. Ibid., 96, 95.

49. Ibid., 46.

50. George Lamming, *The Pleasures of Exile* (Ann Arbor: University of Michigan Press, 1960).

51. Lalla, *Postcolonialisms*, 308.

52. Ibid., 321.

53. Barbara Lalla, *Arch of Fire: A Jamaican Family Saga* (Kingston: Kingston Publishers, 1998).

54. Barbara Lalla, *Cascade: A Novel* (Kingston: University of the West Indies Press, 2010).

55. Mary McIntyre, review, http://maryemcintyre.wordpress.com/2011/01/02/cascade-a-novel-book-review-by-mary-e-mcintyre/, 2 January 2011.

3.

TOWARDS A "WHOLENESS OF VISION"

Criticism Lalla's Way

[JENNIFER RAHIM]

ON THE OCCASION OF A formal retirement, one courts redundancy to begin
with a statement like this: Barbara Lalla is an academic and creative writer of
no small stature. Nevertheless it is a risk worth taking. Her output is incredible;
so is the breadth of her influence as a scholar, teacher and mentor. Her expert-
ise and interests span a broad spectrum of skills and disciplines that encom-
pass linguistics, discourse analysis, literary criticism and (although she may
object) theory, history, cultural studies and imaginative writing. When much
more than duty compels one to gather some thoughts that would express grat-
itude for so valued and admired a colleague as she has been and continues to
be, a certain realization strikes those left behind, so to speak. It is this: We have
no claim to a void. We are the inheritors of an invaluable resource that is as
much a testament to the extraordinary exercise of mind as it is of spirit. So her
leave-taking, much like that of her fellow retirees, Bridget Brereton and Ian
Robertson, lays out the challenge or, perhaps more accurately, the responsibility to begin decoding what that mountain of work has been saying. I firmly
believe such an exercise is necessary for going forward. Already that process is
well on the way. Her scholarship has attracted the lively interest of her peers
and students, both within and beyond the region. This chapter hopes to join
in that dialogue in its consideration of some of the insights her criticism offers
to Caribbean literary and perhaps cultural studies.

A literature is shaped by the sociohistorical and cultural realities of the world
or worlds it addresses and so will necessarily produce a certain quality of critical
sensibility. More than anything, the long interrogation of the identity called

"Caribbean-ness" has been about naming the ongoing development of a particular type of sensibility or feeling. Barbara Lalla is a critic in full possession
of the state of consciousness that gives expression to the as yet little interrogated and relatively new arrival on the global literary scene called Caribbean
criticism. In her groundbreaking magnum opus, *Postcolonialisms: Caribbean
Rereading of Medieval English Discourse*, she writes with the unforced authority
of a lived conviction, "Caribbean criticism is well placed to mediate in the postcolonial debate",[1] a line that will undoubtedly be much quoted and debated.
The groundings of that bold claim lie in her first book, *Defining Jamaican Fiction: Marronage and the Discourse of Survival*.[2] There she mobilizes the trope of
the maroon as an indigenous approach to interpreting Jamaican fiction. For
now, I wish to give some attention to her choice of the word "mediate". It
implies a third-party positioning assigned to an impartial facilitator at once
knowledgeable of the key issues at stake and adept in opening the dialogue to
expand the horizon of understanding of all parties, even pointing the way to
resolution. Caribbean criticism, Lalla asserts, has arrived at a place at which it
can meaningfully participate in the literary academy's most urgent questions.
These include, but certainly transcend, conceptualizations of the nation, aesthetic and identity debates, canonicity wars about inclusion and influence, the
geopolitics of literary production and consumption, and the very nature of postcoloniality itself.

   The first time I encountered the word "mediate" used with any relevance to
Caribbean literary studies was in an essay by George Lamming, entitled "Western Education and the Caribbean Intellectual".[3] Speaking within the context of
the region's emergence from colonialism and the resultant formation of the
colonized by a "Western" tradition of knowledge, Lamming charges the
Caribbean "intellectual" with the responsibility to form a "native" "inventory"
drawn "from within" the shared body of lived experience.[4] Among those he
classifies as the "intellectual" is the "literary critic", whose task is to be a "medi-
ator of the text", that is, to "link the human substance of the text to the collective
consciousness, the continuing social reality which has, in fact, nurtured the
imagination of the writers".[5]

   I bring together these two contexts because Lamming, in a sense, helps to
unlock the significance of Lalla's use of the word to position Caribbean criticism at the helm of the postcolonial debate, which, she is well aware, references
histories and human circumstances engendered by the colonial project and
now form the bedrock of our contemporary postcolonial ethos. By relinking

the literary text, like cultural discourse in general, to the "human substance" of its creation, Lamming rearticulates a wholly *humanizing* facility for which literature has long been valued and positions criticism as a participant in that (re)education process. Caribbean literary production, however, is cited as a formidable "occasion" of challenge to the Eurocentric privilege of its traditions and demonstrates, as Edward Said puts it, how "it is possible to be critical of humanism in the name of humanism".[6] The mediation of the enduring "truths" of this vital conversation between society and its contributing (con)texts is therefore what the Caribbean criticism best serves.

What has this body of literature, drawn from the region's "collective consciousness", been saying about itself? What lessons of sensibility are to be derived from the "human substance" on which the region's literary imagination is nourished? These seem the questions that are criticism's most urgent business, not that they should be addressed once and for all. They form a part of that ever-renewing effort at collective self-understanding that also implies a critique of the course of human relations and the modes of thinking that have impacted attitudes and behaviours. Lalla has been very engaged with these questions. Her enduring interest in reading the literary arts as a story of human confrontations with power, especially those histories in which transcultural merging has destabilized hierarchical convention through processes of resistance and transformation. Although her linguist's formation is ever-present, the inner preoccupation of her criticism is with the implications of having emerged from a civilization like the Caribbean's: the mistakes of "contact", the challenges of old systems of power and privilege, and the recreative outcomes that express how we "make life" together.

Very early, Lalla establishes her interest in identifying an indigenous aesthetic as being integral to the development of a "native" critical language and interpretative perspective. In *Defining Jamaican Fiction*, she therefore gives focus to the "perspective of marronage" as a distinctive feature of that literature.[7] One key aspect of her study is the case it makes for the importance of respecting the integrity of a national literature, a category that can be easily suppressed in a generalized regional rubric like "Caribbean", not to mention the popular transnational configuration of the canon aided by the diasporan trajectory of postcolonial studies. Without denying the existence of trans-island commonalities, she describes the goal of *Defining Jamaican Fiction* as "an attempt to distinguish a national fiction within the Caribbean aesthetic".[8] Further, while acknowledging that the "story of the Maroons certainly seizes on the Caribbean imagination" she notes this is "nowhere more so than in Jamaica"[9] and that the phenomenon of marronage can "supply some of the parameters of a literary discourse characteristic of Jamaican fiction".[10] Such an approach respects historical and sociocultural specificities of the individual nation spaces while acknowledging a regional coherence and thereby impacts how the literary historiography of the Caribbean is mapped.

Lalla's argument is that "Caribbean literature begins with a conscious effort, in Jamaica, to build a national rather than a regional literature".[11] The implication is that a literary criticism propelled by a regionalist thrust, anxious to claim a West Indian or Caribbean literature, can inadvertently suppress the independent nation-building agendas a particular literature served. This had been the case for Jamaican fiction, since what was classified as "West Indian" by critics, such as Kenneth Ramchand, comprised novelists who were, in the first forty years of the twentieth century, overwhelmingly Jamaican.[12] Indeed, there are few anglophone territories to match Jamaica's prominence in the development of West Indian or anglophone Caribbean literature, other than Trinidad and Guyana. The former island, for instance, has a literary tradition that goes back to the nineteenth century, as well as an influential early twentieth-century literary renaissance when magazines like *Trinidad* and the *Beacon* became avenues for literary expression in the 1930s. This creative movement paralleled the growing "anti-establishment" discontent that opened the way to nationalistic aspirations.[13]

To acknowledge the distinctiveness of a Jamaican or Trinidadian fiction, as Lalla rightly argues, "is not intended as a denial of Caribbean literature, of its reality and wholeness".[14] The two realities are codependent. A sense of belonging to a "transnational household", as Lamming argues, is without question a mark of Caribbean-ness that does not threaten allegiances to separate nation-states.[15] Nevertheless, the danger of any umbrella categorization is the occlusion of some of the very local particularities and nuances attributable to the diversity on which cultural enrichment depends – as can happen with critical discourses that apply the broad brush to define pan-Caribbean poetics.

The story of the Caribbean's literary canon is therefore incomplete without giving recognition to the desire for a national literature which existed at its very foundations (and this is by no means an exhaustive way of belonging). Importantly, Lalla by no means skirts the difficulties that attend identitarian claims at both the national and regional levels, particularly for a canon marked by so much variance as well as commonality, and where the borders of home often transcend the island and extend into metropolitan places like the United States and Canada.[16] The vital place of the nation in the literature's indisputable transnational architecture resonates with Sandra Pouchet Paquet's assertion that "the ideal of a national literature has a role to play in the development of a national literature, and that the nation state provides a legitimate legal framework for developing and defending the resources of a community".[17]

Paquet's position is that "Caribbean literary culture" is one that "shifts the focus away from the ideal of a national literature as rooted and self-determining, to focus instead on hybrid cosmopolitan experiences that tend to blur if not erase, the physical boundaries of the nation state".[18] The blurring of the nation space is, however, precisely what Lalla's approach works against, where necessary, as it is a vital shaper of aesthetic and content. Both elements inform how we tell the history of what is called Caribbean literature and so make the case for a paradigm that has an eye for the local within the whole. On the one hand, such an approach resists the de-localization tendencies of postmodern aesthetics and, on the other hand, it is a corrective to literary histories that "present Caribbean literature as beginning with Britain" and the arrival there of writers like C.L.R. James, Edgar Mittelholzer, Samuel Selvon, George Lamming and others.[19]

The validation of cultural and geographic location is an ideological positioning that sees these as central to shaping literary discourse and its poetics, which is well established in both *Defining Jamaican Fiction* and *Postcolonialisms*. The analytical drive of both books affirms locatedness in contrast to theoretical trends that favour dislocation, as had been the case with much of the "posts". Caribbean scholarship and creative writing, for Lalla, cannot be simplistically delimited or authenticated by geography and nationality. She anticipates the need to insist on the importance of these categories in light of the currency postcolonial thought has afforded transnationalism's transitory character. Allison Donnell, for instance, expresses her reservation with the outward movement of the black Atlantic trajectory. Referencing writers like Olive Senior, Donnell argues that in "a critical moment in which the states of in-betweenness, migration and exile have accrued value through postcolonial theorizations to the point where dislocation is regarded almost as a virtue in itself, Senior's writing helps us to explore what it means for those people who have to stay, who choose to stay, or for whom moving on is not moving up.[20]

With the publication of *Postcolonialisms*, the national focus adopted in *Defining Jamaican Fiction* gives way to a more expansive exercise in the unique

Caribbean perspective Lalla brings to the rereading of British Medieval literature. Her discussion of masquerade and the grotesque in the English Middle
Ages, for instance, proceeds from links struck with the "transgressive impulse"
and "carnivalesque disorder" so fundamental to Caribbean culture but also par-
ticularized in relation to the Jamaican Jonkanoo parade and Trinidad and
Tobago's Carnival with its *mas'* and *ole mas'*.[21] Similarly, Lalla draws parallels
with discourse types like Chaucer's "Pardoner's Tale" and Caribbean trickster
discourse, which are evident in the relationship she suggests between Trinidadian "robber-talk" and the Pardoner's posturing.[22]

With Lalla, then, there is a conscious effort to avoid the missteps of a generalized approach to Caribbean cultural expressions given the diversity that
equally comprises the individual, nation and region and so requires the critic
to be attentive to the numerous circumstances that blur the "inner as well as
outer parameters" of such categories.[23] As a result, as with her study of
Jamaican fiction, flattened reductions are avoided without denying the existence of national or pan-Caribbean similarities. Nevertheless, extensive comparative analysis is recommended. The choice to focus on the one "factor of
obvious relevance to the definition of a literature", that is, "the language that
is its medium" is therefore a means to circumvent unproven presumptions
often derived from stereotyping.[24]

Interestingly, Gordon Rohlehr, in "The Problem of the Problem of Form",
argues for the usefulness of a continuum-theory framework to accommodate
the anglophone Caribbean's "literary situation", in which writers routinely nav-
igate an aesthetic that embraces oral and modernist traditions.[25] Lalla takes up
his cue in "Opening *Salt*: The Oral Scribal Continuum in Caribbean Narrative",[26] supporting the applicability of continuum theory to read Caribbean narratives. It is therefore also possible that, in theorizing about the development
of Caribbean literature, such a framework may be helpful to keep faith with distinctions at the level of the national within the regional rubric. Dougla poetics,
for instance, has emerged as a centric aesthetic and political feature of Trinidadian fiction. This term, coined by Shalini Puri in 1994 to describe Indo- and
Afro-Trinidadian relations, is intended to create symbolic resources for concep-
tualizing and negotiating hybridity, with the purpose of generating unity and
unmasking power relations. It points to the influence of demographics on the
politics of nationalism and literary production. The African and Indian Trinidadian interface therefore represents a significant distinction from Jamaican fiction, even as both literatures may intersect on many issues of theme and style

as well as comprise the general category called Caribbean literature. A continuum model facilitates such patterns of difference and similarity.

Lalla, of course, is an innately eclectic scholar but has been especially credited for her role in pioneering the application of critical discourse analysis to Caribbean literature. This is the guiding methodology for both her seminal books of criticism, *Defining Jamaican Fiction* and *Postcolonialisms*. In fact in the latter, in which she brings a unique Caribbean perspective to her rereading of British medieval literature, she admits that her process facilitates a "social, literary and linguistic interaction" that produces a "hybrid discourse".[27] Her linguist's attraction to decoding the language, literature's medium, intersects even if differently, with Lamming's, who positions language at the heart of the evolution of Caribbean civilization. In "Language and the Politics of Ethnicity", Lamming writes: "In order to prepare ourselves for conflict (and conflict must be accepted as a norm and not a distortion), we must remind ourselves of the unique character of this movement of peoples into this archipelago, and remember that in this struggle of finding self through language and discovering language through self, we have a situation in which many contestants are making rival claims on our attention."[28]

Language, then, is that pivotal negotiator of contact and exchange. It is the medium of expression and transgression that records the tense process of insertion undertaken by the many peoples who have contributed to making the Caribbean a home. Further, in marking language as a site of contestation or creative conflict involved in the demand for recognition and space, Lamming simultaneously names it as a key instrument of power. Lalla, in my view, is primarily engaged in mapping this process of insertion and assertion and the destabilization of conventions and transformations that ensue. Caribbeanness has always been wrought through exercises in the reinterpretation of received texts, along with the creation of indigenous oral and scribal modes of communication with the two often intersecting. The election, for instance, to study "the perspectival features associated with marronage" is for Lalla an opportunity to make a unique contribution to the debates on the language of Caribbean literature. She argues that the scholarship at the time was limited to the consideration of "a writer's choice of alternative registers" as in the case of the "authenticity" agenda of "nation language" pursuits and the stylistic approach to defining Caribbean narration.[29] The analysis of perspective of particular character type therefore expanded how Caribbean literary language use was understood and discussed.

Although their publication is separated by a twelve-year span, her two books of literary criticism are testaments, from different vantage points, to her fascination with the formation and evolution of literary discourse as indicators of spatiotemporal data and ideological positions that related to place and time, identity and belonging, survival and the strategic absorptions that transpire in societies, emerging from the collision of unevenly weighted cultures. In *Defining Jamaican Fiction*, her focus is trained on the "maroon" perspective as a distinctive feature of narration. In her study of medieval literary discourse in *Postcolonialisms*, the emphasis is on applying a Caribbean perspective as a reading position or framework that "throws light on evolving connections between the language of a new literature and the sense that literature expresses location in place, of affiliation with a group or with a series of groups . . . overlapping or intersecting in ways that produce distinctiveness or particularity".[30]

The multiple aspects comprising the architecture of meanings that accrue to her careful perspectival analysis of the "maroon" are well documented in *Defining Jamaican Fiction*. My main interest, however, is to consider some of the major aspects of the contribution she makes to the debates in Caribbean literary studies on the articulation of an "indigenous" poetics. Her analysis of the "perspective of marronage" in *Defining Jamaican Fiction* is a key starting point. It lays the foundation for her broader Caribbean framework, which later guides her analysis of medieval literature in *Postcolonialisms*.

In the first instance, Jamaica's history of Maroon slave rebellions, which supplies the concept of marronage, is recognized as having become part of the allegorical framework of Jamaica's fiction in ways that have expanded interpretations of the historical figure. Lalla's objective is therefore to explore the "attributes of the maroon character", which include a range of categories over time from travellers to fugitives, the traumatized, recluses, outcasts and rebels and those in "psychological wildernesses" of various kinds.[31] These include individuals and groups rendered marginal or alien by normalized perceptions of sanity versus insanity, criteria for defining civilization as opposed to barbarism, and experiences of exile and belonging based on gender roles or class hierarchies. In so doing, Lalla achieves a transhistorical and trans-ethnic applicability of an indigenous trope that reconfigures and broadens its usual "restorationist" viewpoint beyond African cultural survival.[32] Further, although recognized as distinctively Jamaican, the relevance to the broader Caribbean and beyond is preserved.

Lalla concurs with established narratologists that perspective is the principal feature of narrative and so allows one to distinguish it from crudely assigned authorial positions as its study attempts a "logical" analysis of a "speaker's orientation to events".[33] The text is addressed as a discursive document through which "different facets of truth" are represented so that "the reader can construct a more holistic vision than was previously available".[34] If, as Lalla claims, "the driving force" of Jamaican fiction is "a commitment to truth" (certainly not an exclusive trait), then that truth is never singular or absolute but rather the sum of the lived realties, offered by a network of shifts in viewpoints the texts offer, as well as the "presuppositions" readers bring to them. In this regard, perspectival analysis is an engagement with the contexts of attitudinal stances, which is always a historically constructed, spatially and socioculturally determined dynamic.

The region's literature, having emerged from the coexistence of diverse and intersecting ways of seeing and knowing marked by ethnicity, geography, gender, language and faith, supplies rich lessons about the politics of cultural fusion and change. A concept like a "marooned consciousness"[35] certainly represents an effort to invent an indigenous critical language. Reading marronage as a feature of narrative perspective, however, is an invaluable testament to the limitations of narrowly interpreted enthnocentric approaches to Caribbean literary and cultural arts. Lalla's primary resource in *Defining Jamaican Fiction*, for instance, is a range of writers from varying backgrounds. These include writers like John Hearne, Erna Brodber, Henry Winkler and Olive Senior. Their narratives reveal how shifting and converging identity positions related to a variety of socially constructed notions of difference and otherness are sometimes easily destabilized.

Lalla therefore notes with respect to the exploration of "feelings of homelessness" within the very Jamaica that should be home, that the fiction "departs radically from simple polarities, such as black/white, exploited/exploiter, and so on that have contributed to stereotyping in Caribbean literature".[36] This breakdown in binaries leads her to the conclusion that "[l]ike the regional literature as a whole Jamaican literature is distinguished from the black writing model in that it is less race centred, less hinged to the philosophy of negritude".[37] Further while the region's commonalities with the postcolonial community are not in question, even those affinities cannot be comfortably accepted unquestioned. She notices, for instance, how Jamaican literature interrupts neat classifications such as the "imperial-colonial dialectic" employed by Ashcroft, Griffins and Tiffin.[38] Using Brodber's "resurgence of voices that have been pressed beyond the boundaries of existence" in *Myal* as an example, she argues that to "speak of a distinctive Jamaican literature is no more to deny its relationship with other literature in English than to deny its closer relationship with English literature of the Caribbean".[39]

The multiple affiliations that inform Caribbean writing will certainly defy any dualistic framework defined too simplistically by margin-centre resistance. The literature's canonical interdependency is but an extension of an identity condition. Lalla finds it necessary to remain open to the way, for instance, Jamaican narratives "depart from regional vision"[40] or how, by giving consideration to the "affinities and differences", texts as diverse as *Wide Sargasso Sea*, *Myal* and the Old English "Wife's Lament", explore "female marronage" and "raise the question of how much British literature should be considered imperial".[41] Intertextuality therefore has to be read not just as imperial canonical resistance but as both "strategy" and "theme", simultaneously "endemic to education and creativity".[42]

One would also imagine therefore that categories given to texts such as "imperial", "postcolonial" and even "Caribbean" are made questionable by the very blanket assumptions that engineer their formulations. Monolithic categories grouping authors and their subjects alike, as well as"two-dimensional" paradigms,[43] are inadequate, as even the question of healing historical injustice returns to a relational or reciprocal formula. A text like *Myal*, for example, "takes current Caribbean preoccupation with neocolonial trauma beyond binarism . . .; shared responsibility for marronage and graded possibilities for locating the consciousness rather than mutually exclusive loci of margins and centres".[44] The analysis of "shifts" in perspective seems a useful way to avoid defining literary cultures as varied and heterogeneous as the Caribbean's in pure or exclusive terms. If not, one would then tend to rely too simplistically on highly politicized and easily misapplied criteria related to race, gender, class, language, nationality and geographical location, categories that are themselves constantly deconstructed. Whether on the basis of the employment of the oral and scribal, the standard and the vernacular, assumed insider and outsider positioning, the literature leads Lalla to the riveting conclusion that Jamaican fiction is a discourse that "redefines civilization. . . to reveal the fluidity of truth about power, reason, and responsibility. In so doing, the discourse replaces stereotypes of past victimization and exploitation with an indigenous vision of essential humanity in a present for which all are responsible and of an untried shore to which it is possible to bring only native abilities."[45]

The very intertextuality that defines a Caribbean canon is a product of the region's identity space and so anticipates Lalla's move in *Postcolonialisms* towards a rereading of the British canon, so foundational to the anglophone Caribbean. Interestingly, her insistence on enforcing a Caribbean-derived approach to rereading that literature actually signals the defining ethic of her critical practice. This ethic, I believe, is embodied by a seminal phrase she supplies in a recent essay, "Metastance and Re-Membering: Caribbean Postscripting of the British Canon": Criticism's function is to be at the service of mediating a "wholeness of vision".[46] This democracy of practice is a sensibility that has been nurtured by the very nature of Caribbean culture and her linguist's fidelity to the words on the page, that is, the language of literature itself.

I say more about Lalla's contribution to the postcolonial debate in "Postcolonialism at the Crossroads: A Precursor to Rerouting Anancy".[47] I wish to add, however, that the Caribbean postcolonial (to borrow Puri's formulation[48]) demonstrates the value in today's global cultural environment for a critical practice that, like Lalla's, is oriented to what is arguably, in the best sense, a universal viewpoint. By this I mean one that balances differences, whether ethnic, attitudinal or otherwise, with the common of the whole. As such, it remains open to an ever-growing understanding of the human condition but at the same time is able to challenge the established parameters (often related to power) that legitimize human experience and indeed what it means to be human. In *Defining Jamaican Fiction*, Lalla's study of the "outsider" in texts like Rhys's *Wide Sargasso Sea*[49] and Winkler's treatment of "madness" in *The Lunatic*[50] are most pertinent.

The special gift of the region's history has been the challenge, to paraphrase Lovelace, of welcoming every Other[51] and the retraining of presumptions that comes with having to accommodate the ways in which variance and heterogeneity push at established boundaries and frames of seeing and understanding. The region's literature is a primary resource for encountering this most profound humanizing exercise of relations. It would be impossible for the inner dynamics of this literature's wrestling with the traumas and transformations that characterize the new world it maps to not shape a critical practice. In *Postcolonialisms*, it is no wonder that she writes with firm confidence that being "well versed in the postcolonial experience" makes "Caribbean criticism well placed to mediate in the postcolonial debate" and further, that the region has a "take or leave it" attitude to postcolonial criticism itself.[52] Her adoption of a Caribbean "metastance"[53] in *Postcolonialisms* is no doubt an extension of her interest in narratology, particularly the investigation of perspective and the active role of the reader as a cultural agent in this regard.

Lalla's deliberate redirection of the authority of the gaze from the colonized to the colonizers testifies to a self-assigned privilege of perspective against a history that denied that right. The privileging of a Caribbean point of view, however, is not a suppression of the so-called master texts or to produce polarized divides between the literary traditions of the colonizer and (ex) colonized. Apart from asserting presence, the primary purpose of enforcing the legitimacy of the historically marginalized "look" is to enrich the process of interpretation by allowing the viewer "to embrace conceptual and attitudinal choices instead of remaining bound by choice-less adherence to convention.[54]

It is always possible to contend that viewers or readers are interpellated in ways of which they are sometimes unconscious and so can inhibit the "transcendence" of fixity that narratology claims to help circumvent. Lalla, however, remains convinced of the benefits. Moreover, she makes a strong case for the Caribbean postscripting of British canonical texts, arguing that it is a "crucial dimension of Caribbean criticism" as it "looks back at matters long regarded as already settled, at material regarded as privileged beyond question, so as to detect and inscribe something more and, probably, something other than the established readings.[55] This approach is far different from the crude subversion of the colonizer's text, as can happen in postcolonial intertextual discourse where it is identified as acts of resistance to the Othering stereotypes and conventions often circulated by the texts of empire. Rather it points to a more interdependent paradigm that impacts canonical as much as identity debates.

In *Postcolonialisms*, Lalla's fascination with the manner in which life, language and literature interrupt binaries to demonstrate the interrelations among similarities and differences that demarcate identities is taken to a different level. There, she self-describes the philosophy of her methodology as a hybrid positioning that locates itself on the "shearing fault line between First and Third Worlds".[56] The radical interfacing of British medieval literature, its aesthetic, linguistic features and sociopolitical concerns, with Caribbean and postcolonial debates closes the distance between their traditions, reconfiguring in the process every possible historical, geographical, linguistic, aesthetic and canonical border.

Ultimately, however, it is the collective human story that infuses Lalla's critical sensibility even as she is committed to validating the cultural context of her Caribbean belonging, in which that story is lived and from which she derives the tropes that mark its distinctiveness. It is this orientation that gives rise to her affinity to humanism as a critical practice. In *Defining Jamaican Fiction,* she therefore argues that "not all traditional humanism need be written off as suburban moral ideology and thus as 'imperial' ", sharing in Terry Eagleton's assertion that it is always the political that gives the fullest meaning to any moral stance.[57] Debunked in the process is the apolitical stigma ascribed to "traditional humanism" by, for instance, postcolonial studies in its eagerness to defend its exclusions and the prejudicial politics of difference. Said however, productively reminds us it is "the abuse of humanism that discredits some of humanism's practitioners without discrediting humanism itself".[58]

Lalla, from this standpoint, sees no contradiction between concerns for the "imperishable truths of the human condition and the uniqueness of the individual" and for the individualism of specific literatures, for example, "Jamaican writing".[59] To advocate a shared human condition is not a denial of the particularities of the lived experience and their contexts. As such, literary and cultural scholarship is freed to admit and establish points of confluence across traditions and nationalities, thereby demonstrating the intertextuality that speaks to the interdependence at the heart of human cultures. Lalla's attraction to postscripting as a strategy for rereading is precisely to take advantage of the opportunity to "bring new sensibility to canonical works".[60] Such interpretations at best complicate understanding in an effort to release that albeit difficult-to-define "we-perspective",[61] possibly evocative of the Hegelian "reciprocal recognitions" to which Fanon was so stubbornly committed. Getting at that "widely inclusive" "voice" is, in essence, a dialectical exercise that interfaces apparent divides and disparate perspectives.[62] Yet this is the sort of criticism our current global order demands and on which criticism as a practice in democracy depends as we try to discern, with greater understanding, the "truth" of who we are.

NOTES

1. Barbara Lalla, *Postcolonialisms: Caribbean Rereading of Medieval English Discourse* (Kingston: University of the West Indies Press, 2008), 22.

2. Barbara Lalla, *Defining Jamaican Fiction: Marronage and the Discourse of Survival* (Tuscaloosa: University of Alabama Press, 1996).

3. George Lamming, *Coming, Coming Home: Conversations II – Western Education and the Caribbean Intellectual* (St Martin: House of Nehesi, 1995).

4. Ibid., 14.

5. Ibid., 16.

6. Edward Said, *Humanism and Democratic Criticism* (New York: Columbia University Press, 2004), 10.

7. Lalla, *Defining*, 3.

8. Ibid., 4.

9. Ibid., 2.

10. Ibid., 11.

11. Ibid., 9.

12. Ibid.

13. Reinhard W. Sander, *The Trinidad Awakening: West Indian Literature of the Nineteen-Thirties* (New York: Greenwood Press, 1988), 28.

14. Lalla, *Defining*, 9.

15. Lamming, *Coming*, 32.

16. Lalla, *Defining*, 8.

17. Sandra Pouchet Paquet, "The Thematics of Diaspora and the Intercultural Identity Question", *The Caribbean Writer* 12 (1998): 229.

18. Ibid.

19. Lalla, *Defining*, 10.

20. Alison Donnell, *Twentieth-Century Caribbean Literature: Critical Moments in Anglophone Literary History* (London: Routledge, 2006), 104.

21. Lalla, *Postcolonialisms*, 235, 237.

22. Ibid., 275.

23. Ibid., 8.

24. Ibid., 9.

25. Gordon Rohlehr, "The Problem of the Problem of Form: The Idea of an Aesthetic Continuum and Aesthetic Code-Switching in West Indian Literature in *The Shape of That Hurt and Other Essays*" (Port of Spain, Trinidad and Tobago: Longman Trinidad, 1992), 3.

26. Barbara Lalla, "Opening *Salt*: The Oral Scribal Continuum in Caribbean Narrative", unpublished book chapter in *Caribbean Literary Discourse: Voice and Cultural Identity in Jamaica and Other Territories of the Anglophone Caribbean*, ed. Barbara Lalla, Jean D'Costa and Velma Pollard (forthcoming).

27. Lalla, *Postcolonialisms*, 322.

28. George Lamming, "Language and the Politics of Ethnicity", in *Beyond Borders: Cross-Culturalism and the Caribbean Canon*, ed. Jennifer Rahim with Barbara Lalla (Kingston: University of the West Indies Press, 2009), 21.

29. Lalla, *Defining*, 11.

30. Lalla, *Postcolonialisms*, 3.

31. Lalla, *Defining*, 2.

32. Ibid., 12.

33. Ibid., 17.

34. Ibid.

35. Ibid., 206.

36. Ibid., 18.

37. Ibid., 94.

38. Ibid.

39. Ibid., 93.

40. Ibid., 94.

41. Ibid., 95.

42. Ibid., 103.

43. Ibid., 94.

44. Ibid., 95.

45. Ibid., 203.

46. Barbara Lalla, "Metastance and Re-Membering: Caribbean Postscripting of the British Canon" (unpublished paper presented at "New Geographies: Studies in Postcoloniality and Globalization" International Conference, University of the West Indies, St Augustine, 25 March 2011), 12.

47. Jennifer Rahim, "Postcolonialism at the Crossroads: A Precursor to Re-Routing to Annancy" (unpublished paper presented at the conference New Geographies: Studies in Postcoloniality and Globalization, University of the West Indies, St Augustine, Trinidad and Tobago, 24–26 March 2011).

48. Shalini Puri, *The Caribbean Postcolonial: Social Equality, Post-Nationalism, and Cultural Hybridity* (New York: Palgrave Macmillan, 2004).

49. Jean Rhys, *Wide Sargasso Sea* (Harmondsworth, UK: Penguin, 1966).

50. Anthony Winkler, *The Lunatic* (Secaucus, NJ: Lyle Stuart, 1987).

51. Earl Lovelace, "Welcoming Each Other: Cultural Transformation of the Caribbean in the Twenty-first Century", in *Growing in the Dark (Selected Essays)*, ed. Funso Aiyejina (San Juan, Trinidad and Tobago: Lexicon, 2003), 163–75.

52. Lalla, *Postcolonialisms*, 22.

53. See Lalla, "Metastance", for numerous definitions of this term.

54. Lalla, *Postcolonialisms*, 5.

55. Ibid., 2.

56. Ibid., 321.

57. Lalla, *Defining*, 4.

58. Said, *Humanism*, 13.

59. Lalla, *Defining*, 4.

60. Ibid., 2.

61. Ibid., 6.

62. Ibid.

4.

CODE-SWITCHING PHENOMENA
IN ORAL AND SCRIBAL DISCOURSE

Lalla's Contribution

[VALERIE YOUSSEF]

IN THE LAST FIFTY YEARS, the range of Creole speech in Caribbean linguistics and in Caribbean literary discourse has been represented with increasing accuracy as its speakers have seized the space to speak for themselves in discourse and as recognition of Creoles as full languages in their own right has grown. Notwithstanding the encroachment of Standard English on the structure of Creoles throughout the anglophone Caribbean, these languages have emerged as literary forces in their own right, even though represented differently by each speaker and writer, even within a single territory. While some writers continue to mute Creole, to have Standard English eclipse it, the majority give it full rein, even allowing it, as Samuel Selvon does, to dominate narrative as well as dialogic space.

The issue of authenticity in language use is now one of intense linguistic inquiry, and Barbara Lalla's painstaking work to establish relative authenticity in textual discourse needs to be recognized and acknowledged in the context of this current focus.[1] Authenticity in the Labovian era of the 1960s and 1970s was understood to entail the use of a "pure" non-standard dialect, the vernacular, the speech of the everyday man and woman in their most natural environment.[2] However, the diversity of cultural, ethnic and class-mixing and -crossing that represents early twenty-first century social reality has led to questioning of this idealistic view.[3]

Within Caribbean linguistics since the late 1950s, there has been a strong and necessary focus on the adequate description of Creole varieties as distinct entities in their own right, a focus on the pure Creole and its validation. Simultaneously there has been the need to construct adequate models for the description of language use in Caribbean speech communities in which variation is acknowledged and has to be effectively accounted for. Consequently, there has been relatively little focus on the speech *range* of anglophone Caribbean speakers as *individuals*, on what I have elsewhere termed *varilingualism*,[4] in accounting for the ordered code-switching that is prevalent in such communities. In her examination of literary discourse, Lalla has also succeeded in more adequately defining the range of Creole speech as she has plumbed the complexity of writer, audience and setting factors that impinge on code choice. The importance she perceives in this voice as deriving purely from the Caribbean becomes clear from her own words (personal communication): "Defining a literature as Caribbean cannot be separated from capturing the Caribbean voice in literature." With this focus, she has homed in on its range in ways that are significant for Caribbean linguistics, as well as literature.

In her chapter in this volume, which was written in the wake of the conference under description, she shifts her evolving profound concerns further to define the complexity of the cacophony of voices that represent diverse Caribbean realities, the challenge for the writer and the illusory status of any single Caribbean voice. Her earlier work, which is discussed in this chapter, demonstrates the Caribbean scribal voice of the late twentieth century to have been more realistic than what preceded it, even in its very diversity. I am here concerned with this earlier explicatory phase and what it contributes to the description of oral discourse.

Summarizing the range of Lalla's contribution to linguistics, we recognize that, in her literary criticism, Lalla has analysed the Creole voice linguistically.[5] In her historical linguistic work, she has searched it out, identified it[6] described its phases of development[7] and provided meaningful linguistic and sociolinguistic criteria by which to situate it.[8] In her own creative work she has represented it through different characters negotiating diverse situations and circumstances[9] and using inevitably that variety that best fits each character's situation and circumstances.

This chapter focuses on the breadth of insight and definition Lalla has brought to the representation of the Creole in scribal discourse to argue ultimately that the written and oral voices, as they interface, complement one another, since both are the output of the same multifaceted Caribbean selfhood

and both are becoming more adequately analysed. Ultimately they are performances also, targeting diverse audiences in increasingly complex ways.

One of Lalla's very particular achievements has been the recognition she
has given to code-switching as a significant feature of Caribbean selfhood as it
establishes and articulates individual and group identities in multilingual
Caribbean spaces. Lalla's work has remapped the scribal manifestations of
Caribbean speech, most specifically Jamaican, not merely acknowledging its
mushrooming into an increasing array of contexts but reflexively engaging
with it and exploring its every nuance and subtlety. In so doing she establishes
standards that can also bring greater accuracy to definition of the oral voice.
Linguistic authenticity today as it is produced by speakers in diverse contexts
is argued to be ever-shifting according to the demands of the situation. This
shifting of itself constrains speakers to levels of stylistic variation that make
each interaction slightly different in its weighting of Creole features. Real
acknowledgement of this phenomenon is found in Lalla's work on scribal
discourse, which coheres with the body of work on spoken and mediatized language use today.

It is necessary to say a brief word first about Lalla's analysis of the emergence and establishment of a Creole voice in Caribbean literature. She has
done this specifically in her best-known native Jamaican variety. Although she
claims in an interview to have felt no need to authenticate the Creole, that work
having substantially been done by Caribbean linguists by the time her own
investigations began around 1980,[10] her work makes it abundantly clear that
she recognized very clearly that what existed in both the historical and literary
record needed to be analysed, named for what it was and dismissed. Always
concerned with ideological perspectives, Lalla needed to expunge from
anything claiming to be a real "Creole" record that which was not, namely the
earliest "inscribers of Creole" who were, as she dismissively and accurately
records, "inventing" it.[11] Always incisive in her criticism, Lalla notes that such
purportedly Caribbean writings as typified the eighteenth and nineteenth century were "clueless voyeur or reporter types" representing a "British adventur-
ing and exploratory perspective".[12] In consigning these to what she describes
effectively as the "Ventriloquist" phase of Creole representation, she dismisses
such texts from anything we would want to consider Caribbean writing. Such
writing neither represented the Creole that its speakers would have used nor
their identities. Indeed, it failed entirely to recognize the Creole as a language
in its own right and, most important, it was ideologically othered: it was one

person writing another, with absolutely no comprehension of that other's lived experience, demeaning and diminishing that person in the process.

Lalla has slightly more positive descriptors for Creole representation in the first half of the twentieth century, noting that it "signals its existence and then effaces itself".[13] Still writing in a colonial era, authors did not attempt sustained Creole representation, perhaps because of an ambivalence towards the Creole language, born of a colonial era that had negated it. At that time, the Creole language often invoked laughter and was included for humorous effect. This phase is, for Lalla, a censorship phase; the Creole is marked, but it can at least now be deployed as "a medium of sensible communication" in characters with "little education". She identifies a third phase beyond the mid-twentieth century as one in which Creole was actually used as the language of choice for such matters as serious political commentary. It became the stuff of "serious artistic endeavour".[14] Although stereotypical perceptions of the Creole continued to be writ large, nonetheless this voice establishes itself and "negotiates for authority". This is a time of profound change, clearly linked to the serious establishment of Creole linguistics over a period of ten years and marked in two conferences held at the Mona campus of the University of the West Indies in 1959 and 1968, respectively.[15]

Down to the present, Lalla faithfully records what she labels as the current expansion phase, and it is here that she perceives an indigenous Creole voice truly emerging across the board in Caribbean literature. Caribbean writers are finally writing themselves and their peers, writing out of a bilingual consciousness and sensibility in both Creole and Standard English, which better comprehends the communal lived experience of postcolonial Caribbean populations. Colonialist writers of former times were inevitably Othered in an ideological sense that made accurate representation impossible. Lalla's tremendous contribution in defining this latter phase of speech representation is the clear recognition that it is not mono-varietal, but rather one that switches constantly between Creole, Standard and mesolectal varieties, even as the characters it belongs to would be bound to do. She writes that "code-switching in the literary discourse has moved away from an externally controlled adjustment prompted by a desire for authenticity but constrained by a desire for convergence with a non-Creole literary audience and moved to an expression of the indigenous voice. Code-switching becomes a mechanism for laying claim to discourse and literary Creole constitutes a mechanism of resistance."[16]

In describing the current phase, Lalla establishes that it may be mere stereotyping for us to regard Creole entirely as a functioning distinct entity, attractive though that variety may be as an effective voice of resistance, and authentic ideologically. It is not just that the language used by fictional characters is reproduced by writers who are inevitably bi-varietal in their own language competence, but, more significantly, it represents characters who would be variously bi-varietal, characters who might be aiming for the Standard and hypercorrecting, characters whose life and vitality draw from their effective code-mixing, as well as characters who would produce Creole fairly consistently. It strikes a chord of recognition with my own experience of the actual oral voice recorded the length and breadth of Tobago in the 1990s and evidencing, in the majority of cases, manifold code-switches.[17]

Lalla notes that, as the authority of the Creole voice grows, so must authenticity, but that there is plurality within. She relates this to the highly complex forging of Caribbean identity in a postcolonial and postmodern time: "Authenticity in Caribbean literary discourse must account for plurality and plurality cannot be extricated from the politics of Caribbean discourse where identity is undergoing construction by a fractured but resilient psyche."[18]

Having established all this, however, Lalla has recognized further that every individual text can usefully be assessed under a number of potentially relevant profiles for us to establish its level of relative authenticity. She establishes distinguishing criteria for text, writer and audience. To take her writer profile as an example (perspective is established by considering whether the writer is a long-term resident, indigenous, frequent or occasional visitor, or foreigner (accepting overlap among these), and by equating each with specific attitudes to the Creole.[19] Their relative linguistic knowledge, social experience and level of information on the Caribbean are similarly taken into consideration. This is important because otherwise one might dismiss as "ventriloquist" a text that is in fact written by a Caribbean person producing the language expected of his time, which would bring respect to the character portrayed. It is thus we might explain the peculiarly Standard English voice of characters in *Rupert Gray: A Tale in Black and White,* which was apparently written by a "black Trinidadian" who trained as a lawyer in Britain.[20] As Lise Winer notes, this kind of usage was not uncommon in British novels of the time, including Thomas Hardy's rustic character Gabriel Oak, whose speech standardizes as he gains more "heroic stature". Our attention to the exact positioning and ideology, not only of the writers but also of their characters, is necessary to attempt to establish a measure of authenticity.

Here I would ground and hold Lalla's contribution to an authentic revisioning of perspective on the representation of the Creole voice. While her own love of literature has caused her to ultimately position herself within that discipline, her acute linguistic ear has encompassed accurately that which holds true for both scribal and oral discourse in the Caribbean at the present time: that the Creole voice is not always one. Rather, it may be two; it may be three. It may be far more than three, and all of these may be present in any single territory. As writers work out their own identity and those of their characters, as they appeal differentially to diverse local and diasporic spaces, there will be as many renditions of that voice, differently mixed with other varieties, as there are characters, but they will be authentic as long as they represent Caribbean identity and experience. Even if the Creole voice appears fogged in some cases, by the need to appeal to metropolitan ears, and perhaps muted by the need to be understood by the non-native ear, code-switching is one of its essential features, even though its extent differs for every individual and in every sociolinguistic setting. This becomes a manifest and lasting contribution to Creole linguistics, for she recognizes the varied repertoire of speakers in a way that mainstream Creole linguists has done less of, because of the need linguists have felt to focus ideologically on the Creole variety in a more singular way.

Now I elaborate on the essential quality of code-switching by drawing from a paper that Lalla produced in 1998;[21] it interrogated language use in Olive Senior's "Zig Zag". In her analysis of this work, Lalla demonstrates how central code-switching is to the identity of Senior's characters and, most specifically, Sadie, the heroine, the younger and darker sister, growing up in a home which is, as so many, mixed racially, and torn between Creole and Standard discourse, both representative of self and each representing a distinct ideological position. In the context of this piece, Lalla defines the necessity of code-switching to the act of characterization. She writes, "It is essential to note that the movement between codes is a fundamental aspect of the Caribbean setting and of Caribbean characterization . . . an essential strategy for perspectival shift on the ideological plane."[22]

Further on, however, Lalla distinguishes it, not just as a literary device, but as typifying real usage: "In selecting codes, . . . the author reflects attitudes to language which have changed considerably over the past two centuries. As a result, code-shifting has increased in ease, frequency and acceptability."[23]

Lalla discusses this at length out of her own concern to explore the challenges to the creative writer of concerns for *legibility* and *authenticity*. Code-switching allows the Caribbean writer to comfortably take on board issues that superficially may appear conflictual: of *legibility* for a varied and not necessarily Creole-speaking public and of *authenticity*, a faithful and legitimate record. She argues that such constraints cast a different light on Braithwaite's label "*nation language*" to which he first referred in 1971 which has traditionally been used in reference to the "pure" Creole but, as she argues, demands extension: "*[N]ation language* embraces not only the Creole but the local version of Standard English that continually interfaces with the Creole."[24] Speaking later of the "double entente" the skilled Caribbean writer achieves in apparently using Standard English but voicing it, phonologically and semantically, in Creole ways, she concludes: "[T]he literary discourse in this way becomes a form of Caribbean language which empowers the Creole by controlling the 'imperial' written code in these very specific ways."[25] In all this there is an issue of validity and of achieving it in scribal discourse, which make Lalla's considerations ultimately significant for the everyday speaker more than she herself concedes.[26]

She has argued that true realism can never be achieved in representation of the Creole[27] that there will always be more or less deliberate choices – of Creole, of Standard, of level of Creole, of which features to use and so on – and this is a fair comment. Ultimately there will always be a consciousness of writing for an audience that is lacking in everyday speech. Further, as noted above, skilled writers may choose a feature for its duality of meaning, because it conveys different things in the Standard and the Creole, and they can draw on each one. The very mergence of features of Caribbean Creoles with Standard varieties, which is characteristic of mesolectal and even acrolectal levels of language use in Caribbean sociolinguistic complexes, lends itself to literary exploitation and depth that many readers may, in fact, miss. Authorial and reader competence in the contact codes and their shifting relationships become issues that determine effective readability of the text. Ideological perspective becomes more nuanced by the potential released by the very existence of language continua.[28]

Elsewhere Lalla has set up templates for "profiling a text" on the basis of a range of "distinguishing characteristics".[29] Ultimately, however, she sees realism as illusory in scribal discourse, constrained by audience variables that the writer must consider, and excepting only "authentic, objective and exact installation of features"[30] which can only be assessed from an accurate sociolinguistic assessment of the text. She declares: "Realism is essentially notional, an illusion constructed of such elements as credibility and objectivity (which in the case of Creole can only be assessed in connection with some profile of the producer of the text) of other elements such as authenticity and verisimilitude (which must rest on analysis of the text itself) and of vividness (which has much to do with the profile of the audience)."[31]

Accepting this, however, people in the real world and the discourse they produce will be analysed and weighed for successful communication in relation to appropriateness for audience and may be more or less weighed for authenticity at the same time, as we all shift our speech style every time we speak in relation to our audience, setting, goals, and even mood. What the writer represents in discourse is an attempt to mirror an increasingly complex reality.

One only needs to consider the respect that has been given to Allan Bell's theory of audience design to recognize that issues of ideological perspective and of responsiveness to complex and diverse audience factors are very much the stuff of everyday discourse whereby individuals negotiate complex interactional spaces.[32] Bell developed his audience-design model to explain the way New Zealand radio station talk-show hosts modified their speech, claiming that they did so according to a complex range of listener and hearer factors, which might include immediate addressee, auditors, overhearers and eavesdroppers, all of which categories he closely defined. Referee design, speech modification for a non-listening audience as for example, a model target group a speaker might aspire to from another territory, was also a concern. It was argued that speakers consider audiences other than the addressee, even as writers consider not just their textual characters' interaction but also the text's audience. Later Bell modified the model to take more account of independent speaker variables, since his model was claimed to be too responsive to the audience at the expense of the expression of self-identity in the speaker.[33] This too is a factor for consideration in scribal as in oral discourse which Le Page and Tabouret-Keller,[34] in their work on acts of identity, brought to the forefront of Creole linguistics considerations.

Bell's model of spoken language has been recently taken up and applied to translations of the Bhagavad Gita[35] with the reader identified as auditor, with foreign readers as eavesdroppers and readers in later times as overhearers. Both the speaker and the addressee are claimed to be represented by the author. In other words, a model introduced solely to describe reception of spoken discourse has been applied to an authored text with audiences absent in time and space. Admittedly, a religious work designed to instruct the followers of that religion is different in its capacity for reception from a novel, but the example does indicate again, and with a different kind of representational focus, the way in which a text can speak to absent reader/auditor in ways that mirror the spoken voice.

Moreover, if we consider dialogue internal to the text and compare it to everyday conversation, other comparative elements emerge. If writers create a specific voice or range of voices through their characters, do not all Caribbean persons create and recreate themselves in the very act of living out daily life, moving through different settings and situations? All individuals have multiple roles in their daily lives, represent themselves differently within those roles and are perceived differently by every person who hears them. Further, no one reading this chapter, for example, would receive it in the same way. Each would receive the words differently and would represent the author of those words differently. The medium can change, and issues of performance can still arise.

My own research in language acquisition has demonstrated that three-year-old children can switch between Creole and Standard language varieties differentially according to the audience to which they are speaking and the setting in which they find themselves; they do not just acquire codes but the knowledge and capacity to switch and mix among them according to audience factors. They have already learnt to perform, with all that this entails. One young man of three admonished his sister to talk appropriately as he had to talk "for Valerie" (myself) in a setting in which I had hoped to capture his most Creole speech.[36] He was one step ahead of me, decided what variety I needed to hear and how it should be enacted, and was well up to the performance. He and his sister became characters in a play being acted out for my convenience, although their stage was the real world.

So then, if I create a character, forged from my own experience of a specific Caribbean sociolinguistic complex, and provided that I am a member of that speech community or of a community of practice within it, am I not just adding one more link in the communicator-receiver, speaker-addressee chain, and if everything that I put into that character comes from my lived experience as a Caribbean person, cannot that person mirror reality quite effectively? While Bakhtin argues that the writer can never produce reality given that "he, as its creator, remains outside the world he has represented in his work",[37] he can, at the same time, create characters whose speech shares the same shifting nuances of stylization as are produced in the real world.

Indeed, today we are faced with mediatized realities in the context of which individuals invent and reinvent themselves many times over, deliberately creating new persona to fit their whim of the day. It is becoming increasingly acceptable in the twenty-first century for a person to adopt a new name as that individual moves into a new context. To become another is acceptable and if acceptable, then that other becomes self, a self that is continuously reconstructed with the validity the age allows and confirms.

Another dimension of the closeness of the scribal world to the real is demonstrated in a series of talks given by Caribbean creative writers as they discussed their art at the 2007 Mona academic conference, "Writing Life". I am not a creative writer myself but always an avid reader, and I recognize the profound effectiveness of fiction to express the individual's real experience in ways that the data of quantitative research methodologies in the social sciences cannot. I was impressed by the extent to which these writers appeared to perceive their work, their characters and their very language as extensions of their own life and experience.

Jean Small recollected the childhood occasion when a male cinema worker took her to a private room where he exposed himself to her. She recollects this, however, in the context of her remembering it only as she wrote, but, in so doing, suddenly being able to explain many of her later behaviours, finding out "why you are the way you are" and being empowered by this experience. She records that "the marking experiences of your life make you what you are", and it is out of those that you write.[38] This is not to contend that every writer merely writes themselves but that they create characters informed by experience and further backed up by intensive research out of the need to be able to mesh that experience with a character whose sensibilities they also understand.

Jean D'Costa,[39] in a piece entitled "Born Inside the Stories", details how her writing, even of children's fiction, was birthed in early childhood experiences that she encoded in thought even before her language experience began. These became the stuff of her later story making. Further, D'Costa, writing of the reproduction of reality, also speaks of the need to produce a range of language varieties in affective writing. Commenting on the need for Caribbean writing to represent the real voices of its characters, she speaks to the code-switching capacity that Caribbean speakers develop:

[A]s children we acquire a variety of language forms each marked for a cultural purpose, each defining a social role. We have varying skills in each form depending on the household into which we are born, our schooling, and our contact with differing aspects of our society. Meaning exists in all these forms, we do not get lost as we shift from patois to standard. We may indeed enjoy the shifting, using it for various effects and advantages.[40]

And it is in this context that D'Costa speaks to a shift among Caribbean writers to being able to use the full range of naturally occurring codes in writing, concomitant with the recognition of the Creole as valid in its own right. It is telling also that she interrogates her own use of Standard English, concluding that she is using it at the time of writing because it was the language she grew up using as appropriate to formal situations. It is as much part of her as the Creole is.

There were other telling accounts at the same conference. Honor Ford-Smith spoke of her writing as having become her way of dealing with violence as it confronted her own life and that of urban Kingston. Stacy-Ann Chin wrote out of a brutal near-rape encounter; Erna Brodber wrote of her so-called fiction as something far different from fiction: the exploration of profound sociological research questions as, for example, on the problem-solving capacities of yard culture, introduced in *Jane and Louisa* and to be subsequently explored in further sociohistorical research.

In drawing the strands of this discussion together, I am led to suggest that the bounds on "reality" are more complex and illusory than the division between the literary and the everyday. If we ourselves are constituted of complex identities played out differentially in the course of our daily encounters, are we not at all times to some extent performers for a specific audience? Our language use, as noted earlier, has shown that to be the case. And are not fictional characters, on occasion, extensions of aspects of the self and others we have known, worked out as effectively as possible by their creators, who use language to differentially characterize them and define their experiences?

In this kind of context and others, Caribbean writing has become multidimensional, needing to evidence code-switching as the languages of its real-world context and differentially intertwine both language varieties entailed to represent aspects of the individual's identity and ideological positioning. In this kind of context, within complex twenty-first century milieux, Lalla's work on defining the Creole voice as peculiarly Caribbean, but nonetheless multidimensional, has such value. It speaks not just for the scribal but also for the oral, not just for fiction but also for everyday life, for after all, are not the borders between these two being broken down in new ways every day?

We sometimes seek more "authenticity", meaning mono-varietal production of the Creole in our writers than we should, considering the speech of real individuals. Merle Hodge[41] for example, has questioned the overuse of Standard English pronouns in Lovelace's representations of Eva's Creole discourse in

The Wine of Astonishment.[42] Perhaps Lovelace may have been accommodating his audience and heightening the legibility of his text, but we may note that it is only the most basilectal Creole speech that retains Creole object pronouns in Trinidad and Tobago today. Rather, they appear to lend themselves to suppression in everyday speech very readily. Are we not perhaps looking for pure Creole where in fact it hardly exists? If this is the case, can we berate writers for not using it? Is not code-mixing the very stuff of the authentic Creole voice today?

I thank Lalla for drawing our attention to these dimensions of the complex and multifaceted Creole voice and for recognizing in a literary context the complex interplay of sociolinguistic factors defining it. This perspective has accomplished much towards enabling us to recognize authenticity in the spoken voice in the real world in the extent of variability that it has achieved. While I have also made a mild case for more authenticity in the fictional world than Lalla would accept, and although she does not entirely share my perspective, I know she will not mind my exploring it in the context of the complexities of present-day experience and self-enactment.

Notes

1. Barbara Lalla, *Virtual Realism: Constraints on Validity in Textual Evidence of Caribbean Language History*, Society for Caribbean Linguistics Occasional Paper, no. 32 (St Augustine, Trinidad and Tobago: Society for Caribbean Linguistics, 2005); Barbara Lalla, "Creole and Respec' in the Development of Jamaican Literary Discourse, *Journal of Pidgin and Creole Languages* 20, no. 1 (2005): 53–64; Barbara Lalla, "Creole Representation in Literary Discourse: Issues of Linguistic and Discourse Analysis", in *Exploring the Boundaries of Caribbean Creole Languages*, ed. Hazel Simmons-McDonald and Ian Robertson, 173–87 (Kingston: University of the West Indies Press, 2006).

2. William Labov, *Sociolinguistic Patterns* (Oxford: Basil Blackwell, 1972).

3. Mary Bucholtz, "Sociolinguistic Nostalgia and the Authentication of Identity", *Journal of Sociolinguistics* 7, no. 3 (2003): 398–416; Nikolas Coupland, "The Authentic Speaker and the Speech Community", in *Language and Identities*, ed. Carmen Llamas and Dominic Watt (Edinburgh: Edinburgh University Press, 2010), 99–112.

4. Valerie Youssef, "Varilingualism: The Competence behind Code-Mixing in Trinidad and Tobago", *Journal of Pidgin and Creole Languages* 11, no. 1 (1996): 1–22; Valerie Youssef, "Varilingualism: A Term for Twenty-first Century Language Acquisition Contexts", *Éducation et Sociétés Plurilingues*, no. 28 (June 2010): 65–76.

5. Barbara Lalla, "Registering Woman: Senior's Zig-Zag Discourse, and Code-Switching in Jamaican Narrative", *Review of International English Literature* 29, no. 4 (1998): 83–98. Republished 2005, *Short Story Collection* 78.

6. Jean D'Costa and Barbara Lalla, *Voices in Exile: Jamaican Texts of the Eighteenth and Nineteenth Centuries* (Tuscaloosa: University of Alabama Press, 1989). This is the companion volume to Barbara Lalla and Jean D'Costa, *Language in Exile: Three Hundred Years of Jamaican Creole* (Tuscaloosa: University of Alabama Press, 1990).

7. Lalla, *Virtual Realism*.

8. Lalla, "Creole and Respec' "; Lalla, "Creole Representation".

9. Lalla, "Registering Woman".

10. Barbara Lalla, interview by Valerie Youssef, May 2011.

11. Lalla, *Virtual Realism*, 57.

12. Ibid., 58.

13. Ibid., 63.

14. Ibid., 65.

15. Dell Hymes, *Pidginization and Creolization of Languages* (Cambridge: Cambridge University Press, 1971).

16. Lalla, *Virtual Realism*.

17. Winford James and Valerie Youssef, *The Languages of Tobago: Genesis, Structure and Perspectives* (St Augustine, Trinidad and Tobago: School of Continuing Studies, 2002).

18. Lalla, *Virtual Realism*, 79.

19. Lalla, "Creole and Respec' ".

20. Lise Winer, *Rupert Gray: A Tale in Black and White* (Kingston: University of the West Indies Press, 2006), 272.

21. Lalla, "Registering Woman".

22. Ibid., 87.

23. Ibid., 90.

24. Ibid., 85.

25. Ibid., 95.

26. Lalla, "Creole Representation".

27. Ibid., 197.

28. Robert Le Page and Andrée Tabouret-Keller, *Vernacular Literacy* (Oxford: Clarendon Press, 1997), 5.

29. Lalla, "Creole and Respec' ", 6, 7.

30. Ibid., 17.

31. Ibid., 17.

32. Allan Bell, "Language Choice as Audience Design", *Language in Society* 13, no. 2 (1984): 145–204; Allan Bell, "Back in Style: Reworking Audience Design", in *Style and Sociolinguistic Variation*, ed. Penelope Eckert and John Rickford (Cambridge: Cambridge University Press, 2001), 139–69.

33. Bell, "Back in Style".

34. Robert Le Page and Andrée Tabouret-Keller, *Acts of Identity: Creole-Based Approaches to Language and Ethnicity* (Cambridge: Cambridge University Press, 1975).

35. Phrae Chittiphalangsri, "Virtuality in the 'Community of Texts': Audience Design in the Orientalist Translations of the Bhagavad Gita" (speech delivered at "Translation and Communities/Traduction et Communautées' Conference", Université de Bretagne Sud, Lorient, 6–8 July 2006).

36. Valerie Youssef, "Children's Linguistic Choices: Audience Design and Societal Norms", *Language and Society* 22, no. 2 (June 1993): 257–74.

37. M.M. Bakhtin, *The Dialogic Imagination: Four Essays* (Austin: University of Texas Press, 1981), 256.

38. Jean Small, "A State of Being", in *Writing Life: Reflections by West Indian Writers*, ed. Mervyn Morris and Carolyn Allen (Kingston: Ian Randle, 2007), 85.

39. Jean D'Costa, "Born inside the Stories", in *Writing Life: Reflections by West Indian Writers*, ed. Mervyn Morris and Carolyn Allen (Kingston: Ian Randle, 2007), 123–37.

40. D'Costa, "Born", 134–35.

41. Merle Hodge, "The Writer in the Caribbean Language Situation", in *Writing Life: Reflections by West Indian Writers*, ed. Mervyn Morris and Carolyn Allen (Kingston: Ian Randle, 2007).

42. Earl Lovelace, *The Wine of Astonishment* (London: Heinemann, 1986).

5.

RESTORING THE SHATTERED NATION-FAMILY IN LALLA'S *ARCH OF FIRE*

[PAULA MORGAN]

All of the Antilles, every island, is an effort of memory; every mind, every racial biography culminating in amnesia and fog. Pieces of sunlight through the fog and sudden rainbows, arcs-en-ciel. That is the effort, the labour of the Antillean imagination, rebuilding its gods from bamboo frames, phrase by phrase.
—Derek Walcott, "The Antilles: Fragments of Epic Memory"

IN ZORA NEALE HURSTON'S *Their Eyes Were Watching God*, Nanny, the maternal grandmother, deeply scarred by enslavement, denigration, rape, brutality and the wreckage of her daughter's life, pleads with her granddaughter as representative of yet another generation to dissuade her from becoming a floor rag for a no-good man to wipe his feet on: "Put me down easy, Janie, Ah'm a cracked plate."[1] The domestic image of marring, fragility, lack of resilience and impaired functionality, intended to convey the jarring impact of historical collisions, resonates with Walcott's figuration of the New World civilization as a "cracked heirloom whose restoration shows its white scars". The traumatizing catalysts generated by the violent encounter between the peoples and social orders that converged at the birthplace of New World island nations have elicited from our creative writers of successive generations, birthplaces and genders haunting repetitious engagements with what Walcott identifies as the "care and pain of the Antilles", the "restoration of our shattered histories, our shards of vocabulary".[2]

This chapter reads Barbara Lalla's *Arch of Fire: A Jamaican Family Saga*[3] as such an act of restoration in relation to the island of Jamaica. The five-hundred-page narrative flirts with and ultimately extends beyond the generic constraints of the historical novel, the plantation novel, the family saga, the psychological thriller, the novel of suspense and the supernatural novel. Based on scribal and oral narratives collected over decades, its epic sweep culminates in the 1980s, the period in which the island was dissolving into the social chaos that motivated the mass exodus of its middle class. Lalla's novel focuses on the sustaining bedrock unity of the society and the fissures along which it threatens to disintegrate. Conceived as backchat to the then-prevalent doom-speaking of the society and filtered through an unflinchingly honest gaze, Lalla's novel lays bare the ugly and the ennobling, the transient and the sustaining, in a quest to ferret out the soul that sustains the nation in crisis.[4] This analysis, a subset of which I have discussed elsewhere in relation to Brodber's *Jane and Louisa*,[5] reads this Jamaican family saga as reflective of the imperative and paradoxes inherent in constructing a Caribbean nation family.

Narrating the Nation

A fair cross-section of attempts by theorists to define the nation proves deficient in terms of illuminating the experiential interface of Caribbean peoples with their island and ancestral birthplaces. To the extent that we accept Anderson's construction of the nation as an imagined community – a system of cultural representation in which persons imagine a shared experience of identification with an extended community – fashioning such a construct is problematized by the rawness, inequities, absence of ancient landmarks and the ancestral loyalties within modern Caribbean societies. Despite reams of scholarship intended to demystify the political and psychic power of the nation, it retains an enduring hold on the psyche, extending sinews of belonging, which remain paradoxically unchallenged by contemporary notions of fluidity, boundarylessness and transnationality. As the impulse towards globalization heightens, anxiety about what the nation is, to whom it belongs, its tenacity and social constructedness, also heightens. As Homi Bhabha argues, "The nation fills the void left in the uprooting of communities and kin and turns that loss into the language of metaphor. Metaphor transfers the meaning of home and belonging across the middle passage . . . across those distances and cultural differences that span the imagined community of the nation people."[6] A major challenge is the evocation of a unifying metaphor that bridges people groups and yet acknowledges the specificities of their histories and their pain.

Ernest Renan,[7] discounting "race, language, material interest, religious affinities, geography, and military necessity" as being adequate explanations for the creation of a nation, argues that "a nation is a soul, a spiritual principle. . . . One lies in the past, one in the present. One is the possession in common of a rich legacy of memories; the other is a present-day consent, the desire to live together, the will to perpetuate the value of the heritage that one has received in an undivided form."[8] For Caribbean writers whose history is littered with manacles, inequities and oppressions and for populations whose tenancy on these islands was initiated by the largest movement of enforced and bonded labour in human history, the rich legacy of memory to which Renan refers is problematic and compromised. Its legacies into the present day, of racism, structural inequities, poverty and oppression take a toll on Renan's second definer: the willingness to live together and the will to perpetuate the value of the heritage. Yet as Lalla contends, Jamaica survives, and Jamaicans exude a fierce loyalty to home and a certain grasp on national identity.

Notwithstanding the meanderings of scholars, in the popular imagination the nation as definer of identity remains tied to primordial connections of blood and tribe; to essentialized and racialized notions of being; to heart attachments to seascapes; to the navel-string-buried umbilical connection to motherland; to the subtle and fluid speaking and understanding of mother tongue; to the cultural moorings of food and drink; and to the visceral call of stance, gesture and embodiment. And this is where Lalla roots her evocation of Jamaicanness.

Narrative is pivotal to the process. The inception of West Indian nation-states coincided with a literary renaissance in the English-speaking Caribbean during the 1950s and 1960s. The early literature tested the potential and reflected muted optimism in relation to West Indian political nationalism. The eventual disintegration of this vision saw younger writers such as Lovelace upholding a cultural versus political nationalism. Arguably the subsequent speaking of the women writers reflects a peculiarly female epistemological interface with history, bringing to the fore submerged domestic and mythic traditions and oral narratives that have been outside the domain of traditional historiography. As Tagoe argues, "in the historical writing of West Indian women, custom, tradition, myth, ritual belief are given new interpretations and meanings in forms that are inextricably linked with the narrative forms of an oral culture and with the language and metaphors of a different cosmology".[9]

Arch of Fire writes the nation as a political entity whose social crisis has brought it to the point of threatened extinction to trace the pathways by which it has arrived. Pivotal to the present time of the narrative (and to the period in which the author was actually writing) is the mass exodus of the middle classes from a society toppling into anomie. It comprises a backward glance and reconstruction of the histories of Jamaica's people groups to simultaneously affirm coherence and to delineate the forces that militate against coherence. In other words, Lalla tests the limits and potentialities of the nation at the brink of threatened social collapse. A linguist by profession, Lalla represents the range of Jamaican languages as she grapples with how to weave a multiplicity of discourses into a coherent whole. Her plea for the (re)construction of national community rests on contentions of shared humanity and interdependence of the human family.

NATION AS HUMAN FAMILY

Narrating the nation as domestic genealogy has strong appeal to Caribbean female writers, whose concerns shy away from the world of public figures and letters to capture the hitherto submerged worlds and voices of women and underclasses. *Arch of Fire* opens with a mnemonic device, which is necessary because of the complexity of the narrative and the diversity of its slate of characters. The standard visual motif of the historical novel – a sprawling family tree – becomes a genealogy that links all of the major characters, all the ethnic groups, despite the hostilities of history and existing relational challenges, into one family. In Lalla's grand saga, all families are traced back to the earliest arrivants on the island to evoke the sense of the interconnectedness of the human family and the interrelatedness of all the people groups that have formed the basis of modern Jamaican society. As the novel weaves backwards and forwards through time, the personal histories symbolize the histories of collectivities and ethnicities: Jews, Scots, Irish, Spaniards, Africans, Indians, Tainos (Amerindians). The present time of *Arch of Fire* conveys the story of Catherine Donalds, a mixed-race woman of Indian and African lineage. She is the daughter of the prosperous and aspiring middle class who falls prey to the sexual advances of a Creole landowner, Stollmeier, and produces a child whom she raises in impeccable respectability. To rise above the position of fallen woman, Catherine must practice invisibility and dissemblance, erase all signs of sexuality and project a super-moral image. The two-member Donalds/

Stollmeier family unit is at the core of the narrative and is the point of interface for all the other families: Castries, O'Reillys, Stollmeiers, Hayneses, Cohons, Lions.

Initially, stark class differentiation dictates that the worlds remain separate except for workers who come and go. Towards the end of the novel, the aging protagonists are isolated by the migration of their community and marooned in an urban cul-de-sac symbolically named Oxford Close. The impoverished black "sufferers" are erupting in a mindless, nonspecific, mass violence – the legacy of decades of denigration, hopelessness, starvation and deprivation – that threatens the entire nation, not only the cultured but essentially exploitative life of the privileged Creole class. The novel also tests the reconstructed plantation as a nurturing place for a new wave of formerly privileged, now-dispossessed, upper-middle-strata urban dwellers. In the final scene, the Creole inheritors of the plantation are driven out of Kingston back to that decaying structure, which provides shelter but externalizes their immoral rootings, their tenacity and their imminent collapse.

In her enquiry into the making of the collective mind of its peoples, Lalla valorizes the traditions and the common humanity of all. Indeed she affirms family as the last vanguard against the hurtling social chaos. The people groups are bound by tight, though often submerged, webs of connection and cause-and-effect relationships. The nation family is also linked by hardship. Each major character encounters a personal debilitating tragedy and casts about for some avenue of transcendence. Even for criminals – who Lalla represents as created by excessive social and psychic violence, deprivation, poverty and abuse, and who, in turn, generate the same – recuperative potential resides in the hope of reintegration into family, even to the human community. Through Les, whom he eventually murders, the clear-eyed don Austin Louis is offered access into a generous and loving family.[10] The motif provides a glimpse of utopic possibility in a narrative dedicated to documenting encroaching social chaos. In Lalla's economy, no social group can live an airtight existence. All must share culpability and credit for the common inheritance.

Women are transcendent within this nation family. Lineage within the dominant, present time frame of the novel is traced through a female genealogy that valorizes women's words and worlds. It is focused on Catherine Donalds, her daughter Stella and her adopted granddaughter Grace. This is the stable centre from which all other worlds are assessed. Female centredness permeates every aspect of the narrative. The text presents a veritable cornucopia of myths and domestic lore, from the hyperbolic lore of Maroon's nanny, who catches and shoots bullets with her buttocks, to traditional recipes for food, drink and curative herbs. In this sense, *Arch of Fire* captures and validates nation as envisioned through a female-centred epistemology and interface with reality. Major historical events are powerfully evoked, or perhaps the better term is embodied. The relentless linear historical events are recorded as they shape the working-out of private histories. Hence the 1907 earthquake in Kingston brings the addition of the kingpin of the family. Again figuring inclusivity, Grace is the baby whom the desperate woman trapped by fire throws into Stella's arms. The famed earthquake does not pass into history; rather, its impact on lived events is as never-ending as the saga itself.

Yet reflecting its ideological bent towards the hegemonic order, the family history is also the history of the patriarchs, deeply rooted in Judeo-Christian symbolism. It is complete with its Abraham, who departs the faith of his fathers and is cut off from its lineage, to take to his bosom a Christian wife and faith. This frames the wandering and loss of all the ethnicities against the quintessential Jewish diasporic wandering. The male lineage is constantly at risk from bitterness, accident, disease and murder. The engrafted Grace, whose name means "divine favour and blessing", possesses unmerited favour that symbolizes the redemptive process that operates inexorably out of the midst of the grimmest human loss and adversity. She becomes the stable centre of the family, the carrier of its lineage and the maternal ancestress of its emotionally disturbed son of promise, who, in turn, symbolizes Jamaica's contradictory, ambivalent future. The complex family structure boils down to a single disturbed child, for whose sake the survivors mobilize an incredible exertion of love, to infuse life and order.

Even for a sensitive female writer, the nation as family trope is problematic. Lalla, in her quest for a metaphor that bridges cultural difference, does not manage to steer clear of traps inherent in engendering history. The originary myth, filtered through the world view of the Taino, is represented as calling the nation out of prehistoric, prelinguistic, chaotic formlessness, into spatiotemporal groundings and representation. In collusion with masculinist terms of discourse of empire, the land, gendered female, is subject to transfer of ownership to new gendered male gods "wearing thunder in their belt".[11] The agency of transfer from Taino male to mulatto male is rape and abduction of the last Taino woman: "And even as the woman screamed and struggled against the muscular arms that locked her safely in front of him on the horse, even as the massive animal thundered towards the trees bearing her away from the sight and memory of her race, even as the smell of blood rushed away on the wind, she knew she was saved by the murderer from the slow death overtaking the tribe."[12] As may well be the case for all good Amerindians, the painful loss of the land for the male Taino is dulled by divine mandate and philosophical accommodation. For the female Taino, rape and abduction are reconfigured into a blessing and her only salvation from death by enforced labour and disease. She may be read as pragmatically washing away her past to ensure the possibility of a future.

The nation as family trope also takes on complex nuances in relation to the modern scenario. Lalla engages with the ongoing discourse in relation to Creole society as the basis for the modern Caribbean nation-state. Theorists have long recognized "a desperate need for a coherent national ideology and cultural identity. The Creole society thesis offers an approach to national integration by seeking to unite people of diverse origins in an overarching ethnicity based on the recognition and recreation of a developing Creole culture."[13] The hegemonic ideology at the moral centre of the novel resides with the middle-stratum Jamaican. The upper stratum – the immediate inheritors of the privileges of the planter class – are steeped in the values of plantation society: mercenary, decadent, lustful, culturally impoverished, greedy, wasteful, exploitative in the extreme and lacking in moral finesse. The Creole intermixture personifies respectability, blending the commonsensical family and community allegiances of the black folk with the civilizing impact of the colonizer. From this dominant Euro-Creole sensibility all other worlds are assessed. These range from the mercenary and irresponsible landowning class of the Stollmeiers to the innocuous Afrocentric domain of Icelin Castries and its evil counterpart in Louise Haynes.

The episodic structure of the narrative, with frequent prolepses, facilitates evocation of a series of distinct worlds and world views and an expression of a multiplicity of discourses. Even characters and people groups that are in intimate daily connection remain compartmentalized. For those like the disgraced Catherine Donalds and her lineage, who set their feet firmly on the pathway leading to middle-class respectability, there is an insistent requirement to forget, sacrificing everything – her parents, her sister and most of all herself – for the child: "It meant unlearning sayings, erasing myths, ignoring old pains. She had to leave the dead unburied, the living unembarrassed, the unborn unencumbered. . . . Some things were best forgotten or left unlearnt."[14]

Numerous persons in the narrative are blood related and in contact with each other, yet they are ignorant of the linkage. The most dramatic example is Stella, who lovingly tends her aunt, whom she knows only as a faithful servant. Even a lifelong family retainer like Icelin, who literally sacrifices herself for her masters, is known only in part. Bound to perpetual servitude though generations, Icelin is so integrally connected with the master that she will work, with or without payment. She eventually sells her soul and sanity (the good servant murders the bad servant) to keep her masters from harm. Class differentiation and conditions of domestic servitude are major deterrents to knowing the person and world view of the other. Indeed, the repressed and subordinated black servant class is represented as superior in terms of their knowledge of the mindset and world view of their masters. Rohlehr reads the diverse forms of compartmentalization, erasure and amnesia as reflective of national soul sickness indicative of dis-eased origins:

> There is the drive to create dynasties; the concern with yet terror of tracing genealogical ties, after a variegated and upwardly mobile middle class has chosen to sever links with the past. To cope with traumatic rupture from familiar traditions and relationships, protagonist after protagonist makes the stoical choice of suppressing and forgetting the past. *Arch of Fire* explores the success or failure of this strategy of amnesia and the hazards that attend both denial and obsessive remembering of the past.[15]

In keeping with Bakhtin's notion,[16] the implied author darts in and out of the respective worlds mapping their interface, their erasures and their exclusions. Although the hegemonic Creole world and world view are clearly at the verbal ideological centre, the implied author is comfortable where all levels intersect. The text is careful to display the self-centred, arrogant, ignorance of privileged upper strata Creoles who determine hegemonic social values. It presents the black working class as being in possession of a viable alternative epistemology in relation to elements such as kinship ties and herbal-healing remedies. Moreover, the novel is careful to rebut the upper-class discourse of racism.

Consider, for example, the portrayal of the Rasta man Matthew Leon, better known as Lion, who is an honourable man of honourable lineage. He and his father are credited with redeeming the lives of vulnerable young boys and restoring them to their families. In Bakhtin's terminology, Lalla's multivalent discourses criticize themselves and the implied author "polemicizes" it with

language, argues with it, agrees with it (although with certain conditions), interrogates it, eavesdrops on it, but also ridicules it, parodies it, exaggerates it and
so forth.[17] In keeping with the numerous worlds that she evokes, Lalla, to borrow Bakhtin's terms, presents character as "ideologically authoritative and independent", that is, as possessing a "fully weighted conception of his/her own"
and not as the object of the author's "finalizing artistic vision".[18] *Arch of Fire* is
indeed polyphonic.

NATION AS PLACE/LANDSCAPE

Landscape plays a pivotal role in this novel's negotiation of complex processes
of forgetting, amnesia, recuperation and recovery. Inscription of multiple
modes of belonging to and interface with the nation as place/landscape serves
to validate the tenancy of each ethnic group, past and present. Insofar as they
all appropriate distinctive notions of place, they come to belong. The diversity
of perspectives, despite the hegemonies and governing epistemes that would
annex legitimacy of place and naming, becomes, in Lalla's evocation, a democ-
ratizing impulse that lends depth of meaning to the Jamaican national motto:
Out of Many, One People. Successive imprintings of belonging creates as it
were a palimpsest – an inscription on a parchment that has been only partially
erased; hence it possesses within it traces of multiple previous inscriptions:
accumulations, accretions, erasures, anomalies and the like. Cultural geogra-
pher Ivan Mitin identifies every concrete landscape as reflecting "coexistence
of several different scripts, implying not just different historical eras, but several historical and contemporary actors as well":[19]

> What happens with every concrete place? It turns from one-layer material land-
> scape into the whole set of numbers of autonomous layers that possesses various
> hierarchy. Each of the layers is firstly, a system of material elements; secondly,
> one of the geographical attributes of a place; thirdly, some (infinite number) of
> spatial ideas (geographical images, spatial myths etc.). A source of plurality of
> the layers and a sense of constructing attributes lie in interpretation realized by
> constant giving of new definitions and meanings to various elements of a place
> (semiosis). We suggest calling such model of a place palimpsest.[20]

Each layer of the palimpsest becomes one of the descriptions of place or one
of the spatial interpretations and myths, that is, one of the multiple contexts,

constructed meanings or realities of a place. The novel foregrounds conquest, placing the account of the imperial enterprise as a violent act of pillage at the beginning of the narrative. Lalla nestles the account of the pre-imperial existence of the land deep within. It is evoked as a pristine, timeless, no-man's-land that is held lightly even by the zemis: the nature spirits to which the indigenous Taino's pay obeisance. Echoing the biblical creation account, at the beginning, "[t]he island hung at the edge of the world. Eternity tossed and swirled formlessly around it."[21] The prelapsarain island body is replete with fecundity, vitality, riotous beauty, playfulness, and in keeping with the ontology of the Taino through whom these perceptions are filtered awe inspiring majesty, languorous circularity, peace and impassivity.

The European conquistador's bid to possess the land as signalled from the opening passage is a study of contrasts:

> Beneath the stony contemplation of the great house, the valley scooped away to a distant edge of deep green coconut fronds parted by pulses of sunlight reflected from the sea. The sky was pitiless at noon, branding the low-lying fields and roads, but at dusk it relented, salving with dew so that nothing really died forever. Even when the hurricane rode in and the wind rose cracking its whip upon the land, twisting, breaking and uprooting, still when the screaming died away the soft shoots sprouted again their chorus of resistance.[22]

Spatiotemporal coordinates that define the imperial gaze economically convey hierarchical power relations reflective of the historicity and social relations inherent in conquest. The landscape is perceived as locked into diurnal and seasonal cycles that delineate the inimical forces metaphorically associated with conquest. The village here, "sun tempered and blood soaked",[23] lies under the gaze of the great house, which occupies an elevated vantage of the hegemonic plantation order. Its stony visage speaks impenetrability, exclusivity and disapproval. Knowledge and appropriation of the landscape by representatives of the colonial order has bequeathed a vantage point so permeated with conquest that a force as unpredictable and uncontrollable as a hurricane becomes a horse-mounted conquistador with the inevitable whip-wreaking wanton violence and destruction on the land. Respite and transcendence come from timeless cycles of regeneration, which ensure that even for the colonized, the earth is never spent. The landscape that refuses to die is emblematic of the collective resistance of the oppressed. For the earliest Spanish inhabitants, for whom the vitality, vast natural beauty and towering vistas of Taino's perception are reduced to the lost dreams of El Dorado, place is reductive: an ugly strip of savannah permeated by the torpor and heat, and time is an unending succession of interminable, oppressive, dusty hours that contextualize boredom, apathy, furtive fornication and incest, creeping insanity and early death.

Lalla's evocation of landscape is a remarkable achievement. In essence, belonging is etched into the landscape through layers of narrative inscription such that it becomes impossible to erase the tenancy of any period or ethnicity; rights of belonging are imbricated onto ways of seeing, possessing and relating to the landscape. By inscribing appropriation and citizenry of every succeeding people group and of their place, the implied author is acting as a synthesizer of meanings of place and presenting a rich and diverse palimpsest, one that includes the deformed and imperfect along with the bright and beautiful. The inscription of successive vantage points and forms of territorial imaging presents a new spatial mythology with which to counteract and challenge the negative speaking over the land.

By the present time of the novel, the plantation as symbol of a stake in the land has been replaced by the urban gardens of the emergent coloured middle class, who have inherited the postcolonial kingdom. Traces of the pristine prelapsarian wilderness survive in its riotous ferns, brilliant, lavish, tropical blooms. The vestiges of plantation life manifest in shrinking potentiality for preservation of a genteel civilized and gracious middle-class existence, with its round of elegant garden parties. The urban front garden leads to the fern-shaded porch, the semi-private space between the public roadway and the house. Catherine Donald's unrelenting middle-strata aspirations are reflected in her Lower King Street dwelling with its humble, lush and beautiful front garden as surely as her lover's social location is reflected in the Stollmeiers' balconied townhouse on Half Way Tree Road and the solid stone plantation rural stronghold called Goldfields. When Reverend Jackman loses Catherine's daughter Stella to Abraham Goldman, his emotional pain, sexual frustration and rupture of his reproductive aspirations are reflected through his perception of the garden as he waits to bless the wedding cake of the newly united couple:

> On the verandah at King Street, the maidenhair fern fluttered on shiny black stems which rose hard and wire thin in a spiny cluster at the base of the pillars. . . . Reverend Jackman alone concentrated on them, forcing himself to notice the uneven line of fine brown seeds which crusted the edges thinly. He studied the wide arch of the fishtails, wondering at their forking stems and peering at tender

shoots, coiled at their ends in pale tight promises of life. He brushed the knuckles of his finger over the transparent green of baby's breath foaming over red clay.[24]

His loss of his pure, virginal love object as the repository for his seed and mother of his progeny is conveyed in veiled sexual imagery. The crystallization of his loss in terms of his minute observation "alone" among the ferns bespeaks his inability as a brown man to appropriate and to plant a stake firmly in the social space characterized by elegant gardens. These are the very gardens that are being threatened by the growing commercialization that is transmuting gracious suburban homes and gardens into paved properties dedicated to business. The overarching impact despite all the change is the evocation of island body that has become tangible, variable, responsive to successive people groups and yet imbued with endurance, everlastingness and transcendence.

What accounts for the substantiality of Lalla's construction of the nation? Larsen argues that the nation remains an object of thinking entrapped in "the oscillation between two forms of cultural mythology: culture as empirical inert given ('rarified object') and culture as purely contingent, absolutely mutable 'effect' of its encoding (mutable subject)". Put another way, current dialogue in relation to nation tosses around the "fallacy of essentialism" and the "fallacy of textualism".[25] This text mediates these positions. Lalla's intensely nostalgic text, nested in the specificities of historical events and triggered by the desire to account for the enduring sense of Jamaican identity, is no mere textual construct. Indeed, it is careful to define identities and cultures as historically rooted and contextually determined. Yet Lalla's indigenous, hegemonic, Creole creation is also intra-group representation within a contested domain. The post-1970, Caribbean textual world has been until quite recently been dominated by Afro-Caribbean narrative self-assertion and exposure of injustices and inequities of the hegemonic Creole world. For Lalla, the evocation of a multi-ethnic family of man within a hierarchical, indigenous, hybridized Creole space proves viable. The hegemonic Euro-Creole sensibility remains firmly entrenched at the centre of the fictional universe against the back drop of a complex ethnically diverse Jamaican family of man, inscribed within visionary (b)orderlands where myth, history and spirituality coincide. This chapter reads Lalla's *Arch of Fire* as evoking the nation family as a fragmented and in need of wholeness, internal integrity, consistency and load bearing capacity – a cracked heirloom so infinitely precious as to be well worth the effort of restoration.

Notes

1. Zora Neale Hurston, *Their Eyes Were Watching God* (New York: Harper and Row, reprinted 1990), 19.

2. Derek Walcott, "The Antilles: Fragments of Epic Memory" (Nobel lecture, 7 December 1992), http://www.nobelprize.org/nobel_prizes/literature/laureates /1992/ walcott-lecture.html.

3. Barbara Lalla, *Arch of Fire: A Jamaican Family Saga* (Kingston: Kingston Publishers, 1998).

4. Barbara Lalla, interview with Paula Morgan, Video Voice Tracks Series, Department of Liberal Arts, University of the West Indies, Department of Liberal Arts, 2011.

5. Paula Morgan, "Historicizing Islands in the Sun: Nation and Beyond in Lalla's *Arch of Fire* and Brodber's *Jane and Louisa*", in *Swinging Her Breasts at History*, ed. Moira Inghilleri (London: Mango, 2006), 61–78.

6. Homi K. Bhabha, "Dissemi-nation: Time, Narrative, and the Margins of the Modern Nation", in *Nation and Narration*, ed. Homi K. Bhabha (London: Routledge), 140.

7. Ernest Renan, "What Is Nation?", in *Nation and Narration*, ed. Homi K. Bhabha (London: Routledge, 1990), 8–22.

8. Ibid., 19.

9. Nana Wilson Tagoe, *Historical Thought and Literary Representation in West Indian Literature* (Gainesville: University of Florida Press, 1998), 225.

10. For fuller discussion, see my discussion of criminal deviance in Paul Morgan, "'Dark and Unfathomable beyond Control': Women Writing the Deviant Male", in *The Centre of Remembrance: Memory and Caribbean Women's* Writing, ed. Joan Anim Addo (London: Mango, 2002), 273–94.

11. Lalla, *Arch*, 59.

12. Ibid.

13. Nigel O. Bolland, "Creolization and Creole Societies: A Cultural Nationalist View of Caribbean Social History", in *Questioning Creole: Creolization Discourses in Caribbean Culture*, ed. Verene Shepherd and Glen Richards (Kingston: Ian Randle, 2002), 29.

14. Lalla, *Arch*, 15.

15. Gordon Rohlehr, *Transgression, Transition, Transformation: Essays in Caribbean Culture* (San Juan, Trinidad and Tobago: Lexicon, 2007), 489.

16. Mikhail Bakhtin, *The Dialogic Imagination*, ed. Michael Holquist (Austin: University of Texas Press, 1981).

17. Ibid.

18. Quoted in Richard Harland, *Literary Theory from Plato to Barthes* (New York: St Martin's Press, 1999), 160.

19. Ivan Mitin, "Mythogeography: A Region as a Palimpsest of Identities", in *Cross-Cultural Communication and Ethnic Identities*, ed. L. Elenius and C. Karlson (Luleå, Sweden: Luleå University of Technology, 2007), 216.

20. Ivan Mitin, "Place as Palimpsest", *Parallel 60 Journal on Cultural Policy and Humanitarian Practice* 4 (December): 13. http://www.journal.60parallel.org/en/journal/200831/295, accessed August 2011.

21. Lalla, *Arch*, 46.

22. Ibid., 3.

23. Ibid.

24. Ibid., 93.

25. Ibid., 87.

6.

IAN ROBERTSON

Re-Visioning the Creole Voice

[VALERIE YOUSSEF]

DURING HIS ACADEMIC CAREER, Ian Robertson contributed significantly to the creation of positive educational experiences for Creole and non-standard dialect speakers in the Caribbean through developing accurate linguistic, sociolinguistic and sociocultural perspectives on their education situation. Moving from his own early academic education, which focused more specifically on English literature, to his career beginnings as a secondary school teacher in Guyana and then further to his academic career in the disciplines of both education and linguistics, he has been able to shape a perspective on language-education policy that has re-visioned the Creole voice in education. His own ultimate concern is that the effective implementation of his suggested policies is lacking but the hope is absolute that, as an increasing number of teachers are trained to teach from a base of critical language awareness, primary-school children and their parents in the anglophone Caribbean and beyond will yet perceive their language situation in a balanced and accurate way. If we ask what is unique to Robertson's perspective on language and language education, it is undoubtedly this emphasis on language awareness. This chapter reflects on his own particular perspectives, which are sometimes obscured in more generalized perceptions of his work, shared by the vast majority of Caribbean linguists, on the validity of Creole and its place in education.

It is important to define what Ian Robertson means by *language awareness* because it is most usually conceptualized in the context of foreign-language learning and the kind of knowledge of form and function relationships that are perceived as fundamental to that context. My understanding, however, has always been that Robertson wanted to inculcate language awareness in the earliest stages of primary school for Creole-speaking students, their parents and their teachers. He felt that an appropriate language-education process could not proceed unless all these stakeholders recognized Creole as a rule-governed system in its own right. Lip service to a belief held by a few linguists would be insufficient; only knowledge that brought conviction would serve to change not just language attitudes and beliefs but also perceptions of self and the capacity individuals have to articulate their everyday experience and be respected for it. To this end, Robertson recently produced a language and language-education policy for Trinidad and Tobago[1] that encapsulated views he has been developing over many years.

In a recent interview, Robertson indicated that when he started out as a teacher he did not know knew whether the struggles of his students related to their language situation or to more fundamental learning issues. While his work convinced him of the former, he found himself ill-equipped to tackle the difficulties they were experiencing in the classroom. He recorded the traditional colonial attitudes to language teaching in the context of which his upbringing had taken place in a document written in 1954 by the director of education in what was then British Guiana; it described English as the "mother tongue" of the colony. In this context the mother tongue was recorded as being reproduced in a "slovenly" way in the "colony", but there was no mention of Creole. It was the invisible language, wrongly constituted as lazily produced English. There was English, there was bad English and there were endangered aboriginal languages.

Two major language conferences took place at Mona, Jamaica, however, shortly after this, the first in 1959 and the second in 1968. The conferences, initiated changes in the perceptions of linguists in recognizing clear structural differences between Creoles and other languages with which they variously interfaced. The important sociolinguistic concepts of diglossia[2] and of the post-Creole continuum[3] were raised at the first conference and were further elaborated at the second. But at that time students of English literature were the ones who taught English at secondary school, and Ian Robertson himself, grounded in a strong literary background, was challenged by the language situation he found in the classroom.

The report on the 1959 conference described the Caribbean language-learning context for the first time as a quasi-foreign language one and acknowledged the existence of separate language systems while simultaneously recognizing that the language situation was neither wholly foreign nor wholly native in relation to English.[4] The overlap between the two language varieties and the non-existence of clear cut-off points between the two[5] made for a paucity of accurate language labels for the situation. The late Dennis Craig in particular worked tirelessly to have the two languages taught in proper relation to one another[6] and with concern for the validation of Creole in the education system.

Robertson's contribution built on these emerging base concepts, but he focused on language education as a tool in general education and set forth the crucial relationship between the two. He recognized "the need for personal development through greater self-awareness and the need to develop a socially cohesive society through the appropriate levels of understanding and tolerance of those members of society who were different".[7] In addition, Robertson challenged the practice of teaching languages separately and with little reference to one another or to any real relevance for those languages in society at large. He argued that "language education must be premised on its potential to contribute to the wider goals of education which may be addressed in a specific way through language. These would include the maximization of individual academic potential, the development of a sensitivity to and a concern for fellow citizens who may be different and the establishment of equity."[8]

In that context language education becomes something different, something more noble, and it was in a humane and humanitarian context that Robertson developed his perspective on the critical need for language awareness as something that should be inculcated from the earliest stages of primary education. It is one thing to tell the world that a language such as Creole is structurally viable; taken as a surface statement this will simply be rejected. But it is something far more to share language awareness. According to Carter, "Language awareness refers to the development in learners of an enhanced consciousness of and sensitivity to the forms and functions of language. . . . Its adherents also stress the cognitive advantages of reflecting upon language, and argue that attitudes to language and to language learning can change as a result of methods which highlight particular language features by actively involving the learner."[9]

Robertson's ultimate goals were:

1. Awareness of the language demographic situation of the Caribbean region and the associated cultures of all its peoples,
2. Competence in the use of the official standard language and at least one other international language,

3. Metalinguistic awareness of the native Creole language,
4. Communicative competence with all that this entails of appropriacy norms in the society,
5. Awareness of "the links between language and social history and organization" and
6. Understanding of "the nature and functions of language".[10]

What Robertson is advocating here then is education in the range of languages in use in the Caribbean, with a corresponding focus on the particular socio-historical and sociocultural contexts in which they operate and all this matched with an understanding of the ways in which social history shapes and determines language as well as perceptions of it. These perceptions demand discussion, as they may well be inaccurate. Such information is to be matched with a clear understanding of what language and language use actually entail and further, the pivotal roles that they play for each individual in the contexts of the range of social milieux encountered. Language is not just for exchanging information but for expressing self and identity, defining oneself and relating to others. Finally, there is language knowledge itself: conscious recognition of Creole as a structured entity alongside the capacity to use the language varieties in the society effectively in the full range of language situations.

Robertson recognized that this kind of knowledge could only come about if inculcated early in the education process, beginning in primary school as most desirable, because it allowed not only for stronger motivation for language learning but also the capacity in the students, parents and teachers to make their own assessments of languages and their speakers from an informed base. In so doing, they would not fall prey to what the power mongers in society might seek to establish. In this respect, Robertson's views seem close to those of Norman Fairclough,[11] who has developed a model of critical language awareness for implementation in schools in the United Kingdom. Fairclough's perception of hegemonic control through discourse, however, is couched in a monolingual framework and pertains to manipulation in political and media discourse, a rather different site of inequity. I note that only today a postgraduate student reported to me that her experience in primary school is of a student population who describes Creole as "poor-people language" despite their own use of it and despite efforts by previous teachers to help them to see the language more accurately.

Not content with this, however, Robertson has been concerned with the implementation of appropriate policies towards which end he has developed courses in educational linguistics at the University of the West Indies and has interfaced extensively with successive ministries of education in Trinidad and Tobago until linguistics graduates became recognized as a significant core of secondary-level language teachers in the country. He has also prepared a national education policy to which I alluded earlier. Formerly, graduates in English literature, as Robertson had been at the beginning, were sent to teach English, both language and literature, in the school system. Out of his own experience, however, he recognized that only a sound knowledge of language, both general and specific, could equip teachers for the task at hand.

A major concern, then, has been the development of an appropriate policy and approach at the primary level and an effective teacher training system, with a concern to foster language development and literacy from the earliest stage possible. Alienation from the education system through maltreatment of the child's home language has been normative in the past, and the recognition that such alienation is counterproductive to the entire educational experience must be impressed upon primary-school teachers, since each one may have the sole responsibility for the instruction of an entire class for all subjects and for an entire year. Not only this, but students go home to parents who often share the wrong attitudes to their own language, which it is so desirable to expunge. Students need a strong grounding in language awareness through the teachers with whom they spend so much time.

Robertson has commented on the disjuncture throughout the region between education policy and practice. He records sound philosophical positions from the Trinidad and Tobago Ministry of Education's white paper on education,[12] which clearly speak to the need for inclusivity:

1. Every child has a right to an education that will enhance the development of maximum capability regardless of gender, ethnic, economic, social or religious background.
2. This right pertains to all children regardless of location or physical or mental ability.

Robertson argues further that goals of social and cultural awareness cannot be achieved without proper language and language-education policies. A corollary to such positioning is a concern that language and not just the official language should be considered in formulating language-education policies. Children should be educated in the language that most fits their circumstances and that may not always be the prevailing standard or official language in their home territory. In his policy document,[13] Robertson notes that early Christian missionaries were quick to recognize the importance of communicating and educating through the individual's home language. He quotes also from Patrick J. Keenan,[14] who wrote in the context of concern for the extension of English competence in a colonial context, that the policy employed at the time fell short of rationality.

Keenan was referring to education in English for children for whom it was clearly a quasi-foreign language. In the same vein, Robertson would ask today what the relevance is of education in English to Guyanese children for whom it is their second or third language. He couches these concerns, not just in terms of ensuring appropriate language development as essential to academic learning, but in terms of the values of "self-reliance, tolerance, equity, respect and integrity".[15] Thus Robertson sees "the selection of language" as concerned to bring about "a positive sense of linguistic self" and "respect" as being engendered by the understanding of the languages used by others, accompanied by the capacity to use that language where possible.

Robertson's recent policy document argues for the use of Trinidad and Tobago Creoles as well as Trinidad and Tobago Sign Language, stating the rights of the Deaf to be taught in their native Sign as a basic human right. Noting that the Ministry of Education's White Paper includes objectives such as "promoting social cohesion, maximizing personal development and ensuring cultural development and sensitivity", Robertson cements his case for the use of local Creole languages in education.[16] He notes that the surveys he has conducted have confirmed that teachers work with Creole in the classroom since they informally recognize English as not entirely native to their students. Our own corpus studies have confirmed this recognition in our teachers at the secondary level, indicating that they use Standard English as their majority code but relate to students and question them in Creole.[17] Robertson aims to render all citizens secure in their communicative and metalinguistic competences and states, as objectives for all, competence in a local Creole, as well as in English, Spanish and Sign. Awareness and sensitivity to the language situation of the territory remain paramount. Policy changes involve making both English and Sign Language official languages and the two Creoles of Trinidad and Tobago's national languages. Heritage languages also are to be properly documented and capable of access in the schools where there are significant numbers of children of a particular background. An institute for language education, as well as local centres concerned with language and education, would be established to support teacher and school development. Stakeholders throughout the system should be brought to clarity on the significance of mother-tongue education for all speakers in the establishment of literacy and positive learning.

OVERVIEW AND SUGGESTIONS FOR DEVELOPMENT

The linking of human values to language concerns in education are then Robertson's most lasting legacy, his views in the 2010 language-policy document being the culmination of his work in this arena. The implementation strategies he recommends may not be introduced, not because of a lack of respect for the views they express, but because they may be regarded as unrealistic for a territory where Creole and Standard are gradually merging and where the forces of globalization will continue to dictate a premature obsession with the attainment of English competence. Parental views in particular will be difficult to change to a full acceptance of Creoles alongside Standard varieties.

From an implementation perspective, what is still lacking is a set of clear statements as to how Creoles will be integrated into the education system. Accepting that standardization, codification and elaboration may be achieved, how will the Creoles be actually used "to facilitate education and learning"?[18] To say that "the roles of Trinidad Creole and Tobago Creole in education must be properly determined"[19] is to leave more to others than they may be able to handle. Is it that there will be a policy of transitional bilingualism whereby students start their education in Creole and achieve literacy in it, while taking English as a subject until such time as their knowledge renders it capable of becoming the education language? If this is the case, how will this be worked out in a society in which all individuals' relative knowledge of Creole and of English is a little different from the next and their code-mixing equally personal?[20] I myself find useful the following suggestions taken from the Jamaican Language Education Policy of 2001,[21] which elaborates on transitional bilingualism as follows:

Language Instruction
In the early years (up to Grade 4) teachers should . . . operate on the principle of transitional bilingualism which entails:

- acceptance of children's first language;
- flexibility; using children's first language to facilitate comprehension;
- extensive use of communicative strategies such as role play for practicing forms (structures) of English, particularly those which differ from Creole forms;
- comparison of Jamaican Creole and Standard Jamaican English structures (contrastive analysis) and other bilingual teaching strategies;
- employ strategies of immersion in English through the wide use of literature;
- content-based language teaching (integration across curriculum areas);
- modelling of the target language in the classroom.

Regarding the last point above, I feel it is time to make a different space for English in the curriculum from both the traditional one and that of an official but alienated tongue. It is detrimental for us to shift from regarding this global language as a first language that we speak badly to regarding it as a language that belongs eternally to the Other but never to ourselves. Our university students and many other members of Caribbean societies acquire fluent English as a native variety, albeit a language that develops later than the Creole for the majority. To maximize classroom use of it in a non-censorial frame that fully demonstrates its native functions in a Caribbean world is a particular implementation strategy that we may embrace practically.

Re-visioning the Creole voice demonstrates once and for all its absolute value to Caribbean societies, its absolute integrity and its absolute creativity; it also gives space to the potential bilingualism of its speakers, whose voice it has been Robertson's distinctive contribution to establish beyond question. Linguistic sensitivity and respect are cues for all learners rather than just a few to become successful additive bilinguals. It has been proven in numerous language situations that learners acquire a second language variety successfully only when their home variety is valued in the society in question. Since we have been brought close to proper respect for Creole and the Creole speaker, we can expect students to learn Standard English more successfully as long as we use appropriate Caribbean role models who already use the Standard as their own. The two language varieties, already manipulated and mixed in many language contexts, can be even more successfully embraced if they can be perceived as belonging to each Trinidad and Tobago national. If we are to become truly postcolonial as a society, the notion of English as exclusively foreign-owned must be eradicated.

Notes

1. Ian Robertson, "Language and Language Education Policy" (report to the Seamless Education Project Unit, Ministry of Education, Trinidad and Tobago, 2010).

2. Charles Ferguson, "Diglossia", *Word* 15 (1959): 325–40.

3. David De Camp, "Towards a Generative Analysis of a Post-Creole Continuum", in *Pidginization and Creolization of Languages*, ed. Dell Hymes (Cambridge: Cambridge University Press, 1971).

4. Dennis Craig, "Education and Creole English in the West Indies: Some Sociolinguistic Factors", in *Pidginization and Creolization of Languages*, ed. Dell Hymes (Cambridge: Cambridge University Press, 1971), 371–92.

5. Richard Allsopp, "The English Language in British Guiana", *English Language Teaching Journal* 12, no. 2 (1958): 59–66.

6. Craig, "Education and Creole English"; Dennis Craig, *Teaching Language and Literacy: Policies and Procedures for Vernacular Situations* (Georgetown, Guyana: Education and Development Services, 2006).

7. Ian Robertson, "Linguistics and the Reform of the Caribbean Language Curriculum" (mimeo, Faculty of Education, St Augustine, University of the West Indies, 2009), 4.

8. Ibid.

9. Ronald Carter, "Language Awareness", *ELT Journal* 57, no. 1 (January 2003): 64–65.

10. Robertson, "Language Education Policy", 6.

11. Norman Fairclough, *Media Discourse* (London: Edward Arnold), 1995.

12. Trinidad and Tobago National Task Force of Education, "Education Policy Paper, 1993–2003", Ministry of Education, 2004, http:www.nalis.gov.tt/Education/EducPolicy_Philosophy.html, quoted in Robertson, "Language Education Policy".

13. Robertson, "Language Education Policy".

14. Patrick J. Keenan, *Report upon the State of Education in the Island of Trinidad* (Dublin: Alexander Thom, 186), quoted ibid.

15. Robertson, "Language Education Policy", 39.

16. Ministry of Education, quoted ibid., 42.

17. Valerie Youssef, "The Varilingual Language Use of Trinidadian Teachers" (paper presented at Third International Conference on the Linguistics of Contemporary English, St Mary's College, University of London, 15–18 July 2009).

18. Robertson, "Language Education Policy", 55.

19. Ibid., 47.

20. Valerie Youssef, "Varilingualism: The Competence behind Code-Mixing in

Trinidad and Tobago", *Journal of Pidgin and Creole Languages* 11, no. 1 (1996): 1–22; Valerie Youssef, "Varilingualism: A Term for Twenty-first Century Language Acquisition Contexts", *Éducation et Sociétés Plurilingues*, no. 28 (June 2010): 65–76.

21. Ministry of Education, Jamaica, "Youth and Culture 2001 Language Education Policy", section 8.4, 25.

7.

POSSIBLE CARIBBEANS

Assembling the Fictional Voice

[BARBARA LALLA]

> facts lie behind the poems which are true fictions
> – Mervyn Morris, "Data"

THE CARIBBEANNESS OF OUR discourse lies both in our way of seeing and in our way of voicing what we see, but perhaps the truest fiction in Caribbean literature may be the Caribbean voice itself. Although Genette clearly distinguishes voice from perspective[1] – who speaks rather than who sees – he provides relatively little information on how voice is conveyed, and most of our understanding of voice has developed subsequently, for example through reference to Bakhtinian polyphony. Our understanding of voice in Caribbean discourse has much to gain from discussions that have drawn on Bakhtin's view of the multi-voiced and dialogic nature of utterances generally, and from his understanding of texts in which many independent and equally valid voices are heard.[2] Despite Genette's distinction between who speaks and who sees, the operation of voice parallels that of perspective in that polyphony or heteroglossia can convey multiple and conflictual ideological views, which are granted equal validity.

All that is conveyed in creative discourse is channelled through the literary persona that is contingent on voice – the proposed source (in answer to our question: *Where is this coming from?*). If the voice that proposes a text world set in the Caribbean is a Caribbean voice, we tend to assume that this enhances truth and, with truth, realism. In assuming this, we tend to overlook the extent to which this Caribbean voice is itself a construction and to forget that the relationship between narrator and narrated (which hinges so delicately on perspective) is similarly a fabrication contrived through this fictional voice.

POSSIBLE WORLDS: POSSIBLE VOICES

Without becoming overly embroiled in the place of fiction within theories of logic, I want to locate my comments within a possible-world frame. The treatment of fiction as mimesis rests on a relationship between the invented world and actual prototypes, and the credibility of a fictional Caribbean world involves extrapolation from prototypes in the actual Caribbean to another possible world. The complex language situation in the actual Caribbean increases the slipperiness of the fictional Caribbean. Even in relation to less fraught circumstances than our own, only minor variations tend to be sufficient to alert readers to the fact that the writer is evoking social groups different to our own.

Doležel supports Kirkham in explaining that "a *possible world* is a hypothetical entity postulated as an aid to talking about and studying the various ways the universe might have been different".[3]

Possible worlds proposed in creative literature constitute a fictional universe that may resemble the actual world or operate on entirely invented principles laid out in propositions that are consistent and persuasive in the internal logic of that set of propositions. Alexander Pruss demonstrates available ontologies.[4] The possible world encountered in literature can only be fabricated through language, and writers sometimes carry this fabrication into the realm of language itself. Obvious cases spring to mind, like the narrative of Anthony Burgess's *A Clockwork Orange*, but the inventiveness of invented language in fiction is perhaps scalar. (One has only to consider the distinctions between dialogue and actual conversation in the most traditional texts.)

In the Caribbean, writers of what would be viewed as realistic fiction fabricate narrative voice to perhaps a greater extent than is normally acknowledged. Doležel explains that "fictional worlds are ensembles of non-actualized possible states of affairs",[5] and he links fictional persons with any actual prototypes they may have by *transworld identity*. Presumably, fictional voices may also be ensembles. The transworld identity of which Doležel speaks is a consequence of the contingency of worlds in which characters and their situations may occur in different versions or guises. Unless there is a *rigid designator*, like a proper

name, fictional versions and their actual prototypes may only be related in fragile ways; so the links between one fictional version of a character and another
must, therefore, be even more tenuous. There is also a rather delicate connection between fictional voices of Caribbean speakers in the literature and the
linguistic prototypes in the real Caribbean. The consolidation of voices, based
on prototypes from individual territories, into one representative voice requires
more extensive invention.

The Caribbean constructed in literature is peopled by characters, some of
which have prototypes or versions elsewhere, versions connected by transworld
identities. The husband of Rhys's Antoinette, for example, is connected by a
transworld identity to Brontë's Rochester. But Caribbean literature relates to
other discourses in ways other than through transworld identities. The
Caribbean is a location that has long been represented or mentioned in literature, and the Caribbean that is now constructed in Caribbean discourse has
been constructed in other discourses in the past, such as British canonical discourse. In distinguishing Caribbean discourse, it seems reasonable to identify
a Caribbean perspective and Caribbean voice as crucial indicators of the discourse. It is questionable, however, whether what we might refer to as the
Caribbean voice in our literary discourse has any actual prototype. It may be
an ensemble of non-actual, possible states of affairs, an alternative Caribbean-
language situation.

The true Caribbean voice in literature can only be fictional, *fictional* here
being used for poetic as well as prose composition. This is so not only because
the faithful record effect is only an effect, and realistic representation of speech
can only be fallacious,[6] but because Caribbean speech can only be authenticated by reference to specific, although highly diverse, voices from individual
territories. The Caribbean voice is identifiable in relation to territory (1) apart
from whatever it conveys of social variables (like ethnicity, gender, class or age)
that may be appropriate to that territory and (2) however this voice shifts
between language varieties in the territory, according to whatever rules govern
such choices in that territory. The abstraction – Caribbeanness – is ideologically
prompted and is itself indicative of a conceptual point of view. The Caribbean
voice is a construction that is politically governed, fabricated with a view to
redistribution of power, to solidarity, and to validation of a group ensconced
in the space and set of circumstances we call *Caribbean*.

How is such a fabrication – Caribbean voice – achieved? Voice, as a function
of *who speaks*, is most usually associated with the narrator or central conscious-

ness. Yet *who speaks* is not always ascribable to narrator or to character exclusively. The speech of characters in narrative fiction is either represented through the narrator's voice or through the voices of the characters that the narrator presents to an audience. The narrator's voice tells us that speech has occurred or that a speech act (like an order) has occurred. The narrator may offer additional information regarding the manner of delivery, code choice and so on. The narrative voice may also offer some of the content conveyed by the speech through indirect speech, in the narrator's own words. On the other hand, a character's speech involves actual original words and sentence structure – direct speech – rather than a narrator's representation of the original by way of the narrator's reporting clause, such as, "she said".[7] In this most nearly unfiltered representation of speech, the centrality of the character's voice is foregrounded in that what is said has main clause rather than subordinate status.

It is true that, in contrast to indirect speech , a more faithful representation of the character's voice by the narrator can be achieved through free indirect speech, in that what is said has main-clause rather than subordinate-clause status and in that reporting clauses are suppressed. However, in free indirect speech, tense, pronouns and other deictic markers relate to the narrator rather than the character. Indirect speech, free or otherwise, reveals the narrator assimilating others (the characters) to himself or herself (the narrator). While free indirect speech shows relatively little interference from the narrator, the effect remains mimetic to an extent; meaning remains under the control of the narrator, so narrative authority is maintained. In addition, in some discourse the language may remain closer to that of the narrator's voice and in so doing diverge somewhat less from Standard English for the convenience of a wider audience. Genette follows Plato in identifying two strictly textual mimetic factors "the quality of narrative information . . . and the absence (or minimal presence) of the informer – in other words, of the narrator", so that mimesis is "defined by a maximum of information and a minimum of the informer".[8]

This means that the more palpable the narrative control, the more filtered the voice of the character – unless the narrator is a character (homodiegesis) or unless a series of narrators are characters in the work. This makes the representation of Caribbean voice in narrative and in characterization extremely complicated (in view of the complexity of the Caribbean language situation) and demands extensive contrivance on the part of the creative writer.

One way forward has been for Caribbean literary discourse to exploit a range of homodiegetic narrators such that narrative authority is surrendered to characterization. Any of these characters can speak in the real variety of a Caribbean territory or area of the diaspora, and this polyphony can suggest the composite Caribbean voice. Generally speaking, in fact, I believe it is more the characters' voices that are cast as specifically Jamaican, Barbadian, Guyanese, Canadian, Trinidadian or what have you, in keeping with their characterization. Detailed representation of regional differences between Creole varieties may be suppressed in the interest of a wide audience, but the odd signal establishes the source territory, like Jamaican's notorious non-phonemic [h]. "They push me hup to a place in Scotland," says Naipaul's Jamaican in *The Middle Passage*.[9] The relative precision with which the voices of different territories is represented in characterization versus narrative calls for survey and analysis, but general observation suggests that regionality, Caribbeanness, is more often, although not exclusively, the province of the narrator.

Unless this narrative voice belongs to a character, it is the (heterodiegetic) narrator who discerns these characters and presents each, voice and all, operating in relation to events that the narrator unfolds, framed in relevant circumstances that the narrator proposes, and (1) the voice of each character is in a sense released by the narrator; and (2) what the character says, in a sense, is selected or has been identified as significant enough to convey by the narrator and (3) how the character says it partakes, at least implicitly, of the narrator's rendering (or at least permission). The muting of the narrator's presence through free indirect speech or in dialogue-packed fiction that comprises mainly direct speech does not eliminate narrative perspective and can only tone down rather than eliminate narrative voice, whether this voice remains consistent or shifts within the discourse.

Narrative voice, to whatever extent it is audible, can only be Caribbean (regional) in a fictional sense in that either (1) regionally shared features are selected and distinctions suppressed, or (2) the variety of one territory is presented as representative or (3) features of different varieties are sampled and combined.

Meanwhile, all this is fluid. The Caribbean voice in literary discourse is not only a selection from or a composite of many voices but has been evolving, over the years, in its scribal representation. Elsewhere I have traced the development of Creole representation in Caribbean literary discourse as initially *ventriloquist* (invented by the non-Caribbean and non-Creole-speaking author and placed in the mouth of a Caribbean character); then more authentic but *censored* (represented by the Caribbean author or the author who knows Creole and placed only in the mouth of characters clearly defined according to class, ethnicity, education and so on); then accurately spoken by characters but *alternating* with the narrator's Standard English; and finally *expanded* in function (used for narrative as for dialogue and no longer sealed off from Standard English but shifting and mixing).[10] This development reflects an evolving view of the Caribbean speaker as having an authentic voice and reflects an evolving empowerment of the Caribbean writer to represent this voice. Current representation of the Creole voice in literary discourse nevertheless remains partial despite the accuracy of the selected features and is thus still a construction of Caribbean speech, recognizable but manageable to a varied readership. Moreover, the intermediate voice achieved through partial representation is an authentic variety of our range along the continuum. Despite this authenticity, Caribbeanness is still very much a construction, still fictional, whether the narrator is more audible or less so, allowing the characters' voices to take over and project Caribbean polyphony.

Authorial presence tends to be likewise muted for the discourse to assume "genuine Caribbeanness", that is, objectively render the "real" Caribbean. Such an impression of objectivity in imaginative writing consists of a sense that important aspects of the work have a reality not fabricated by the author. The impression of the real in fiction is achieved through facts assembled and presented devoid of emotion that might detract from them as facts, by meticulous attention to setting, by construction of characters that fit "types" enough to be recognizable but which surprise through their complexity and contradiction. This sense of reality, however, emerges not only through geographical and historical accuracy of setting, event and characterization but through representation of speech and thought within the setting, through representation of characters' language and through discursive strategies for conveying their attitudes and ways of knowing.

Yet there is a limited degree to which any author can construct a fictional world. Indeed most of the world, although invoked by the author, is constructed by the reader on the basis of shared knowledge between author and reader, including sociohistorical context, intertext and other such information. Writer and reader, as participants in the discourse world, collaborate in constructing the text world through what Joanna Gavins calls world-building elements and function-advancing propositions.[11] Fictional worlds are always incomplete reflections or constructions; and they are reflections or constructions in the sense that texts are world-imaging or world-constructing. Voice is a central attribute both of world-imaging and of world construction, and the reality of the fictional world rests on the readers' impression of authenticity in the fictional voice.

The Caribbean imaged and/or constructed in Caribbean literature comprises a set of alternative possibilities, and the term Caribbean, whether used by the writer or inferred by the reader (as in the case of Shani Mootoo's *Cereus Blooms at Night*[12]), is loaded with potential ambiguity. This ambiguity multiplies possibilities of meaning (as is the way of ambiguity anyway); multidimensional or alternative Caribbeans are thrown up, for example, through such linguistic and discursive situations as code ambiguity and intertextuality.

The complex language situation in the actual Caribbean increases the slipperiness of the fictional Caribbean. Even in relation to less fraught circumstances than our Caribbean-language situation, language variation need only be slight for readers to infer social distinctions. Postcolonial projects of historical revisionism naturally complicate our discourse in sensitizing readers to hitherto submerged local voices. The fabrication of an imaginary world that satisfies as having "reality" depends on authenticity of voice, and since Caribbean reality is culturally composite, the fictional Caribbean that has "reality" must be polyphonic.

Sociolinguists measure authenticity quantitatively, for example in such terms as deletion or retention rates of [-t#] or [-d#] in a specific variety of Creole. But linguistic authenticity is, ultimately, not just one dimensional. Gregory R. Guy and Celia Cutler point out that, in one direction, being an authentic speaker of a variety means approaching or achieving the rates of use of linguistic variables that are typical of that variety but, in another dimension, being an authentic speaker means changing one's usage (even through massive style shifting) if required.[13] Particularly interesting is the light thrown on authenticity by different artists' perceptions of what authenticity entails, for example by the degree to which authenticity in the discourse of hip hop is "about emulating African American gangsta rappers from their attitudes and gestures to their speech patterns".[14] Mary Bucholtz notes the movement in sociolinguistics away from the concept of a genuine speaker associated with some isolated, "pure" form of a language, of monolingualism as the unmarked,[15] towards a more complex concept of authenticity. Similarly, Christian Mair and Véronique Lacoste explore authenticity as a relational concept, noting the importance of context (social, cultural or stylistic) in establishing authenticity.[16] While Mair and Lacoste relate authenticity to locality (for example, Jamaican Creole located in Jamaica), they recognize that authenticity of the Creole in a globalized world may involve linguistic adjustments in contexts beyond the local, and they observe how in an international context the language of performance may move away from mimetic representation of the Creole that would be found locally.[17]

The Caribbean voice in our literature is characteristically composite, the fictional Caribbean comprising alternative worlds between which there is constant slippage in terms of shifts between English and Creole, as in Mervyn Morris's "Eve":

a proper paradise until she buck up on a serpent talking nice.[18]

Here, the inversion of experience, from divinely achieved paradise to dystopia, is conveyed through Creole phrases that comprise words originally English but distinctly Caribbean in meaning. *Buck up on* speaks to the unexpected encounter with the deceiver, the stumbling over evil, the halting in one's tracks by the interloper, while *talking nice* conveys not only verbal elegance of the tempter but the Caribbean persona (the man of words) and a Caribbean discourse type (for example, *mamaguy*). All this apart from the subtle metadiscursive thrust at traditional distinctions between the good and bad speech of colonizer and colonized. Ansgar Nunning points out the self-reflexive nature of metadiscourse, which comprises comments that refer to the discourse itself rather than the story, whether these comments authenticate, elicit empathy, or parody.[19] In Caribbean literary discourse, the *discourse* is not only the subject of comment (*talking nice*) but is often part of the *story* (*a serpent talking*). Authenticity involves multilingual competence closely associated with slippage between narrative levels.

To recognize metadiscourse as characteristic of creative discourse from the Caribbean is to say that Caribbean creative discourse is often in one way or other about Caribbean creative discourse, as demonstrated by innumerable characters (like Naipaul's Ganesh, Selvon's Moses and so many others[20]) who are intent on writing. There are, however, other less-explicit examples of the impulse to discourse on discourse. In the construction of Caribbean text worlds a choice frequently seized on by Caribbean literary artists is that of calling attention to the process of fabrication. This fabrication is a central topic of much of the discourse, and much work remains to be done on the scholar-artist and the occurrence of metalepsis. Metalepsis effects a transfer between the hierarchical levels of narrative production, enabling (according to John Pier) a "short-circuiting" of levels, an intrusion of the narrator into the story world, crossing the boundary between the telling and the told. This effaces, as Pier explains, "the line of demarcation between fiction and reality" and constitutes a transgression of thresholds.[21]

Edward Baugh's "It Was the Singing"[22] may be read as a metadiscursive poem on the redemptive potential of the Caribbean voice. A sacramental immersion in the chorus of disparate voices is conveyed through the river metaphor (*greater than paper-money overflowing; the sadness and the glory, wave after wave*). It is explicated as well in references (*Gertie and me by the river*) and simile (*the singing/ was like a wide water and Gertie laughing/and waving to me from the other side*). It describes the experience of the receptive consciousness: moved, filled and satisfied by that collective voice; raised more by this than sermonizing; lifted more than by comedy or example of fortitude and independence; sensitized beyond physical vision to tragedy and glory; probing depths and departures (through the descant), to account for an outpouring of wealth greater than money. Verbs of perception and cognition convey this deepening sensibility (*hear . . . how Gertie was a rebel; feel the sadness and the glory; know we was a people together*). The metadiscourse actually projects a sense of language failing on the individual level – *I can't too well describe it* – and the sense of a collective voice outweighing the individual – *The singing was bigger than all of we*. Transportation, the narrative effect that moves the reader from the actual world to the possible, is attributed to the singing that lifts participants to a place in which temporal affairs are immaterial. This possible world is not only that peaceful afterlife but a peaceful version of this world, *where gunman and drug addict don't haunt*.

The whole is framed within specific, stipulated circumstances in memory and forecast, which are reinforced by intertext, particularly through the embedded lines of a well-known hymn, "How Great Thou Art" (*then sings my soul . . .*). This is a popular version of an English translation of a Swedish hymn, said to be inspired after its composer experienced a violent thunderstorm followed by subsequent calm and the tolling of church bells. Various additions and innovations to the song have been associated with work among oppressed or dislocated peoples, like the expelled Polish community in England, and the song was subsequently popularized by Billy Graham who was revered in Jamaica, which he visited in his Caribbean tour in 1958. The speaker's concluding proposition, *if they sing me home*, defines peace in possible worlds here and beyond as a basis for the outcome celebrated in the embedded text, *then sings my soul.*

The mesolectal discourse of "It was the singing" facilitates a range of possible readings in Jamaican, but for the most part it is as easily readable by other voices, enabling an understanding of it as "Caribbean". In this sense the homodiegetic account is not only composite but ambiguous. Such ambiguity of code in the fabrication of the Caribbean voice enables complex interplays of meaning, and slippage between codes is widely played on by Caribbean artists (investigated elsewhere in specific works, as in Lalla 2000).[23]

Louise Bennett supplies a good example of ambiguity in English terms and ambiguity through slippage between Jamaican and English in "Colonization in Reverse".[24] Journey and migration, the latter not always forced, are central to Caribbean experience, and the circumstances of Jamaicans *going foreign* prompt a set of core propositions in the text world through which Bennett rehistoricizes mass movement to and from Jamaica. To achieve this, she manipulates ambiguity, sometimes playing on key words that have separate meanings in English and Jamaican. The verse plays on terms like *bound* in describing Jamaicans as England bound, to exploit both the obvious meaning, "on the way to", "pointed in the direction of", and the less obvious, "tied, constrained", which underlies the grip of England as colonizer as well as its tug as perceived motherland. These are plays on English meanings, and (curiously) the more obvious meaning is in fact the non-literal, and the less obvious is the literal. But never mind that. The inversion of Jamaica's sociohistorical background is not only explicated in the theme of colonization in reverse, which turns history *upside dung* (Jamaican pronunciation of the English phrase) but implicated in possible ambiguities of code – for does history, as meted out by the colonizer, get upturned as crap (the English meaning of [dʌŋ])?

Further inversion is implicated in reference to a perpetuation of economic exploitation of Jamaicans by Jamaicans, but the overall shift of agency to Jamaicans is both explicit (in the opening of a cheap-fare-to-England agency) and implicit in the operation of transitivity in the text. Jamaica people colonize, pour, plan, get settled, pack, turn, ship off, immigrate, populate, live, box, seek, look, stay and read. *Jamaica people live fe box bread outa English people mouth.* They are ever the agents of action unless exploited by their own people or unless they settle for the dole and so choose to become patients of an action profitable to themselves (*paying she*).

All these characteristics of the text are as Caribbean (and, often, English) as they are Jamaican, but in further ways the poem distinguishes the voice as specifically Jamaican. It is true that sometimes attributes of the text flag linguistic differences to the eye only, like *wat*. This spelling throws in your face how normal pronunciation (even by Standard English speakers) has long dispensed with the [h] in *what*. At the same time, the poem dismisses any pretension of consistently close sound representation, for example spelling "joyful" as in English regardless of the range of vowel choice possible, because that is the point: There are options that Jamaican readers (and Caribbean readers in general) will make automatically to suit themselves. The selection of *I* rather than *me* for subject in the same line as *me* rather than *my* for possessive reinforces this issue of choice.

However, the text clearly indicates Jamaican phonology in *gwine* and, probably, in *burs*. The way is left clear for the reader to pronounce burs as [bɜʳs] or [bʌs] to rhyme with *reverse* or *worse*, accordingly. The orthography of *burs* as distinct from *buss* is convenient to the English reader, and the implied pronunciation [bɜʳs] is just as Jamaican as [bʌs] – indeed more so because the latter, the more basilectal form, is used elsewhere in the Caribbean, while the former, more mesolectal, is characteristically Jamaican. *Gwine* stands out because it incorporates many features: [ŋ>n] as in the more legible *colonisin* but also a number of vowel changes, including syncopation and compensatory labialization [w] to produce a single-syllable word. However, [ŋ>n] and other well-known characteristics like [Θ>t] and [ð>d] as in *thousand* and *de*, as well as the reduction of consonant clusters in *boun* and *burs*, are regional features of the anglophone Caribbean. The manoeuvring between English and Creole is as Jamaican (and Caribbean) as Creole itself and throws up the world of the England-bound Jamaican even as it subtly sideswipes English.

Not only is voicing the Caribbean achieved in a variety of ways, such as Creole representation, metadiscursive commentary, code-shifting and code ambiguity, but this fictional voice is constructed for interface in the literature between worlds, now and beyond, home and foreign, here and elsewhere.

(IM)POSSIBLE CARIBBEANS

So far we have considered the Caribbean voice through which we encounter fictional worlds that compare relatively closely to the actual Caribbean or Caribbean diaspora. The inevitable intersections of possible worlds with each other are voiced in ways that project contact and contestation, like code shift and intertext. As is often the case in fabricated worlds, the fictional Caribbean is often angled to complement some other *inner* world.

Simpson quotes Vološhinov[25] as reminding us that "existence reflected in the sign is not only reflected but refracted".[26] In representing a Caribbean voice and mind, the author becomes engaged in wording a consciousness in mechanisms by which the internal states of others, their interior landscapes, may be inferred. It is widely recognized that such a Caribbean consciousness is by no means unitary. Stuart Hall's theory of diasporic identities draws on the enigmatic nature of Caribbean identity as based on origin elsewhere and on the violence and rupture through which these identities are assembled.[27] The Louise Bennett example earlier in this chapter demonstrates how ambiguities of code enable plays on meaning, and how orthographical flexibility facilitates the reader's fluid movement in the continuum that projects this multiple, shifting and enigmatic consciousness. Indeed the awareness of a riven self, the sense of one's own identity as Other (and as other than real), emerges again and again. Often, as in Merle Hodge's Tee in *Crick Crack Monkey* and Olive Senior's Sadie throughout her progress in "Zig-Zag",[28] it is a complicating factor of individual maturation and its mirror image, national development.[29]

So far we have considered the representation of Creole and the slippage between Creole and English involved in voicing the Caribbean. We have also taken account of intertextual relationships between (on the one hand) European, African and Indian texts and (on the other) Caribbean texts. At this point I would like to turn to intertextual relationships between earlier and more recent Caribbean texts, and, after that, to peer past metadiscursive obsessions with the character as writer to the more speculative metadiscursive construction of a governing discourse that orders existence in outlandish Caribbean worlds.

Elsewhere I have remarked on Nalo Hopkinson's rewriting of Derek Walcott's *Ti-Jean and His Brothers* in *Brown Girl in the Ring*, especially through the revision of the horizontal connections of three brothers to the vertical connections between grandmother, mother and daughter.[30] Walcott having drawn on existing folktale, Hopkinson draws on Walcott, but each creates a new text world extrapolated from (yet distinct from) its prototypes along lines that specialists in narrative logic term *transduction*.

Hopkinson constructs a world that purports to be in Toronto with the CN Tower at its centre, but the core of this area, the Burn, is Caribbean inner city.

Doležel defines *transduction* as taking the literary work "beyond the communicative act into an open, unlimited chain of transmission" without the duty (which the translator would have) of preserving the fictional world of the original.[31] The dual nature of rewriting, as marking not only the difference from but the connection with the past,[32] enables what Doležel identifies as postmodern re-evaluation – though I cannot for the life of me see why he limits it to the postmodern, as similar re-evaluation is clearly apparent in earlier literary periods.[33] Doležel argues that this re-evaluation takes three forms:

- Transposition, which relocates the main story to a different setting in time and space and is parallel;
- Expansion, which fills gaps and is complementary;
- Displacement, which redesigns the prototype to a radically new version and is polemical.

Doležel demonstrates how Jean Rhys goes beyond transposition and expansion through multiple shifts in the fictional world made possible by the polyphonic narrative. In *Brown Girl in the Ring*, however, Hopkinson pushes the edge of her fictional world further away from its (Walcott) prototype and closer to rupture.[34] The shockingly alternative guise of its characters goes beyond Ti Jeanne's transformation as third-generation woman, protected by African divinities, to the transformation of the devil from white planter to Caribbean don. Exploitation of the Caribbean poor is not only gendered but perpetrated by black Caribbean characters on each other in a fallen first world space: privileged Toronto demoted to dystopia. In Hopkinson's version of dystopia, unlike Morris's, the serpent does not even pretend to be *talking nice*.

This *im*possible world is fabricated as a possible Caribbean space through constructions of voice that are impossible in the Caribbean itself but possible in a time and space where language mixing (of varieties of anglophone Caribbean Creole) could have occurred. The situation proposed extrapolates from the Caribbean diaspora in Canada.

In this contrived setting, Rudy's voice is mainly Jamaican Creole. "Bloodfire!" is his opening curse – appropriately in view of his control of the Burn through such characters as the blood-drinking ball of fire, called the soucouyant in Eastern Caribbean style versus Ole Haig, the Jamaican term. He establishes the distribution of power in Jamaican with himself as deictic centre: "Is we a-rule things here now".[35] However, while he commands his human underlings and manipulates the English-speaking Baines in Creole, he controls the zombie-like Melba in Standard English: "Keep on dusting, Melba".[36] At the same time, his language also contains characteristics of anglophone Creole other than Jamaican, such as *does* (habitual) and *she* (object) familiar in Trinidadian. This construction of a Caribbean elsewhere in a voice more code-mixed than code-shifting, is taken further in Hopkinson's *Midnight Robber* – ultra way out and way in – to a different planet and to the inner space of the womb.[37]

All this is a very recent development in Caribbean literature, but how new is speculative discourse regarding the Caribbean? When we in the Caribbean world of letters began to re-cast the colonizers' constructions of ourselves, we tried to convey actual communities. In these instances, we were representing Caribbean prototypes as we knew them, and our approach was mimetic. Then (not instead of, but in addition to such constructions) we began to conceive alternatives for European literature, enabled by Caribbean ideology: Antoinette's incendiary response to betrayal and confinement in Rhys's *Wide Sargasso Sea*, Jimmy's warped self-image of himself as Heathcliff in Naipaul's *Guerrillas*, Cesaire's *Tempeste* and Walcott's Odyssean sailor, to name a few. Finally, in such work as Hopkinson's, we conceive of radical alternatives to our own constructions. Yet our suppositions of even the most impossible of other Caribbeans are still based on extrapolation.

Joanna Russ calls science fiction a discourse whose subject matter does not exist.[38] However, although the circumstances that leap out at us cannot possibly exist in our own world, they are embedded with circumstances that do, and all these circumstances are framed in an imaginary world that makes them not only possible but inevitable, allowing us to systematically and rationally explore them in that context. This alternative world offers what Darko Suvin calls *cognitive estrangement* in rejecting mimesis in obvious ways, but it does not reject mimesis in every way, for cognitive estrangement requires similitude as well as dissimilitude.[39]

Our own construction of possible Caribbeans through cognitive estrangement is peculiarly ironic because in the eighteenth and nineteenth century British world of letters, the physical West Indies was a space for speculation, a space so distant and known so little that any version might do and the briefest reference might trigger wonder, might stimulate the reader to grapple with the impossible. In the world of nineteenth-century British imperialism, narrative construction of the rational order of things partook of and reinforced an essentially bureaucratic ethos, that of the empire's work as the exercise of power over far flung peoples.[40]

The West Indies in British fiction was the unknown and (as outer chaos) to some extent the unknowable, the problematic. It offered a degree of unrepresentability, and it was so located as to awaken speculation. Seo Young-Chu proposes scales of estrangement,[41] and in a continuum of high or low intensity in the estrangement offered by fiction the shifting between worlds that occurs in *Midnight Robber* produces intense estrangement. But it may be that we have underrated the intensity of estrangement offered in nineteenth-century British literary references to journeys to the West Indies and to the hybrid nature of Caribbean reality where Others seemed as wildly suspect and threatening as Hopkinson's douens do to the tall people of her far-flung Caribbean worlds.

What happens if (knowing what we do about extrapolation) we not only go back to tamper with early British constructions of ourselves but (based on our own knowledge of our actual worlds) we postscript these constructions by inferring the significance of the West Indies in the British construction of its own identity? Perhaps we unmask in canonical texts the underlying yearning (not so dissimilar to our own) for self-definition, a yearning behind the setting up of margins. For these margins, in delimiting the known and "civilized", account for difference by locating the unfamiliar beyond borders. These margins account for gaps in information by associating the gaps with periods of absence from within the borders. If so, these margins are there to validate what lies within by defining some Other from which to mark off the British self-under-construction. British inventions of the West Indies then contribute to a discursive construction of Britishness.[42]

In this sense, British inventions of the Caribbean and Caribbean speculative fiction relate curiously, almost like mirror images. British constructions do not distinguish the different territories of the West Indies beyond naming the odd island, just as Caribbean futuristic settings amalgamate and re-mythologize Caribbean origins. Caribbean science fiction proposes permutations through which issues in our known world can be examined anew through cognitive estrangement, in relation to which Maill and Kuikon ,[43] David Herman[44] and Fiona Doloughan[45] all refine on earlier scholarship on defamiliarization.[46] Caribbean science fiction not only extrapolates from known issues but rewrites the historical past to a speculative future history: the migration of Caribbean peoples in great ships from Earth to the planet of Toussaint in *Midnight Robber*, and the reconfiguration of societies and landscapes by a violently intrusive governing force in *Brown Skin Gal*. The folklore/science fiction/fantasy triad in Caribbean speculative fiction inverts a triad that underlies British canonical texts with their strong vein of allusion to the myths privileged in their own belief systems and literary traditions; with confidence in the advanced nature of their own society, as a point of departure in travel literature; with the realism that mimesis implies in drawing from prototypes in British society and through vague fragmentary reference to other far-flung places designating these as unknowable.

In Caribbean discourse, the fictional voice is as incomplete as the fictional world and requires the audience to fill in along the lines of cues provided in the text and context. But this interaction of reader and writer raises further challenges in the production of a viable fictional voice. Norman Fairclough points out that the flows, networks and interconnections that characterize globalization "include flows of representations, narratives and discourses".[47] Caribbean writing is being produced in an increasingly globalized world, even as Caribbean hypersensitivity persists regarding our own formative sociohistorical circumstances. Increasing cultural and linguistic interface between the Caribbean and elsewhere runs alongside growing recognition of the crucial role of Caribbean discourse in identity formation and affirmation of selfhood and accommodation of the multiple interfaces within the region.

The fictionality of the Caribbean voice is, therefore, particularly complex because of several circumstances operating at the same time: the Caribbean language situation entails multivocality, and what we may term our discourse situation fosters metadiscourse and metalepsis. Thus, the interface between Caribbean writer and international readership is fraught with linguistic choice and intertext. Moreover, the role of Creole in the Caribbeanness of the discourse is associated with resistance to standardizing forces and embrace of individual expression (complicating considerations of legibility with principled *faceTiness*), and the individuality itself displays a dialectic of regional and I/land consciousnesses.

British imagining of the Caribbean not only occurred in English that had already developed to a highly codified and increasingly international language, but developed in the framework of British thought; and British imagining of the Caribbean no doubt furthered construction of a framework of British thought, although British imaging of the Caribbean voice could only be inaccurate. However, Caribbean imagining of a Caribbean voice, even in a text world closely assembled from prototypes in the actual Caribbean, is by no means straightforward. Caribbean imagining of a voice for another Caribbean, one that is experienced through intense cognitive estrangement, is yet more fraught. The Nanny song that orders existence on Hopkinson's Toussaint has an equally fictional equivalent in the language of narration delivered by the raconteur's Caribbean voice, assembled from actual linguistic fragments made credible by the imaginary context and studded with cues for readers to fill out from their individual linguistic experience.

But with all these permutations in the imagining of worlds and of journeys to New and newer W/worlds, and with the concomitant permutations of convincing narrative voices for conveying these experiences, who is to say which are the truest fictions, or whose cognitive estrangements are most intense? In any case, the extrapolations that are involved rest on a discursive dimension, on the fabrication of a composite and conflictual voice; on the drawing on linguistic prototypes even while engaging with the non-existent entity. The im/possible world or universe of discourse requires an invention of a context in which it all not only can but must come to pass, the forming of a proposition that it has and the fabricating of an appropriate discourse out of this world.

Notes

1. Gérard Genette, *Narrative Discourse*, trans. Jane E. Lewis (Ithaca, NY: Cornell University Press, 1980), 186.

2. Mikhail Bakhtin, *Speech Genres and Other Late Essays*, trans. V.W. McGee (Austin: University of Texas Press, 1986), 92; Mikhail Bakhtin, *The Dialogic Imagination*, ed. Michael Holquist, trans. Caryl Emerson and Michael Holquist (Austin: University of Texas Press, 1984), 67.

3. Lubomir Doležel, *Heterocosmica: Fiction and Possible Worlds* (Baltimore: Johns Hopkins University Press, 1998), 13 and n.19; Richard Kirkham, *Theories of Truth: A Critical Introduction* (Cambridge, MA: MIT Press, 1992), 11.

4. Alexander Robert Pruss, "Possible Worlds: What Are They Good For" (PhD diss., University of British Columbia, 2001). http://www9.georgetown.edu/faculty /ap85/papers/PhilThesis.html#_t 0c515941279.

5. Doležel, *Heterocosmica*, 16.

6. M. Toolan, "The Significations of Representing Dialect in Writing", *Language and Literature* 1, no. 1 (1992): 29–46; Brian McHale, "Speech Representation", in *The Living Handbook of Narratology*, ed. Peter Hühn et al. (Hamburg: University of Hamburg Press, 2009), http://hup.sub.uni-hamburg.de/lhn/index.php?title= Speech_Respresentation&oldid=1495, accessed 23 Oct. 2011; Barbara Lalla, "Reg-

istering Woman: Senior's Zig-Zag Discourse, and Code-Switching in Jamaican Narrative", *A Review of International English Literature* 29, no. 4 (1998): 83–98.

7. See also Genette, *Narrative Discourse*, 171–72.

8. Ibid., 166.

9. V.S. Naipaul, *The Middle Passage* (Harmondsworth, UK: Penguin, 1969), 245.

10. See Barbara Lalla, "Creole and Respec' in the Development of Jamaican Literary Discourse", *Journal of Pidgin and Creole Languages* 20, no. 1 (2005): 53–64.

11. Joanna Gavins, "Text World Approach to Narrative", *Routledge Encyclopedia of Narrative Theory*, ed. David Herman, Manfred Jahn and Marie-Laure Ryan (New York: Routledge, 2005), 596–97.

12. Shani Mootoo, *Cereus Blooms at Night* (Vancouver: Press Gang, 1996).

13. Gregory R. Guy and Celia Cutler, "Speech Style and Authenticity: Quantitative Evidence for the Performance of Identity", *Language Variation and Change* 23, no. 1 (March 2011): 139–62.

14. Ibid.

15. Mary Bucholtz, "Sociolinguistic Nostalgia and the Authentication of Identity", *Journal of Sociolinguistics* 7 (2003): 398–416, http://www.linguistics.ucsb.edu/faculty/bucholtz/articles/MB_JofS 2003.pdf.

16. Christian Mair and Véronique Lacoste, "A Vernacular on the Move: Towards a Sociolinguistics of Mobility for Jamaican Creole", *Cahiers de Linguistique* (forthcoming).

17. Ibid., 17.

18. Morris, "Eve", in *I Been There, Sort of: New and Selected Poems* (Manchester, UK: Carcanet, 2006), 18.

19. Ansgar Nunning, "On Metanarrative: Towards a Definition, a Typology and an Outline of the Functions of Metanarrative Commentary", in *The Dynamics of Narrative Form: Studies in Anglo-American Narratology*, ed. John Pier (Berlin and New York: Walter de Gruyter, 2005), 11–58; and see Monika Fludernik, *Towards a "Natural" Narratology* (New York: Routledge, 2003); Dole ž el, *Heterocosmica*, 145–68.

20. V.S. Naipaul, *The Mystic Masseur* (London: Deutsch, 1957); Samuel Selvon, *The Lonely Londoners* (1956; repr. Harlow, Essex: Longman, 1985).

21. Genette, *Narrative Discourse*, 234–37; David Herman, "Towards a Formal Description of Narrative Metalepsis", *Journal of Literary Semantics* 26, no. 2 (1997): 132–52.

22. Edward Baugh, *It Was the Singing* (Toronto and Kingston: Sandberry Press, 2000) 36.

23. Investigated elsewhere in specific works, as in Barbara Lalla, "Conceptual Perspectives on Time and Timelessness in Martin Carter's 'University of Hunger' ",

in *All Are Involved: The Art of Martin Carter*, ed. Stewart Brown (Leeds, UK: Peepal Tree Press, 2000), 106–14.

24.   Louise Bennett, *Jamaica Labrish* (Kingston: Sangsters, 1966).

25.   V.N. Vološhinov, *Marxism and the Philosophy of Language*, trans. L. Matejka and T.R. Titunik (New York: Seminar Press, [1930], 1973), 23.

26.   See *A Reader in Discourse Stylistics*, ed. Ronald Carter and Paul Simpson (1989; repr. London: Routledge Taylor and Francis, e-Library, 2004), in reference to Vološhinov, *Marxism*, 23.

27.   Stuart Hall, "Negotiating Caribbean Identities", in *Postcolonial Discourses: An Anthology*, ed. Gregory Castle (Oxford: Blackwell, 2000), 283–84.

28.   Merle Hodge, *Crick Crack Monkey* (Oxford: Heinemann, 1970), 61–62; Olive Senior, *Discerner of Hearts* (Toronto: McClelland and Stewart, 1995).

29.   See Barbara Lalla, "The Validity of Cross-Disciplinary Analysis: The Language of Collapsing Certainty in the Novels of Merle Hodge" (paper presented at the Seventeenth Conference of West Indian Literature, University of the West Indies, Mona, Jamaica, 5–9 April 1998); Barbara Lalla, "Registering Woman: Senior's Zig-Zag Discourse, and Code-Switching in Jamaican Narrative", *Review of International English Literature* 29, no. 4 (1998), 83–98 (republished 2005, *Short Story Collection* 78).

30.   Barbara Lalla. "The Facetiness Factor: Theorising Caribbean Space in Narrative" (keynote address, Twenty-ninth Conference on West Indian Literature, University of the West Indies, Mona, Jamaica, April–May 2010).

31.   Doležel, *Heterocosmica*, 205.

32.   L. Hutcheon, "Historiographic Metafiction: Parody and the Intertextuality of History", in *Intertextuality and Contemporary American Fiction*, ed. Patrick O'Donnell and Robert Con Davis (Baltimore: Johns Hopkins University Press, 1989), 5.

33.   Similar re-evaluation is clearly apparent in earlier literary periods as I have argued throughout Barbara Lalla, *Postcolonialisms: Caribbean Re-reading of Medieval English Discourse*. (Kingston: University of the West Indies Press, 2008).

34.   Nalo Hopkinson, *Brown Girl in the Ring* (New York: Grand Central, 1998).

35.   Ibid., 3.

36.   Ibid., 5.

37.   Nalo Hopkinson, *Midnight Robber* (New York: Warner, 2000).

38.   Joanna Russ, "Speculations: The Subjunctivity of Science Fiction", in *To Write Like a Woman: Essays in Femininity and Science Fiction* (1973; repr. Bloomington: Indiana University Press, 1995), 16; Seo Young-Chu, *Do Metaphors Dream of Literal Sleep? A Science Fictional Theory of Representation* (Cambridge, MA: Harvard University Press, 2010), 77.

39. Darko Suvin, "Metamorphoses of Science Fiction: On the Poetics and History of a Literary Genre (New Haven, CT: Yale University Press, 1979), 8.

40. This is extensively worked out in Daniel Bivona, *British Imperial Literature: Writing and the Administration of Empire* (Cambridge: Cambridge University Press, 1998).

41. Young-Chu, *Do Metaphors*, ch. 1.

42. In doctoral research now underway, Rhonda Harrison relates the development of Romance fiction in imperial literature to interests in the West Indies ("Configurations of 'Romance' and Sexual Power in West Indian Fiction in English, 1827–1917", St Augustine, University of the West Indies).

43. David S. Miall and Don Kuiken, "Foregrounding, Defamiliarization, and Affect Response to Literary Stories", University of Alberta. *Poetics*, 22 (1994): 337.

44. David Herman, *Story Logic: Problems and Possibilities of Narrative* (Lincoln: University of Nebraska Press, 2002), 23, 270.

45. Fiona Doloughan, *Contemporary Narrative: Textual Production, Multimodality and Multiliteracies* (London and New York: Continuum, 2011), ch. 1.

46. See W. Iser, *The Act of Reading: A Theory of Aesthetic Response* (Baltimore: Johns Hopkins University Press, 1978).

47. Norman Fairclough, *Language and Globalization* (New York: Routledge, 2006).

PART 2

TRAJECTORIES OF CREOLIZATION

8.

FRAGMENTS, CENTRES AND MARGINS

[LISE WINER]

LIKE MANY PEOPLE, I BECAME interested in Creole languages, and specifically Caribbean Creole languages and cultures, through experiences in education. In my case, this took place in the early 1970s, when I was a volunteer tutor for the Jamaican Association of Montreal. I became aware of the misunderstandings and missed opportunities for so many Caribbean-background children in Canada. In 1971, Bernard Coard responded to the overrepresentation of West Indian immigrant children in the United Kingdom in special-education classes for the "sub-normal" by explaining the terrible consequences of viewing Creole speakers as people without a "proper language": "A man's language is part of him. It is his only vehicle for expressing his thoughts and feelings. To say that his language and that of his entire family and culture is second rate, is to accuse him of *being* second rate."[1] Lest this attitude of miscomprehension and discrimination be attributed only to colonial ignorance and prejudice in the metropole or to various colonial elements and influences within Creole systems, up until the 1980s and 1990s or later, or indeed even now, many locally born and raised educators, not to mention parents and the general public, in the Caribbean would have generally concurred with this view, only differing in considering it "bad" or "broken" speech rather than not language at all.

Surely that was then, and we are more enlightened now. Nevertheless, in 2009, a highly trained and experienced children's literacy specialist in New York told one researcher that the immigrant Guyanese students in her classes spoke in a manner that was "only one step above grunting". Has any progress been made? Has the *will* to make any progress changed? Extensive research has indicated ways of improving the language and language-related education of Caribbean children, and a slow steady progress is better than none.

Studies of Creole languages, which began seriously in the late nineteenth century, boomed from the 1970s onward. It was a pioneering, groundbreaking discipline of research, both for the elevation of its target of study to "legitimate" languages and for the methods by which these were investigated. The common language – spoken and written – of a Creole society such as Trinidad and Tobago is not monolithic and cannot be characterized by one set of features or rules; neither can the speakers of these languages be divided and classified into neat categories. Because both English and English Creole speech are found in Caribbean English Creole situations, often in the same speaker, they gave rise to the concept of the *Creole continuum*, with the *basilect* – the Creole variety farthest from English – at one end, and the *acrolect* – a local but standard international English – at the other. In between is the *mesolect*, speech varieties that appear to have characteristics of both end *-lects* and a large amount of variation. Although the continuum is not a precise framework, it is, as Lawrence Carrington has noted, "a convenient inexactitude".[2]

The theoretical impact of Creole studies in other disciplines was impressive. The scholarly world was full of papers on such topics as "The Vernacular Architecture Continuum" – which incidentally fit the model better than language did – and you could not turn around without someone in science education or cultural studies or composition theory referring to any variation in terms of "basilect, mesolect and acrolect" or the "creolization" of vernacular culture.

The original concept of the Creole continuum was fairly lockstep and viewed as progressive, that is, progressing from the "low" to the "high", from the margin to the centre. However, this linear representation makes it difficult to view the continuum as multidimensional. Lawrence Carrington has proposed that we consider metaphors of "Creole space" that include the idea of "multisystemic repertoires".[3] One such metaphor is "an integrated mass of soap bubbles, each of which has the unusual feature of a penetrable skin", with bubbles of varied and changing shapes and sizes; "the overall shape of the mass . . . arbitrary and irregular". Carrington claims that Creole space "coheres because networks of communication overlap" in a way that may be "neither constant nor systematic".

Another excellent Carrington metaphor is the marble cake, in which different flavours make different colours of batter, which both combine into a coherent whole – the cake – and retain their coherent shape and shades in contrasting swirls. And, while a Standard English marble cake is only and always chocolate and vanilla – brown and white – a Creole marble cake is more often green or red and white. A metaphor of mine is that of the artistic technique of pointillism, in which all you can see close up is apparently random dots of colour; move back, and you see that there are more dots of some colours than others; move farther back, and as you lose the distinction of all but the most salient dots, they can be re-visioned as constituting other, unforeseen yet increasingly recognizable shapes.

A major contribution of Creole language studies has been its comparative and cross-sectional focus. On the one hand, the Society for Caribbean Linguistics considers any and all languages in the Caribbean, whether indigenous or imported, "real" or "Creole", allowing comparison across a particular geographical, historical and social context. On the other hand, the Society for Pidgin and Creole Linguistics focuses on languages anywhere in the world whose processes of formation derived from a similar history and whose characteristics appeared more similar than not. However, the very concept of Creole has always come with a lot of inherent confusion – that word has the highest number of senses of any word in my dictionary. Some creolists, like Derek Bickerton, working from the then-popular universal and innate models of development, posited that Creoles were invented by children, begging the question of how hundreds and thousands of linguistically competent adults hardly spoke to any other adults until their children grew up and could translate for them.

Furthermore, "Creole", as a type, category or kind of language, was being defined according to a specific kind of historical process by which it had developed, rather than by its resultant linguistic characteristics. Gillian Sankoff and Suzanne Laberge, in their article "On the Acquisition of Native Speakers by a Language",[4] in reference to Tok Pisin, noted that *linguistically*, it was not possible to distinguish the language as spoken by native or second-language speakers. Having raised Creole languages to new heights, we have welcomed new examples but still jealously guarded the portals. Nowadays, against the popular embrace by media and academics of anything called "Creole", creolists fight to keep English itself from being considered a Creole, rather than a language that has borrowed, begged or stolen words, sounds and structures from many other languages, also under some contexts of conquest, but not parallel to those we associate with Creole development.

This perspective gave creolists a framework within which to compare both language and context, and while Creole studies began by focusing on the language itself, by the mid-1990s it had become *de rigueur* to talk about historical sociodemographics. Historical perspective is crucial for Creole languages because their very definition depends on knowing their history, their earliest and more recent pasts determined only by reassembling the fragments that we have.

Language is a particularly rich and fruitful area for the study of "retentions". In Melville Herskovits and Frances Herskovits's work in Trinidad in 1939,[5] they cited rituals, customs and language that they attributed to African origins; Maureen Warner-Lewis's work *Central Africa in the Caribbean* is a fine example of what can be done by a scholar well versed in both the Creole river, although removed in time if not space from the original headwaters, and in its tributaries.[6]

As linguists became dependent on or considered themselves demographic social historians, they took advantage of older sources and newly available online historical databases. We wanted to know, for example, where exactly people had come from, so that we could infer their original languages and therefore check our etymologies. This did not, of course, prevent some scholars from choosing one founding people or language and allowing no others – a counter-intuitive idea for the very discipline that should seek to include as many voices as may possibly be relevant. The first and best example of what can be done to reconstruct, re-assemble and re-analyse these voices is, of course, the kind of work included in Barbara Lalla and Jean D'Costa's twin books on *Voices in Exile*[7] and *Language in Exile*.[8]

PARADISE LOST: THE REAL CREOLES

Another influence of the Creole continuum on Creole studies, in a bitterly ironic reversal of the colonial-centres' view of some languages as "real languages" in contrast to, for example, Creoles, which are not "real" languages, was the tendency to rank Creole languages themselves by their linguistic status as "more" or "less" authentic . Some Creoles are "real" – which must mean that some Creoles are not. "Decreolized" Creoles are not "real" anymore. And thus the Caribbean becomes the subject, or perhaps the object, of a process of re-centring and marginalization, with Jamaica, Guyana, Tobago and especially Suriname re-imagined as a kind of their languages Paradise Lost, considered sorts of Ur-Creole conferring higher professional status on its scholars.

This view is popular with some people because Creole languages – and Creole peoples – in the modern world as we encounter them are far too difficult to deal with: They are not neatly encapsulated, they are messy and variable, the speakers are not using their "proper" grammatical particles. Because they are obviously trying to "talk Standard", they are no longer genuine and legitimate subjects. They are not allowed to be normal, complex, ambivalent, modern human beings.

This is the view that scholars like Valerie Youssef have countered with the model of variation as "normal".⁹ Establishing standards of what is "normal" – as, for example, Kathy Ann Drayton's work on assessing language disorders in an English Creole context,¹⁰ presented at the "Reassembling the Fragments" conference – is important not only for this context, but – in what Louise Bennett would call "colonization in reverse" – perhaps even more important for the worldwide communities who cannot afford to ignore that they are no longer the homogeneous pure centres that they never really were in the first place. As the world becomes a "global village", the centre must adapt and enlarge itself to hold; if not, it will either disintegrate or try in vain to eject what it sees as a threat.

In at least two cases that I know from personal experience – Barbados and Trinidad – many creolists, from both inside and outside the region, persistently refused to recognize that "real" Creoles exist there; in fact, they insisted that these places had *never* had a real Creole. This self-deception was maintained by refusing to explore historical evidence or by ignoring historical evidence that did emerge. It only takes two minutes of standing at the bus terminal in Bridgetown to recognize that what is in the air is Caribbean English Creole; even though some of the particles have changed their clothes, they are the same underneath. In sweeping statements about the nature of Barbadian language in its apparently formative years, some creolists based their theories on a single line or two of secondary evidence, privileging theory over description, syntax over lexicon, and analysis over data, against the insistence by scholars like Ian Robertson on the necessity of adequate amounts of field-collected speech. (And with Robertson, fieldwork is in a real real field!)

In a post-modern world, culture has become self-conscious. For many Trinidadians, and for many people all over the region as well as the "developed" world, it is important that there be a reservoir of traditional culture, a festival-based museum-type encapsulation of all those things older folks remember fondly but never firmly inculcated in their children, too distracted were they by modern lures. Somewhere – in the country, in the bush, in the deep bush, in a Golden Age – are all those aspects of the trope of our "rich cultural heritage": foods, toys, customs, manners. (Our historian colleague Bridget Brereton reported that in 1990 a young American woman came to her office at the University of the West Indies, wanting to know where she could find a population of Amerindians who had "not yet had contact" with European culture in Trinidad.)

Of course, finding "uncontaminated" social groups is not possible now – if it ever was. Is there any "pure" culture that is not some kind of mélange or that did not result from a mixture as basic as Cro-Magnons and Neanderthals? Media accessibility, schools, transportation have permeated everywhere. Yes, there are things you can find in the countryside that you cannot find in the city. But there are things you can find just as easily two steps from the university. Many traditions are simply gone. Many others have segued into new forms. A (Creole) language, a (Creole) discourse, a (Creole) culture do not depend merely on grammatical particles. As Velma Pollard showed me in Jamaica, you can now pay your *susu*[11] hand by cheque.

I would now like to turn explicitly to the theme of this conference, "Reassembling the Fragments", from Derek Walcott's Nobel lecture.[12] The relevant paragraph reads:

> Break a vase, and the love that reassembles the fragments is stronger than that love which took its symmetry for granted when it was whole. The glue that fits the pieces is the sealing of its original shape. It is such a love that reassembles our African and Asiatic fragments, the cracked heirlooms whose restoration shows its white scars. This gathering of broken pieces is the care and pain of the Antilles, and if the pieces are disparate, ill-fitting, they contain more pain than their original sculpture, those icons and sacred vessels taken for granted in their ancestral places. Antillean art is this restoration of our shattered histories, our shards of vocabulary, our archipelago becoming a synonym for pieces broken off from the original continent.[13]

I would like, as we say these days, to interrogate this metaphor, mostly by positioning it side-by-side with the previously mentioned metaphors of soap bubbles, marble cake and pointillism, and also with some additional metaphors, thereby accumulating greater resonance by force of sheer quantity.

The next metaphor is scientific. Georges Cuvier, a brilliant naturalist and paleontologist of the early nineteenth century, analysed Indian and African elephants, as well as mammoths and mastodons, and greatly developed the study of comparative anatomy. It was said of Cuvier that he could imagine the entire animal from a single piece of bone. This is Cuvier's principle of the correlation of parts:

> [A]fter inspecting a single bone, one can often determine the class, and sometimes even the genus of the animal to which it belonged, above all if that bone belonged to the head or the limbs. This is because the number, direction and shape of the bones that compose each part of an animal's body are always in a necessary relation to all the other parts, in such a way that, up to a point, one can infer the whole from any one of them and vice versa.[14]

Here we have real fragments being recombined. In this type of case, fossil reconstruction, it is presumed possible to determine whether or not the re-assemblage is correct, no matter how bizarre or unexpected the result. Well, eventually anyway: A popular, although apocryphal, story tells of Cuvier himself once combining the bones of a plesiosaur and an apatosaurus in creating – under the rubric of reassembly – a four-legged creature that would not have been able to move on land *or* in water.

But the fragments that we are referring to in this region are not fossil bones. To make another scientific metaphor with parallels to "fossilized items" in second-language acquisition, can we perhaps consider Caribbean fragments "living fossils", like the coelacanth, thought to be extinct for sixty-five million years and pulled up from a fishing net in 1938? The coelacanth surely never considered itself to be anything other than "living" and its context anything but water, although the water conditions have changed somewhat. The major difference and similarity between a fossil reassemblage and the reassemblage of the fragments we have all been discussing is that while the reassembled fossil beast lacks flesh and skin and breath, but maintains a true likeness of part of what it once was, we cannot reassemble lives or languages or cultures or histories back into what they were without using liberal amounts of inference and imagination.

Or, take Walcott's archaeological metaphor. The vase that is reassembled is often made with missing pieces, even if it is just missing the dust along the cracks and cuts. It is reassembled without our having a picture of the original to which to refer or without our being able to truly replicate or even understand the process by which it was originally made, and the place or the image/object in its original context. It is like trying to assemble a jigsaw puzzle with a missing box cover and after Tobi Le Bec, my Senegal parrot, has been at it: pieces missing, pieces of pieces missing, chewed-up pieces and pieces with the picture layer peeled off. Nonetheless we try, both because of interest, love and honour, and because, as Walcott says, it seems to be an Antillean mission.

CENTRES AND MARGINS

> Things fall apart; the centre cannot hold;
> Mere anarchy is loosed upon the world,
> The blood-dimmed tide is loosed, and everywhere
> The ceremony of innocence is drowned.[15]

William Butler Yeats wrote this in the poem, "The Second Coming", in 1919, just after a devastating world war. The context is quite different from the use of the famous phrase as the title of Chinua Achebe's 1958 novel *Things Fall Apart*. As Paul Brians notes, in his portrayal of traditional village culture in Nigeria, perhaps as a conscious antidote to Joseph Conrad's *Heart of Darkness*, Achebe is "not only trying to inform the outside world about Ibo cultural traditions, but to remind his own people of their past and to assert that it had contained much of value. All too many Africans in his time were ready to accept the European judgment that Africa had no history or culture worth considering."[16] However, both the poem and the novel refer to the disintegration of previously integrated civilizations that seemed coherent, and even if oppressive, workable.

When the centres that had held for a considerable length of time began to fall apart both from internal and external forces, growing global independence movements for colonial societies presented pressure from the margins. Prior to this, say, throughout the previous few centuries, the nexus of colonial force came from the centres, the metropoles, pushing through the margins like a hurricane blowing all before it. The result of this fracturing force was the fragmentation of the margins themselves – both at the original marginal sites and in the resulting fragmented marginal sites. During the next while, even after independent political sovereignties were established, the globe resembled a dance of the spheres, the sun in the centre of the centre, surrounded by circles of planets, with asteroids zooming through the interstices both individually and in grappes. But even the hierarchy of the galaxy is not immutable. The king of the underworld lost his planetary status when Pluto was downgraded from a planet to a dwarf planet and further: "according to the new rules, Pluto is not a planet. It's just another Kuiper Belt object."[17]

RESPONSIBILITY OF THE MARGINS

These sometimes-broken, sometimes-fragmented margins stayed in the margins, re-marginalized around new centres, or became centres of their own. At the University of the West Indies, Caribbean scholarship has *centred the margins*. This is most obviously seen in the subjects of scholarly attention. When there was some interest in the colonial centres about Caribbean topics from botany to the oil industry, based on pure academic inquiry or corporate imperialism, it was still generally marginal. Titles of publications from Caribbean publishers such as the University of the West Indies Press, or Ian Randle, contrast to some extent with metropolitan postcolonial publishers like Peepal Tree Press, and both contrast heavily with mainstream publishers' content orientation.

The idea that there is one homogeneous "insider" view in any fragment – or a (re-)centred margin – is untenable, as Jean D'Costa pointed out so ably for Jamaica in her plenary address at the "Reassembling the Fragments" conference. Lawrence Carrington has described Trinidad and Tobago as not a country, but a context of operation (personal communication), and perhaps we can extend that to the Caribbean as a region. Trinidad and Tobago in this view includes not only Scarborough, Tobago, but Scarborough, Ontario – and do not forget the Danish National Steel Orchestra.

It is the responsibility of the margins, by choice or default, to pay attention to their own topics. Like other parts of the marginal world, the dimensions of our contexts must not *only* be mapped by outsiders, whoever those are, and given the porosity of the walls that divide us, they must not *only* be mapped by insiders, however they are defined. Anyone who has been in a marginalized power situation knows that you cannot count on the outsider, let alone the oppressor, to pay attention to your concerns. The endless annoyance of the centres by the nagging of the margins will be a presence until the *centres and the margins* become *centres and centres*. The fluidity of Creole space should be reflected in the types of academic attention that will be paid to it.

NOTES

1. Bernard Coard, *How the West Indian Child Is Made Educationally Subnormal in the British Educational System* (London: New Beacon Books, 1971), 29.
2. Lawrence Carrington, "The Challenge of Caribbean Language in the Canadian Classroom" *TESL Talk* 14, no. 4 (1983): 15.
3. Lawrence Carrington, "Images of Creole Space", *Journal of Pidgin and Creole Linguistics* 7, no. 1 (1992): 93–95.
4. Gillian Sankoff and Suzanne Laberge, "On the Acquisition of Native Speakers by a Language", in *Pidgins and Creoles: Current Trends and Prospects*, ed. David De Camp and Ian F. Hancock, 73–84 (Washington, DC: Georgetown University Press, 1974).
5. Melville Herskovits and Frances Herskovits, *Trinidad Village* (New York: Alfred A. Knopf, 1947, repr. 1976, New York: Octagon Books/Farrar, Straus and Giroux).
6. Maureen Warner-Lewis, *Central Africa in the Caribbean: Transcending Time, Transforming Cultures* (Kingston: University of the West Indies Press, 2003).
7. Jean D'Costa and Barbara Lalla, *Voices in Exile: Jamaican Texts of the Eighteenth and Nineteenth Centuries* (Tuscaloosa: University of Alabama Press, 1989).
8. Barbara Lalla and Jean D'Costa, *Language in Exile: Three Hundred Years of Jamaican Creole* (Tuscaloosa: University of Alabama Press, 1990).
9. Valerie Youssef, "Varilingualism: The Competence Underlying Code-Mixing in Trinidad and Tobago", *Journal of Pidgin and Creole Languages* 11, no. 1 (1996): 1–22.
10. Kathy-Ann Drayton, "Assessing Language Disorders in English-Creole–Speaking Children" (paper presented at the conference Reassembling the Fragments, in honour of Bridget Brereton, Barbara Lalla and Ian Robertson, University of the West Indies, St. Augustine, Trinidad and Tobago, 25–27 August, 2011).
11. *Susu* is an informal cooperative savings plan.
12. Derek Walcott, "The Antilles: Fragments of Epic Memory" (Nobel lecture, 7 December 1992), http://www.nobelprize.org/nobel_prizes/literature/laureates/1992/walcott-lecture.html.
13. Ibid.
14. Georges Cuvier, 1798, cited in Martin J.S. Rudwick, *Georges Cuvier, Fossil Bones, and Geological Catastrophes* (Chicago: University of Chicago Press, 1997), 36.
15. William Butler Yeats, "The Second Coming", in *Michael Robartes and the Dancer* (Churchtown, Ireland: Chuala Press, 1920).
16. Paul Brians, *Chinua Achebe:* Things Fall Apart *Study Guide* (2003). http://public.wsu.edu/~brians/anglophone/achebe.html.
17. http://www.universetoday.com/13573/why-pluto-is-no-longer-a-planet/#ixzz1yAP-mvMHI.

9.

A COMPARISON BETWEEN THE DEVELOPMENT OF PALENQUERO CARIBBEAN CREOLE AND SWAHILI-SPANISH INTERLANGUAGE

[M A R Í A   L A N D A   B U I L]

INTRODUCTION

THIS CHAPTER COMPARES SOME developmental features of Palenquero's noun phrase with the data of the Spanish Interlanguage (IL) of four Swahili speakers. Palenquero is a Creole language with Spanish as its lexifier and Bantu as its substrate. Part of the originality of this work comes from comparing a Creole and an IL that share lexifier/target language (Spanish) and substrate/first language (a Bantu language). Authors such as Bickerton[1] consider that the passage of pidgin to Creole happens when children acquire the pidgin as their first language (L1). Lefebvre et al., Mather and Mufwene believe that Creole formation is a special case of second-language acquisition (SLA) and can be explained by transfers from the L1, relexification, reanalysis and fossilization.[2] The aim of this chapter is to observe whether, in a situation of similar languages in contact, adult second-language learners will put to work similar mental processes and create a grammar similar to Palenquero's grammar. We will be observing the development of the noun phrase, trying to find in the IL the absence of grammatical gender and the presence of postnominal determiners and prenominal plural markers.

SLA AND CREOLIZATION STUDIES

The academic community that investigates the origins of pidgin and Creole languages has been divided for many years between those who believe that the substrate languages have the primary role in the formation of the new languages,[3] those who give the most important role to the lexifier[4] and those who believe that language universals have the real responsibility for the main features.[5] We believe that all of them, substrate, lexifier and language universals, play an important role in the creation of pidgin and Creole languages, and excluding any of the three will present problems when trying to account for all the features of a given Creole language.

For other authors, however, the real question is whether a process of L1 acquisition or SLA is responsible. Bickerton[6] in his bioprogramme model distinguishes between pidginization and creolization, believing that the first is a case of SLA with restricted input, while the second is L1 acquisition with limited input. Against this, other authors such as Lefebvre et al. and Mather consider that the creation of a Creole language is more likely a case of SLA.[7] For them the question will be, what is the role played in creolization by language universals and language substrate?

The attempt to establish a relationship between the study of SLA and those of creolization and pidginization is not new. According to Siegel, the possible connections have been discussed for more than one hundred years.[8] Schumann applies the theory of pidginization to the acquisition of second languages in his analysis of the data from the English learner, Alberto, a Hispanic who emigrated to the United States.[9] Alberto's reduced and simplified English shares some features with pidgins. This author also argues in his study that pidginization could be a universal first stage in SLA. In line with Bickerton and his bioprogramme hypothesis,[10] he notes that pidgins and other varieties of incomplete competence (child language, SLA, bilingualism and aphasia) might reveal structures and universal processes that underlie linguistic ability more directly than natural languages by themselves.

Andersen[11] compared the work of Bickerton and Odo[12] based on twenty-four Hawaiian Pidgin English speakers and the research of Schumann on Alberto,[13] and finds the following similarities:

1. Dependence on word order and not inflection to express grammatical relations
2. Coexistence of native language transfer and standard English usage with respect to word order
3. Sporadic appearance of preverbal markers coming from lexical verbs reinterpreted as auxiliaries

4. Use of the basic pidgin negation
5. Lack of subject/verb inversion
6. Prevalence of verbal forms without inflection

Andersen concludes that pidginization is a characteristic of all types of SLA.[14] The author believes that researchers on pidgin and Creole languages and SLA are actually studying the same phenomenon, but from a different perspective.

Andersen goes a step further in trying to explain the internal-processing mechanisms occurring in second-language (L2) learning.[15] In his proposal, he distinguishes between processes of "nativization" and processes of "denativization". The process of nativization is related to Piaget's concept of assimilation: the learner makes the input conform to an internalized vision of what constitutes the system of the L2. As Andersen states, creolization, pidginization and the creation of an IL in the early stages of the acquisition of L1 and L2 share one thing: the creation of a linguistic system that is at least partially independent of the input used to build such a system.[16] This system can be considered native to the individual, as it is the mental capacity of the individual that builds the linguistic system, making it possible to form a new "native: language. The opposite process is called denativization: During this process, the learner adjusts the internal system towards the external input: "[Denativization occurs] when circumstances cause the learner to rebuild his IL to better suit the input (of the target language), to dismantle parts of his 'native' system (the system that he had previously built or is in process of building) . . . decreolization therefore, depidginization and advanced stages of acquisition of first and second languages are types of denativization."[17]

The concepts of nativization and denativization are used in the Andersen model to differentiate between the stages in which the learner constructs his IL, first by internal processes and then by trying to adjust his IL to the target language. The nativization process is consistent with natural acquisition processes and the restrictions imposed by perception and production. In the case of the learner, denativization invalidates the natural processes of acquisition to approach the target language. Andersen argues that nativization is a result of restricted access to input from the target language. With time and increased exposure to target-language input, Andersen argues that the learner's IL will begin to resemble the structure of the target language.

Valdman also notes parallels between creolization and SLA.[18] Although creolization is a phenomenon that can occur over more than one generation and among many speakers whereas ILs are created by individuals, the author argues that these two processes do not differ substantially from a psycholinguistic point of view. Both processes involve the operation of linguistic and cognitive universals but differ only because of social circumstances that variously promote or retard the acquisition of the target language. According to Valdman, the process of creolization occurs when social conditions cause the learner to develop a language that is partially independent of the target language.[19] This new language will become stable while being used as the main means of communication and cohesion of this recently emerged community. In contrast to this are the social conditions of SLA, which usually help the development of an IL closer to the target language.

Valdman accepts Andersen's notion[20] of nativization and argues that this is the process in which, at least in the early stages of SLA, learners develop relationships between form and meaning that differ from those of the target language. This is where the author finds the similarities between SLA and the process of creolization. Valdman argues that the same laws operate in SLA and creolization, such that the differences would be only in the amount of nativization that takes place: in the cases of SLA and creolization, the first being low and the second much higher.

This difference according to this author is only due to social factors. Valdman[21] disagrees with Bickerton and his bioprogramme hypothesis. Bickerton asserts that adults lack the ability to create parts of a language not available in the target language and only children can be responsible for the creation of a Creole language through processes of L1 acquisition. Valdman[22] and Andersen[23] argue that adults are able to restructure and therefore create a Creole language through a long process that involves several generations. According to this version, the Creoles are the results of the gradual expansion of a pidgin language, for instance through the speakers of pidgin as L2 over several generations, and are not only the result of a sudden acquisition of pidgin as a L1 by the children of the L2 speakers.

Currently, the dialogue between the two disciplines is undergoing a revival with volumes such as *Studies in Second Language Acquisition*,[24] or the volume edited by Lefebvre, White and Jourdan[25] aiming to re-establish the dialogue between second language acquisitionists and creolists, and gather the most representative works of the time. As the editors explain in the introduction, the articles in the latter book deal with scenarios in which speakers must find solutions to situations of language contact. Although language-contact situations in which pidgin or Creole languages are created and those that lead to "normal" L2 show many differences, these authors propose in their introduction that the cognitive processes involved in both cases could be similar or at least comparable. These processes would include simplification, relexification and transfer in the initial stage, restructuring and re-analysis during development, and fossilization in the final stage.

Although authors like Kouwenberg have argued that SLA and the development of Creole languages are responses to completely different mental processes, because of the influence of substrate languages in the Creoles and of L1 transfer in SLA,[26] others, like Mather,[27] note that such statements ignore the distinction between mental processes and language outcomes and fail to take into account that L1 transfer has a great impact in the early stages of the learners' IL grammar. What Mather[28] finds particularly relevant is the difference between the mental processes involved in acquiring a L2 (related to the internal language)[29] and the linguistic outcome of this process (external language). The distinction between I-Creole and E-Creole was earlier also made by DeGraff.[30] According to Mather, internal language in creolization can largely be explained by processes of SLA.[31]

Mather states in his article that while one may not completely agree with Bickerton,[32] it is clear that the processes used for pidginization and creolization are the same as those used in SLA and L1 acquisition, respectively, although the end result might not be the full acquisition of the lexifying language due to the extreme historical and social contexts of acquisition. For Mather there is a difference between the mental process of the SLA (related to the internal language) and the linguistic result of this process (external language).

The objective of SLA is the target language (L2), but often the end product is a fossilized IL. There are many factors that affect and influence the varying success of the acquisition. We must take into account the learner's personal motivation and psychological and social distance.[33] SLA in the classroom means, according to Mather, transfers from the L1 and the "mistakes" of other learners, universal processes of SLA, availability of a standard variety that acts as a model and the teacher's corrections.[34] The origin of pidgin and Creole occurs, according to this author, in situations in which the learner appears in a new society without motivation to learn the L2, receiving no formal education and limited access to input. For Mather,[35] creolization can be seen following Bartens,[36] as an unguided process of SLA where L1 is relexified with L2 vocabulary. According to Bartens, varied results are achieved in creolization, although there are similarities among different Creoles that may have to do with the internal structure of the substrate language(s) or the common cognitive processes and universal principles of SLA. In his article, he presents casestudy examples of SLA learners of French in which structures are common with those of French-lexified Creoles. According to Mather, these examples should not be taken as identical to those of the Creole but as possible input that would be restructured and re-analysed generation after generation along the lines of Arends and Chaudenson's gradualist model.[37]

The evidence presented for cases of SLA is as follows:

- word order possesses
    o   postponed definite article
    o   other determiners (oblique form of the personal pronoun) postponed
- clitic pronouns: SVO regardless of whether O is a noun or pronoun
- absence of copula with predicate adjectives or locative
- reduplication of adjectives
- reanalysis of the pronominal article as part of the root of the noun
- absence of grammatical gender
- no movement of the verb
- preverbal markers of time, mood and aspect

According to the author, some of these cases are explained by L1 transfer or influence of the substrate; others, like the absence of grammatical gender, however, appear to be universal in the processes of SLA.

THE STUDY

The current work draws on all previous authors and appears in this new phase of dialogue that has been opened between SLA and creolization studies. It is a longitudinal study in which speech samples of four students of the BA in Spanish at the State University of Zanzibar (SUZA), whose native language is Swahili, were recorded over twenty-five months. The four students had studied English, so that Spanish would be their third language (L3).

Study participants were selected through a general-information questionnaire that was distributed to the entire class in the second semester of the beginners' course. When the longitudinal study started, the students had completed six months of formal education in Spanish, with seven contact hours per week. They had never studied Spanish before, and exposure to this language was reduced to the contact hours in the classroom. Due to various religious festivities and the closure of the university caused by the complicated presidential elections, the total number of contact hours was approximately 140. Ten participants were selected from the questionnaires, taking into account different variables. These included

- the number of second languages spoken (those selected only spoke English),
- the level of English (we looked for participants who had similar levels of English),
- the origin of parents and African languages and dialects spoken at home (selected participants who only spoke Swahili),
- stays in other regions of Tanzania and Africa (selected participants had always lived in Zanzibar; therefore their exposure to other African dialects was reduced) and
- extralinguistic factors such as willingness to participate in the collection of monthly data.

All students participated regularly during the two years of the data collection. The interviews began on 25 April 2006, during the second half of the first year of Spanish. Study participants who had not had previous contact with the Spanish language began to communicate with single words, word lists, and some simple isolated phrases. Data collection ended with interview 14 on 14 May 2008. It was the end of the students' third and final year of Spanish.

To develop the linguistic corpus, the production of four of these students, two men and two women, aged between twenty-three and thirty-six years, was codified and analysed. We chose the four with the highest level of English and with the greatest degree of participation and attendance at the interviews and, therefore, the greater volume of linguistic production. To maintain their anonymity three letters will be used to refer to each of them: The three letters match the headers that mark their interventions in the transcripts. In the corpus created, we have analysed noun phrases, searching for examples that reflect morphosyntactic features that occur in a Creole language (Palenquero), namely prenominal plural markers, lack of gender markers and postnominal determiners.

While Mather (2006) compared Creole languages and an IL that only share French as the lexifier/L2, the novelty of our study is that our languages share not only Spanish as the lexifier/L2 but also a Bantu substrate/L1. A comparison of the two languages in contact situations can be seen as follows:

L1 Swahili	Bantu substrate
Interlanguage	Palenquero
Spanish L3/target language	Spanish lexifier/ superstrate

Figure 9.1

The Bantu language group consists of a set of five hundred languages spoken in Africa; it constitutes a branch called the Benue-Congo subfamily of Niger-Congo languages. They are spoken in a vast area that includes southern Cameroon, Gabon, Congo, Democratic Republic of Congo, Uganda, Kenya, Tanzania, Angola, Zambia, Malawi, Mozambique, Zimbabwe, Namibia, Botswana and South Africa. Twelve of these Bantu languages are spoken by more than five million people. Guthrie classified all the Bantu languages and tried to reconstruct the proto-Bantu and proto-language of this language family.[38] He argues that the Bantu languages originated two thousand years ago in eastern Nigeria and Cameroon, from where they spread to South and East Africa. Most of the languages of this group form a sentence by following the basic order: subject verb object (SVO).

The most prominent grammatical characteristic of Bantu languages is the extensive use of prefixes and infixes. Each name belongs to a class, and each language may have about ten classes of nouns in total. For some authors such as Vicki Carstens, these classes are actually grammatical genders.[39] Gender is indicated by a prefix in the name, as well as adjectives, determiners and verbs that agree with it. The plural varies for each gender and is indicated by a change of prefix.

If the characteristics of the noun phrase of the IL coincide with those of Palenquero, our data would support the thesis of Mather, which argues that the process of creating a Creole is a particular case of SLA and can be explained by processes of SLA: L1 transfer, relexification and reanalysis.[40] With a fairly large degree of idealization, given that the situations differ (the intrusion of English, the different context of creation/acquisition), we could propose that, when similar languages are in contact, adult speakers would use similar processes and create a similar grammar. This would argue in favour of the importance of the substrate in the creation of pidgin, Creole and the L1 in the case of SLA.

But we do not pretend to claim, as Mather does, that everything in the creation of a Creole language can be explained by processes of SLA.[41] One of the differences between IL and a Creole language is the variability and instability of the first since, although Creole languages also show a certain degree of variability, the IL shows it in a higher degree. As noted by Bickerton, children, in the process of acquiring an L1, may be needed to regulate it.[42] SLA could have an important role, but it seems that an L1-acquisition process had to be involved for the Creole language to become stabilized. Below we introduce the research question and the hypothesis of this work.

RESEARCH QUESTION

Is there a similarity between the noun phrase of our learners' IL and that of Palenquero?

HYPOTHESIS

The noun phrase of the IL of our students shares features with the noun phrase of Palenquero because of the role played by the Bantu substrate. Therefore in our IL we will find the following features: (1) absence of grammatical gender, (2) prenominal plural marker and (3) determiner postposed.

After analysing the data, the hypothesis has been proven false for (1) and (3) but true for (2). With respect to (1), our IL seems to show, with a degree of variability and instability, the presence of grammatical gender. The four participants in the study show a sensitivity to gender features; there is a high degree of gender agreement between the noun and the determiner, as well as between the noun and the adjective. It is important to mention that the vast majority of errors of gender were overgeneralizations of the masculine.

In figure 9.2 the statistics show that the proportions related to the percentage of gender agreement errors for each constituent of the noun phrase are not equal, so we must observe these proportions separately.

Rows: gender agreement Error Columns: Noun phrase Constituents

	Adjectives	Determiners	Nouns	All
Hits	202	1022	2671	3895
	218.9	1128.7	2547.4	3895.0
	1.31	10.09	6.00	*
Errors	29	169	17	215
	12.1	62.3	140.6	215.0
	23.68	182.72	108.67	*
All	231	1191	2688	4110
	231.0	1191.0	2688.0	4110.0
	*	*	*	*

Cell contents: Counting

Expected count

Contribution to chi-square

Pearson Chi-square = 332,465, df = 2, P value = 0.000

Chi-square likelihood rate = 333,892, df = 2, P value = 0.000

Figure 9.2. Tabulated statistics: gender-agreement error noun-phrase constituents using frequencies in Count 2

In figure 9.3 we see that, with 95 per cent confidence, the error rate of gender agreement between determiners and nouns is less than 16.5 per cent.

Test p = 0.165 vs. p <0.165

P Value Limit

Sample X	N	Sample p	above 95%	exact
1	169 1191	0.141898	0.159605	0.016

Figure 9.3. Test and CI for a proportion of gender-agreement error between nouns and determiners

In the case of gender-agreement errors between adjectives and nouns, the percentage is higher: with a 95 per cent confidence, the error rate of agreement will be less than 17.5 per cent (see figure 9.4).

Test p = 0.175 vs. p <0.175				
P Value Limit				
Sample X	N	Sample p	above 95%	exact
1	29 231	0.125541	0.167207	0.026

Figure 9.4 Test and CI for a proportion of gender agreement error between the adjective and the noun

With respect to (2) in the hypothesis, generally the plural is marked with the morpheme -s postposed, but more than half of the cases in which the plural is not marked by an -s are actually cases of prenominal marking. This can occur through the marking of the plural with an -s in the determiner placed before the noun, as in the case of "todos" (all) in (1a) or through the use of a determiner that, although not marked for plural, denotes plurality as in the case of "mucha" (many) in (1b). Most of the prenominal marking of plural occurs with the use of quantifiers. In (1c), we see two cases in which the determiner is a numeral quantifier.

(1) a. *MUS: porque *todos persona* en Zanzibar tienen cosas como casa.
    Because *every person* in Zanzibar has things like home.

   b. *MUS: *mucha persona* ahora <usar> [//] usan tus tiempo para educación.
    Many people now <usar> [/ /] use your time for education.

   c. *AMI: en la pictura veo *dos* estudiante y *tres* niño.
    in the picture I see *two* student and *three* child.

In figure 9.5 it can be seen that, with 95 per cent confidence, 51 per cent of cases of plural-marking error are actually cases of prenominal marking. Both Swahili (learners' L1) and Palenquero have prenominal plural markers.

With respect to (3) in the hypothesis, in our data, we did not find any case of determiners in postnominal position. Our data seems to show an influence of the Bantu substrate/L1 for prenominal plural marking, but not regarding the position of the determiners.

Test p = 0.51 vs. no p = 0.51				
P Value Limit				
Sample X	N	Sample p	CI 95%	Exact P value
1	151 298	0.506711	(0.448449, 0.564839)	0954

Figure 9.5 Test and CI for a proportion prenominal plural

Our data reinforces the notion that although transfer seems to play an important role both in SLA and in the creation of Creole languages, it seems to happen in a different way in each. The target language in SLA has a greater role in the adoption of vocabulary and structures than the lexifier in Creole formation. Mather, Sprouse and Lefebvre explain this by saying that access to the input of the lexifier is restricted in pidginization and creolization due to very particular historical circumstances and is not a proof that creolization and SLA are different mental processes.[43]

Kouwenberg, who is not a language acquisitionist, sees two different processes.[44] She states that in the formation of Creole languages, in contrast to SLA, the transfer ceases at the moment when the lexifier no longer has a significant direct role in the creative process; that, for her, is the point at which SLA processes are no longer relevant in the creation of a Creole language. In addition, Kouwenberg argues that the transfer processes observed in the creation of Creoles, such as the allocation of new grammatical functions to the superstrate material, are not seen in SLA. For all these reasons, she states that transfer of L1 in Creole-formation processes and in SLA differs in terms of quantity and quality of the transfer and that the properties of Creole languages that are related to their substrates should not be taken as an indication that SLA is an important process in the formation of Creole languages.

In our data, we found cases of prenominal plural marking that could be considered cases of functional transfer. Siegel defined *transference* as a form of interlinguistic influence found in SLA in which learners use their L1 linguistic features in the IL; these may be phonemes, grammar rules, meanings or functions of a particular word.[45] Traditionally, this transfer was defined as positive when the feature matched that of the L2 and interference but negative transfer when the feature did not match. Siegel distinguishes between *syntactic* and *functional* transfer, the first being the transfer of the word order of the L1 and the second the use of forms of the L2 with grammatical properties of the L1. This second type of transfer resembles what Lefebvre calls relexification.[46] Kouwenberg believes that what Siegel calls functional transfers do not occur in the SLA but happen in creolization.[47] However, we believe that the data from our IL (prenominal plural marking) would contradict this assertion.

If the prenominal plural marking of our data is indeed a case of functional transfer, this would present a problem to Siegel, as he argues that the phenomenon of transfer that occurs in SLA is only syntactic transfer.[48] For cases like that in our data where functional transfer is evident, although with great variability, he argues that there is a production problem, which is not a true reflection of competence. It is difficult to see how one can be sure that this is not part of the competence of learners.

Siegel believes that word order is a feature easily accessible to consciousness, and therefore the slightest exposure to the lexifier's language data could cause restructuring, making it harder to find the word order of substrate languages in Creole languages. An exception to this is the noun phrase with a possessive determiner where Palenquero has maintained the Bantu word order. Functional transfer, according to Siegel, would need much more positive evidence to be restructured. In the case of pidgin and Creole formation, access to the lexifier input was quite limited, and therefore these transfers remain in the Creole languages.

Although we found examples of prenominal plural marking in the IL of our students, a phenomenon that also occurs in Palenquero, it is important not to forget the large variability among individuals, as well as within each subject. The IL of our students is the product of a single grammar with a very high level of instability.

Lardiere studied data from Patsy, a US immigrant whose first language was Mandarin Chinese, and concluded that adults seem to feel comfortable with variability.[49] It appears to be children who, when faced with variable input, regularize. Lardiere also concludes that adults may have introduced new language structures but,[50] as stated in Bickerton, children acquiring the pidgin as an L1 are necessary in order to regularize it.[51] Other models do not see L1 acquisition as the only way to Creole formation. Smith, Robertson and Williamson study the creation of Berbice Dutch and argue in favour of the hypothesis that Eastern Ijo was replaced by Berbice Dutch under the influence of (Creole) Dutch.[52] This scenario suggests a long-term development of the Berbice Dutch Creole, rather than a single-generation creation through Lı acquisition. The evidence of substrate influence in this Creole is also very strong.

Arends proposes for the case of Sranan a transgenerational gradual model of creolization that accommodates both a population of L2 learners and an element of Lı acquisition by the children of those L2 learners.[33] He believes that, while Bickerton's model of Creole formation may account for Hawaiian Creole, each Creole formation is a different case with a different linguistic scenario and should be assessed on a case-by-case basis.

When comparing an IL and a Creole language, one has to be cautious. While we believe that SLA may have an important role in Creole formation, either an Lı acquisition or a transgenerational gradual process or both have to be involved for the Creole language to become stabilized. Therefore what might be said, with a fairly large degree of idealization as the situations differ, is that when similar languages are in contact, adult speakers who created the pre-Palenquero pidgin would have used mental processes similar to those used by our students and created structures like the ones we have observed, and these would have become the base of the Creole language. This would argue in favour of the importance of the substrate in the creation of both pidgins and Creoles.

NOTES

1.   Derek Bickerton, "Pidginization and Creolization: Language Acquisition and Language Universals", *Pidgin and Creole Linguistics*, ed. Albert Valdman (Bloomington: Indiana University Press, 1977), 49–69.

2.   C. Lefebvre, L. White and C. Jourdan, eds., *L2 Acquistion and Creole Genesis: Dialogues* (Amsterdam: John Benjamins, 2006); P.A. Mather, "Second Language Acquisition and Creolization: Same (-i) Processes, Different (e-) Results, *Journal of Pidgin and Creole Languages* 21, no. 2 (2006): 231–74; S. Mufwene, *The Ecology of Language Evolution* (Cambridge: Cambridge University Press, 2001).

3.   Bettina Migge, "Substrate Influence in Creole Formation: The Origin of Give-Type Serial Verb Constructions in the Surinamese Plantation Creole", *Journal of Pidgin and Creole Languages* 31, no. 2 (1998): 215–66;

4.   R. Chaudenson, *Créoles et enseignement du français* (Paris: L'Harmattan, 1989).

5.   Bickerton, "Pidginization".

6.   Ibid.

7.   Lefebvre et al., *L2 Acquisition*; Maher "Second Language Acquisition".

8.   J. Siegel, "Links between SLA and Creole Studies: Past and Present", in *L2 Acquisition and Creole Genesis: Dialogues*, ed. C. Lefebvre, L. White, and C. Jourdan (Amsterdam: John Benjamins), 15–46.

9.   J. Schumann, *The Pidginization Process: A Model for Second Language Acquisition* (Rowley, MA: Newbury House, 1978).

10. Bickerton, "Pidginization".

11. R. Andersen, "Two Perspectives on Pidginization as Second Language Acquisition", in *New Dimensions in Second Language Acquisition Research*, ed. R. Andersen (Cambridge, MA: Newbury House, 1981), 165–96.

12. Derek Bickerton and C. Odo, *Change and Variation in Hawaiian English: Final Report on National Science Foundation Grant No. GS39748* (Honolulu: Social Sciences and Linguistics Institute, University of Hawaii, 1976).

13. Schumann, "Pidginization Process".

14. Andersen, "Two Perspectives".

15. R. Andersen, *Pidginization and Creolization as Language Acquisition* (Towley, MA: Newbury House, 1983).

16. Ibid., 11.

17. Ibid., 12.

18. Albert Valdman, "Creolization and Second Language Acquisition", in *Pidginization and Creolization as Language Acquisition* (Rowley, MA: Newbury House, 1983), 212–35.

19. Ibid.

20. Andersen, "Two Perspectives".

21. Valdman, "Creolization".

22. Ibid.

23. Andersen, "Two Perspectives"; Andersen, *Pidginization*.

24. J. Siegel, "Substrate Influence in Creoles and the Role of Transfer in Second Language Acquisition", *Studies in Second Language Acquisition* 25 (2003): 185–209.

25. Lefebvre, White, and Jourdan, *L2 Acquisition*.

26. S. Kouwenberg, "L1 Transfer and the Cut-Off Point for L2 Acquisition Processes in Creole Formation", in *L2 Acquisition and Creole Genesis: Dialogues* (Amsterdam: John Benjamins, 2006), 205–19.

27. Mather, "Second Language Acquisition".

28. Ibid.

29. Noam Chomsky, *Knowledge of Language* (New York: Praeger, 1986).

30. M. DeGraff, ed., *Language Creation and Language Change: Creolization, Diachrony and Development* (Cambridge, MA: MIT Press, 1999).

31. Mather, "Second Language Acquisition".

32. Bickerton, "Pidginization".

33. Schumann, "Pidginization Process".

34. Mather, "Second Language Acquisition".

35. Ibid.

36. A. Barten, "Phonologische Merkmale atlantischer Iberokreols", *Lusorama* 29 (1996): 73–88.

37. J. Arends, "Syntactic Developments in Sranan: Creolization as a Gradual Process" (PhD diss., University of Nijmegen, Netherlands, 1989); R. Chaudenson, "Créoles françaises et variétés de français", *L'Information Grammatical* 89 (2001): 32–37.

38. M. Guthrie, *The Classification of the Bantu Languages* (Oxford: Oxford University Press for the International African Institute, 1948).

39. Vicki Carstens, "DP in Bantu and Romance", in *The Bantu- Romance Connection: A Comparative Investigation of Verbal Agreement, DPs, and Information Structure*, ed. C. De Cat and K. Demuth (Amsterdam: John Benjamins, 2008), 131–65.

40. Mather, "Second Language Acquisition".

41. Ibid.

42. Bickerton, "Pidginization".

43. Mather, "Second Language Acquisition"; R. Sprouse, "Full Transfer and Relexification: Second Language Acquisition and Creole Genesis", in *L2 Acquisition and Creole Genesis: Dialogues*, ed. C. Lefebvre, L. White and C. Jourdan (Amsterdam: John Benjamins, 2006), 169–81; Lefebvre, White and Jourdan, *L2 Acquisition*.

44. Kouwenberg, "L1 Transfer".

45. Siegel, "Links".

46. C. Lefebvre, Creole Genesis and the Acquisition of Grammar: The Case of Haitian Creole (Cambridge: Cambridge University Press, 1998). Lefebvre proposes the relexification hypothesis, which states that, in the creation of pidgin and Creole, features that correspond to lexical entry in the substrate are assigned to another lexical entry of the superstrate language.

47. Kouwenberg, "L1 Transfer".

48. Siegel, "Links".

49. D. Lardiere, "Comparing Creole Genesis with SLA in Unlimited- Access Contexts: Going Beyond Relexification", in *L2 Acquisition and Creole Genesis: Dialogues*, ed. C. Lefebvre, L. White and C. Jourdan (Amsterdam: John Benjamins, 2006), 401–27.

50. Ibid.

51. Bickerton, "Pidginization".

52. N. Smith, I. Robertson and K. Williamson, "The Ijo Element in Berbice Dutch", *Language in Society* 16 (1987): 49–89.

53. Arends, "Syntactic Developments".

10.

POSTCOLONIAL HISTORIOGRAPHY

Brereton and Naipaul Documenting Ethnic Histories over and against National Paradigms

[NIVEDITA MISRA]

"IN CHASING A NATIONAL IDENTITY after the fact", Bridget Brereton and V.S. Naipaul write histories for a "historyless" nation, Trinidad.[1] Rather than using the Caribbean as a showcase or a case study, Naipaul and Brereton attempt to place Trinidad at the centre, the beginning.[2] This chapter stems from an interest in the contestation between ancestral ethnic identities and national Creole identity in Trinidad. I locate Naipaul as a historian despite his more dominant public persona as a writer and Brereton as a littérateur despite her work as a social historian, and trace their attempts at documenting the life of a nation. In this exploration of divergent approaches using scribal and oral sources for constructing historical narratives, I will be looking at three concerns upon which both Brereton and Naipaul focus: early Trinidadian history before emancipation, interpretations of the black power movement in Trinidad in the 1970s and construction of Indocentric narratives. This comparison interposes my own understanding of history in India, where I have recently emigrated from, and serves as a gateway to understanding how hegemonic narratives on historical events have worked to curb the voices of the disenfranchised and underprivileged sections of society.

History writing in postcolonial states is fraught with problems of authenticity and finding a voice, a vantage point and documentary evidence. Unlike official historiography, which exercises its hegemony on records and documents, postcolonial historians across the world struggle to record, or more likely "construct", the events after they have occurred based on patchy or non-existent documentation. From the perspective of postcolonial Indian history, this involves the work of subaltern theorists in the 1980s striving to "unearth" evidence of how locally led revolts during the 1930s and 1940s were co-opted by the nationalist leadership under Mahatma Gandhi and Jawaharlal Nehru to give indigenous perspectives on a nationalist revolt against the English rule. Through this process, the subaltern theorists undermined the grand narrative of Indian history. However, as Gayatri Spivak, a contributor to the subaltern-studies project, critiqued, the subaltern loses voice in metropolitan discourses through a methodology of co-optation.³ Although the subaltern-studies project in India has been sensitive to the fact that such a positioning places those who have been denied voices on the periphery, it has nevertheless been deemed instrumental in expressing voices from the so-called margins of society. Thus, co-optation of the subaltern in colonial or nationalist history has often been either denied due to barriers of caste, class, gender and language; or accepted and marginalized within official historiography.

Most postcolonial positions question not only the project of history writing but also take issue with who writes, for whom, for what purpose and to what end. This concern acts as a gateway to our understanding of the postcolonial scholars and writers who rewrite the project of history. As Richard Eaton has expressed, postcolonial theory has positioned Indian history (or for that matter, all history) around a single axis of time: pre-colonial, colonial and postcolonial.⁴ Thus, history writing becomes an exercise in rewriting differential perspectives that may give significance to different events at different points in time.

A characteristic example of this was the manner in which British Oriental-ists stretched India's history back to the Indus Valley civilization in order to promulgate the myth that the Muslim invasions and Mughal rule had destroyed India's true wealth and that English colonial rule was in fact its true custodian. Even a cursory understanding of Indian history reveals that the Indus Valley civilization was itself a product of Aryan invasion of Dravidian land.

Another characteristic example from the work of postcolonial historians is to label the 1857 revolt in India as the First War of Independence. In the Caribbean context, most colonial histories posit the "discovery" of the Caribbean by Columbus in 1498 as a marker of the beginning of time and place. The earlier existence of the islands under the Caribs, the Arawaks and other tribes is superseded by Columbus's "discovery".

Brereton devotes a chapter in her *A History of Modern Trinidad: 1783–1962* to this early history.[5] Naipaul devotes an entire book, *The Loss of El Dorado*, to this period of early history.[6] Brereton references Naipaul in her text: "The citizens of St. Joseph were left in drunken isolation, to use V.S. Naipaul's phrase, intriguing against the governor . . . doing nothing."[7]

The Loss of El Dorado is important for it records not just the English takeover of Trinidad but details how aspects of social and legal life were affected by these changes in governance. Naipaul documents how the English takeover of Trinidad did not change the cruelty enacted upon slaves but, like in Picton's case, the governors were charged with dereliction of duty, for supporting such practices. Naipaul interweaves material from archives, diaries and court records to document a phase in Trinidad's history when its strategic positioning as an offshore base was of less importance than the legend it afforded. The legend of El Dorado fed upon the greed of successive conquistadors and agents of the Spanish and English kings, whose aim was to further the myth of the land of gold in order to preserve their own heads. However, the sparseness of accounts from this period may account for Brereton's reliance on Naipaul's creative documentation of the response of the citizens of St Joseph.

While diaries have been acknowledged as important documents, court records offer a rich source of challenge to the prevailing system of the times in interrogating colonial authority. The fact that atrocities against the slaves are recorded in the court registers either as lawful punishment or as petitions for justice point to the necessity of gathering alternative sources of information from which an archive could be built. While by and large the history of Trinidad from the early period until the seventeenth and eighteenth centuries has been about the struggle of the Amerindians and their almost complete extermination from Trinidad, it is available to the postcolonial researcher only through records meant for the colonial king and not inscribed in the landscape in the form of ruins or in the archival records. *The Loss of El Dorado* is about that period that lies in colonial records as a part of the expanding empire. While these records now form a rich source of documentation for contemporary scholars, for Naipaul their discovery was revelatory. As he indicates in his Nobel acceptance speech, the discovery of Chaguanas in the records at the library was significant because it occasioned memories; it spoke to him of a real time and place and people: *need* of documentary sources in addition to mythic and imaginative *re*-sources.

Besides the sparseness of archival material, a major challenge to this "construction" is the selective nature of individual and collective, social and cultural memories. Derek Walcott, in his Nobel acceptance speech, surmises that the Ramayan being played out in the cane fields had a purpose for those who performed it; there was a connection to their pasts, their traditions, their India from whence their own journey had been final. Given the cyclic framework of mythic re-enactment, Walcott sees Western history as problematic because it conceptualizes reality in linear time: "In an oral tradition the mode is simple, the response open-ended, so that each new poet can add his lines to the form, a process very much like weaving or the dance, based on the concept that the history of the tribe is endless."[8]

However, the re-enactment of ethnic folk drama as a mode for capturing the past is different from the process used by a historian in the academy. Like creative artists, historians contextualize their work by grounding it in social patterns. Thus, in a sense, history has been rewritten or reimagined in the Caribbean by a greater grounding in knowledge of past and present traditions, cultures, religious practices, utensils, food and household items. This approach to social ethnography is similar to the quest of the creative artists for a muse and for the relevance of art to life, specifically in relation to the traumatic journey to the Caribbean, which creates an ongoing imperative to connect the fragments. Moreover, historians in the Caribbean have always worked in tandem with creative artists to record history, and it is not odd to find references to Naipaul in the works of most historians in Trinidad, pointing to the fact that creative works have often been used as documents of social history.

Naipaul revisits this issue in *A Way in the World*.[9] The quest for self is searched and re-searched in colonial archives, literature, touristic images, history, nation and lived experience; an outsider's lens is used to view events that have already been refracted through the insider's viewpoint. It is not the anthropologist or the ethnographer who records history but the traveller who imagines the narrative of the events of history. Naipaul constructs historical rampages that have traditionally taken up just a few lines in Western history books as consequences of lost people and their lost intents. Columbus in 1498, Raleigh in 1595 and Francisco Miranda in 1806 had each led unsuccessful campaigns that each recorded. However, Naipaul delves into the archives to "construct" a view of history/story of persons and of places and of himself. While history in its grand march is a political force, for Naipaul it is always a question of personal involvement and personal records. The landscape, the relics, the forts and the documentation reveal little of a broader reality that then has to be *pieced together* from varying sources and points of view. "How could a writer write about this world, if it was the only world he knew?"[10] Yet for Naipaul, Western metropolitan history is nothing beyond the record of whims, fancies and actions of those in command. Though seemingly he endorses this personality-centric view, he aims to fill the gap between individual and community consciousness of the past through a creative understanding of individual and community response to this history.

Although he has often been censured for his statement that "History is built around achievement and creation; and nothing was created in the West Indies",[11] his repeated attempts at writing Trinidad's history, from the early *The Loss of El Dorado* to the more recent *A Way in the World*, document the centrality of history to his concerns. His one attempt at writing a truly historical account, *The Loss of El Dorado* is about how the legend became bigger than what it offered, how greed and ego did not let the legend die and how individual ambition overshadowed events that should have ended the legend long ago. His interventions are in fact based upon the tacit belief that history needs mediation to make sense and that the people of the Caribbean are not "historyless".

Arguably, despite this conviction, he is unable to forge a relation with any of the other populations – Amerindians, French, English, Spanish, Africans or Chinese. His Othering of people, groups and ethnicities is reflected in attitude, tone and voice used in his texts. Sandra Pouchet Paquet discerns a change in Naipaul's attitude towards Amerindians from Guyana when he ascribes no intelligence to them (*The Middle Passage*), to when he individualizes them, recognizing that to them he is an outsider, one of the many travellers who have frequented their territories over the years in *A Way in the World*.[12]

This individualization means recognition of their struggles against the Spanish and the British as part of the claim to "owning" lands. Naipaul's personalized inscription of history makes him comment upon the uselessness and worthlessness of the Amerindians and Africans in accepting the state of things. This sense of acceptance and non-action that generated Naipaul's anger can be traced to his Hindu upbringing and the disjunction between the philosophy of karma and Western education. Naipaul comes to an understanding of the disjunction between traditional beliefs that demand unquestionable adherence and the imposed Western colonial education that demand belief in individuality, rationality and action. However, this sense of knowing one's existence in "two worlds" does not bring Naipaul closer to understanding and acceptance of the African heritage in Trinidad.

Naipaul's early works, like *The Mystic Masseur, The Suffrage of Elvira* and *A House for Mr Biswas*, can be read as rich sources of the social history of East Indians in Trinidad. However, the Indocentricisms of these texts point to the separation of Indo-Caribbean lives from a national or Afro-Caribbean space. Brereton in her more recent work has highlighted how an Indocentric narrative has developed out of a perceived yet real sense of marginalization of East Indians from the political reformation of Trinidad as an independent political entity. Brereton reminds us that in such cases of political reformation "family and community goals were frequently given priority over individual advancement, or perhaps the distinction was simply irrelevant".[13] These communal ties are sometimes given precedence over class alliances, race alliances and religious alliances. According to Brereton, the Indocentric narrative begins with

> the vast majority of immigrants being deceived, tricked or forced to offer themselves to arkatis, . . . a horrific suffering on the long voyage across the kala pani to Trinidad . . . appalling conditions of working and living in Trinidad . . . [and how] they endured and overcame all the hardships, and through their discipline and hard work, they "saved" the local sugar industry. The Indocentric narrative continues with a story of more persecution and discrimination by colonial authorities, by Christian missionaries who attacked Hinduism and Islam and used unfair means to secure conversions, and, increasingly after World War II, by the Creoles who were beginning to dominate the civil service and the government as well as further triumphs. Indo-Trinidadians endured, persevered, and rose on the socioeconomic scale through hard work, discipline, frugality (at times to excess), strong family support, faith in their ancestral religions, and a commitment to deferred gratification in the interest of the next generation. Largely shut out from the public services and government . . . Indian families stressed schooling and professional training for their sons and increasingly their daughters too, as well as entering commerce and industry, becoming by the 1980s well represented in the latter, and probably overrepresented in law and medicine.[14]

However, as Brereton points out, Hinducentric, Islamic, and Christian Indian narratives among many others challenge this mainstream Indocentric narrative. One such theme in the Indocentric narrative, the practice of extreme frugality that ensured business success at the cost of individual ambitions, is highlighted by Naipaul in *A House for Mr. Biswas*.[15]

    A House for Mr. Biswas can be said to be a classic, not only from the point of view of literature, but as a record of the early social history of the Indo-Trinida-dian community, its life and aspirations, its sense of community and restric-tions, its caste and Brahmanical outlook, its compromises and individual rebellion. Naipaul's text delineates the way a community or family can be extremely restrictive and alienating to someone born with individual aspira-tions. Even though Biswas marries into a "good" family, his financial situation demands that he never really breaks free from his emotional, physical and financial dependency on them.

Commenting upon realities between his own upbringing at Lions House and Hanuman House in Chaguanas, Naipaul makes a clear division between the world of his grandmother's house in Chaguanas and the world outside the corrugated iron gate. Much like his idea of having two notions of history (chronological and cyclical) and time (calendrical and mythic), Naipaul sees the world through a bifocal lens in which the division between short sight and long sight reveals more about Trinidad than his avowed vision of "two worlds".[16]

This presentation forms a dual perspective that marks Naipaul's early texts, which present a veritable account of social lives among the Indian communities of the 1930s and 1940s. These accounts also challenge the stereotyped charac-terization of Indians as frugal enough to build "coolie houses", presenting the quest for a house in atypical terms of individual struggle. This is in opposition to the rather nostalgic picture of success being presented in the Indocentric narrative. From this standpoint, ethnic histories that record community lives and lies play an important role. It is not that such histories do not reflect nation-alist feelings, but that the space they claim is distinctive and preserved, outside of contact with other classes and ethnicities.

Both Brereton and Naipaul treat the Afro-narrative in a similar way. The Black Power movement galvanized ethnic identity formation among the Africans and East Indians in Trinidad alike. The movement in its heyday of the 1960s and 1970s challenged the Creole nationalist narrative, accusing the People's National Movement of being neo-colonialists who denigrated African elements in favour of a Creole mix. Brereton outlines the Afro-narrative as giv-ing precedence to enslavement "as the formative experience of the nation's past" with "drumming, African stick-fighting and related forms of song and dance; calypso . . . and traditional elements in the annual Carnival . . . rapso . . . Orisha, Shango, Shouters, Kambule" being emphasized over the more com-monly Afro-Creole sphere of Carnival, calypso,[17] steelband music, Christmas

and Easter and Best Village performances.[18] It is important to note that both
the Indo- and Afro-narratives are written against the national Creole narrative
and not necessarily in opposition to each other.

Naipaul's take on the Black Power movement, like his analysis of events of
pre-English rule of Trinidad, is marked by the rise and whims of prominent
personalities. In *The Return of Eva Peron with the Killings in Trinidad,* he reduces
the Black Power movement to the life of Michael X. Naipaul undercuts all
appeal that the movement had for the poor blacks and the political oppor-
tunists, let alone the general population. Filtered through Naipaul's vision, the
focus is on "[r]evolution, change, system: London words, London abstractions,
capable of supporting any meaning Malik . . . chose to give them. . . . It was in
London that Malik became a Negro. . . . He was shallow and unoriginal; but
he sensed that in England, provincial, rich and very secure, race was, to Right
and Left, a topic of entertainment. And he became an entertainer."[19]

Naipaul recalls having gone to visit Michael X's "home" in Arima in
Trinidad after it was mysteriously burnt and the movement had lost its
momentum. His method is to read carefully the autobiography of Michael X
to intercede that account through the accounts of others whom he meets on
that visit. But in so doing, Naipaul undermines the appeal and political
momentum of the movement.[20] The Caroni march organized in support of
the movement had the support of Indians as well. And the fact that the Eric
Williams government had to forcibly stop the movement, characterizing it as
anti-national, presents a very different scenario from that of Naipaul. In fact
in an essay, "Power", Naipaul equates the Black Power movement with the
energy and useless display of anarchistic tendencies displayed in Carnival. For
him, Carnival represents an African identity and not a Creole national image.
The images of Carnival highlight African-inspired elements like the steel band
and calypso from which Naipaul feels totally alienated.

In fact, any claim to a Creole/dougla[21] identity as the national identity has
always been contested in the social and political arena although finding itself
highly privileged in the domain of identity discourses in Trinidad. Privileging
certain ethnicities over others in the Creole model has been a cause of disagree-
ment as well as the fact that certain ethnicities or classes have not had either
representation or voice in identity politics. However, it is also true that the writing of an ethnic history is deeply steeped in inter-ethnic relations and is
dependent upon survival of a history of hostility between ethnicities. Moreover,
the competing political forces within Trinidad call for the dissolution of a

singular, even hybrid, Creole identity in favour of preserving their own ethnically charged accounts of their contributions to the nation of Trinidad.

Brereton pointed out in *Race Relations in Trinidad: 1870–1900*, that interaction between the Afro- and Indo-populations had been coloured with an overlay of caste and race perceptions. While the African population saw Indians in lower-class terms, Indians saw Africans as lower in caste terms, since they are darker in colour than Indians.[22]

However, as is the case with all generalizations, the reality is not as simple. The perceived general wealth of the Indian population, along with their social and cultural revival, has continued to engender interethnic rivalry. These have been countered with Afro-Trinidadian emancipation celebrations. Africans see Indians as unjustifiably seeking greater command over the country's resources, while Indians see Africans as parasitically seeking to live off the government. The presence of strong, ethnically charged narratives within political parties espouse their ethnic links notwithstanding their claims to be proletarian and egalitarian. This presence of Indo- and Afro-narratives characterize Trinidad's racial politics.

However, on the streets and in our homes, Creole food, culture and families have found an acceptance far beyond that accorded to them in these ethnic narratives. Even participation in Divali and Carnival, often projected in images as East Indian and Creole spaces, is more inclusive than how these are constructed in the respective Indocentric and Afrocentric narratives.

The existence of ethnic narratives points to persistent feelings of marginalization that the respective communities harbour within themselves, which in turn influences competition to inscribe their own constructions of history into the national narrative.[23] Although this phenomenon is not specific to Trinidad,[24] it needs to be documented. Brereton herself recognizes the presence of these oppositional narratives as they have emerged "in the domain of 'public history' rather than in formal historiography".[25]The distinction is important because it points to narratives that already exist, as opposed to being "created". The attempt to document them is also to point to the fallacies within such narratives that continue to reflect and generate hostilities. This ethnic perspective also details how deeply divided the nation of Trinidad is, not only from Tobago, but from within its many populations.

Most postcolonial scholars offer a blend of the oral and written, mythic and real history as opposed to the layout of dates, times and events of Eurocentric metropolitan accounts. Unlike the ideological investment in the sovereignty of the self that underlies metropolitan discourses, postcolonial identities always have been marked at community, caste, race and class levels. This is not to say that metropolitan discourse does not deal with these issues, only that it locates itself at the centre of an individualistic, progressive enlightenment philosophy that characterizes teleological history writing. Bringing such self-awareness to history gives history a formative role and engages with the very process of writing history.

However, paradoxically this owning of history in postcolonial states is wrapped in discourses of identity. Moreover, such an "owning" entails privileging one's location in the land of one's birth, irrespective of the multinational legacies that are carried in the memories of the ancestors. Yet at the same time, in this quest, Caribbean history has to lay a claim upon the history of the white conquistadors, the exterminated Amerindians, the enslaved Africans and the Indian indenturers among many other discourses that circulate in the Caribbean. This dual perspective of ownership and accommodation is due to the dynamic nature of each ethnic incursion that has accrued over a long period of time and to contest the little space accorded to such histories in the hegemonic colonial accounts.

Recent forays into ethnic history by Brereton point to the existence of *literatures* that have maintained a separate identity outside of the official rhetoric. Narration and authorship are prioritized in these accounts. This interest is in line with Brereton's analysis of Naipaul advocating "self-examination" and "self-awareness" for the community to move out of its self-absorbed and static world.[26] It documents not only what needs to be documented but what is indeed the groundwork of newspapers, lectures, preaching, ideological positions, appeals towards those ideological positions and support for those ideological perspectives that often shape our thinking and actions. It signals the coming of age of postcolonial discourses of identity that emphasize contextualization and continuation outside the bounds of predefined fields of enquiry. It also signals how prior written records often become institutionalized (as in the case of Brereton's *A History of Modern Trinidad: 1783–1962*) to such an extent that they command their own hegemony. Scholarship demands that we constantly view and review the hegemony of the written and in the case of ethnic histories, the spoken word.

Notes

1. Brereton herself uses this phrase from Timothy Brennan's "The National Longing for Form" (in *Nation and Narration*, ed. Homi Bhabha [New York: Routledge, 1990], 58) in her essay "Contesting the Past: Narratives of Trinidad and Tobago History", *New West Indian Guide* 81 (3–4): 1–-28.

2. Though Brereton has been more inclusive of taking into account Tobago's history as distinct from Trinidad's in terms of its annexation, its importance as a transit point, its colonial history, its revolts, its bicameral system etc. this paper focuses upon Trinidad since most East Indians came as indentured labourers to Trinidad.

3. Gayatri Spivak, "Can the Subaltern Speak?", in *The Postcolonial Studies Reader*, ed. Bill Ashcroft, Gareth Grifiths, Helen Tiffin (London: Routledge, 1995), 24–28.

4. Richard Eaton, "(Re)imag(in)ing Otherness: A Postmortem for the Postmodern in India", *Journal of World History* 11, no. 1 (2000): 57.

5. Bridget Brereton, *A History of Modern Trinidad: 1783–1962* (Kingston: Heinemann, 1981).

6. V.S. Naipaul, *The Loss of El Dorado: A History* (London: Deutsch, 1969).

7. Brereton, *History*, 8.

8. Derek Walcott, "The Muse of History", in *Is Massa Day Dead?*, ed. Orde Coombs (New York: Anchor-Doubleday, 1974), 11.

9. V.S. Naipaul, *A Way in the World* (London: Heinemann, 1994)

10. Ibid., 27.

11. V.S. Naipaul, *The Middle Passage: Impressions of Five Societies – British, French, and Dutch – in the West Indies and South America* (New York: Vintage Books, 1981), 28–29.

12. Sandra Pouchet Paquet, "V.S. Naipaul and the Interior Expeditions: 'It Is Impossible to Make a Step without the Indians' ", *Anthurium: A Caribbean Studies Journal* 5:2 (2007), http://anthurium.miami.edu/volume_5/issue_2/V5I2index.html, accessed 27 July 2011.

13. Bridget Brereton, "Family Strategies, Gender and the Shift to Wage Labour in the British Caribbean", in *The Colonial Caribbean in Transition: Essays on Post-Emancipation Social and Cultural History*, ed. Bridget Brereton and Kevin A. Yelvington (Kingston: University of the West Indies Press, 1999), 77–107.

14. Bridget Brereton, "Ethnic Histories: The Indocentric Narrative of Trinidad's History" (paper presented at the Global South Asian Diaspora Conference, University of the West Indies, St Augustine, 1–4 June 2011).

15. V.S. Naipaul, *A House for Mr. Biswas* (London: Deutsch, 1961).

16. V.S. Naipaul, "Two Worlds" (Nobel lecture, 18 June 2012), http://www.nobelprize.org/nobel_prizes/literature/laureates/2001/ naipaul-lecture.html.

17. Calypso figures in both categories: the more traditional elements being emphasised over the more merry making elements in the national paradigm.

18 Bridget Brereton, " 'All ah We Is Not One': Afrocentric History in a Pluralist Nation", *Global South* 4, no. 2 (2010): 232.

19. V.S. Naipaul, *The Return of Eva Peron with the Killings in Trinidad* (New York: Knopf, 1980), 28–30.

20. For a more detailed discussion, see Selwyn Ryan and Taimoon Stewart, *The Black Power Revolution 1970: A Retrospective* (St Augustine, Trinidad and Tobago: Institute of Social and Economic Research, 1995)

21. Dougla refers to offspring of Indo-African unions. The term in Hindi or Bhojpuri carries the connotations of impure breed, bastard and deceitful person.

22. Bridget Brereton, *Race Relations in Colonial Trinidad 1870–1900* (New York: Cambridge University Press, 1979).

23. Anton Allahar points out that ethnic histories are not written against national interests but rather within nationalist spaces. Anton Allahar, "Class, 'Race', and Ethnic Nationalism in Trinidad", in *Ethnicity, Class and Nationalism: Caribbean and Extra-Caribbean Dimensions*, ed. Anton L. Allahar (New York: Lexington Book, 2005), 229–59.

24. India is divided along caste lines and language barriers while Africa is divided along tribes. European nations themselves are divided along religious and ethnic patterns as well

25. Brereton, "Ethnic Histories".

26 Brereton, "Naipaul's Sense of History". *Anthurium: A Caribbean Studies Journal* 5, no. 2 (2007), http://anthurium.miami.edu/volume_5/issue_2/V5I2index.html, accessed 25 April 2011.

11.

THE ROLE OF SOCIOHISTORICAL FACTORS
IN THE PROCESSES OF CREOLIZATION

Evidence from Amerindian Languages

[IAN ROBERTSON]

THE SINGLE MOST SIGNIFICANT issue which Creole linguistics has had to address throughout virtually all of its history is the definition of Creole languages. Jacques Arends points to the fact that the lack of agreement on the precise definition of Pidgins and Creoles as well as on the question of which languages properly qualify for this classification is one of the issues that the field has to address.[1] Donald Winford comments on the considerable range of contact languages to which the term is applied.[2]

Peter Roberts carefully documents the rather specific circumstances in which the term is used in the earliest studies.[3] It is easy to read into Roberts the implication that linguists have been too cavalier in assigning Creole status. Many of the languages of the world assigned Creole status are sufficiently different from the languages identified by Roberts for questions to be raised as to the validity of the classificatory system used. Apparent contradictions in the work of some linguists have not helped. John Holm and Francis Byrne, for instance, questions the classification of Berbice Dutch as a Creole on the basis of the profound influence of a single language, Eastern Ijo, on its development.[4] The fact is that we do not "fully understand" the genesis of Creole languages either or there would be no issue of appropriate or inappropriate classification. At any rate, Robertson has clearly demonstrated that Berbice Dutch derived from socio-historical conditions which are largely similar to those which created the other Creoles of the Caribbean and that it shares all the more widespread linguistic features associated with the Creoles of the Caribbean.[5]

Arends refers to the tendency to distinguish between different types of Creole languages and to focus on the plantation, fort and Maroon Creoles as arising out of different sets of socio-historical conditions.[6] Holm and Byrne argue that theories must take account of the reality of the very diverse circumstances in which such languages were established.[7]

The relevance of socio-historical factors to the definition of Creole languages has itself been challenged by a number of linguists. Derek Bickerton makes the important point that any theoretical discussion of a linguistic phenomenon ought to be premised on a reasonably clear characterization of that phenomenon itself.[8]

Attempts by linguists like Bickerton, Douglas Taylor and Talmy Givon to identify these essential linguistic features have not gained general acceptance thus far, both because such attempts have been shown to rule out a priori some languages that are clearly Creole and because they have included languages whose Creole status may be challenged.[9] Given the essential arbitrariness of language itself, it may be too much to expect that the mere possession of a set of features could more than increase the probability of typological identity, for, as Mervyn Alleyne points out, the mere presence of identical features in two languages does not constitute a conclusive argument for their relatedness.[10]

Holm and Byrne's dictum, noted earlier, indicates the need for the social and historical factors to be clearly understood and this, perhaps, has never been thoroughly done for any set or subset of Creole languages. One reason for this failure is the fact that creolists accept general considerations provided by historians without carefully scrutinizing their specific relevance to the processes of creolization.

Creolists assume, quite correctly, that new languages would only emerge when persons develop some sensitivity to the inadequacy of the means available to them for fulfilling their communication and other linguistic needs. Such recognition of the need for a new communication medium is central to the development of Creole languages. Since persons with a common medium would have no need for such a medium, linguistic mixing of slaves would provide precisely the kind of motivation for developing Creole languages.

This has led to the general acceptance of the mixing of slaves as the critical motivating factor in the development of the plantation Creoles of the Caribbean area. In short, linguists have found a good explanation for the kind of motivator for the development of Creoles. But it is not the mixing that is critical. It is the sense of linguistic inadequacy that motivates persons to craft a move to a more satisfactory communication medium. Mixing is one good way to motivate such changes but there are others and certainly the prevailing socio-historical conditions deserve to be considered as well.

In accepting ethnic mixing as the critical motivating factor for creolization, linguists have merely accepted, without the necessary critical sensitivity, the position of historians whose interests, concerns and focus do not necessarily coincide with those of the linguists themselves. One major consideration would have to be the timing of the mixing of the slaves. This would determine whether or not such mixing as occurred did so at the right time and in the right places to promote the sense of inadequacy noted above. A careful reading of the work written on Berbice Dutch,[11] Jamaican Creole English,[12] Sranan Tongo[13] and Haitian[14] would encourage suspicion about the timing of the mixing of the slaves since they all point to evidence suggesting strong inputs from a restricted set of substrate languages.

Ironically, while the issue of heterogeneity of input from the substrate languages may be challenged in some instances of creolization, so too may the assumption of linguistic homogeneity among European planters, managers and overseers. In several instances in the Caribbean, the politically dominant group was not the numerically dominant one. In the Danish West Indies the numerically dominant were the Dutch. In the Dutch colony Demerara, it was the English. Somewhat later, in Trinidad, this Spanish colony was peopled mainly by French colonists. There is also evidence that in some territories, Berbice, for example, there were speakers of several European languages. As in the case of the non-European languages the issue is one of ensuring that the proper time considerations are taken into account.

Bickerton and Givon are right to assert the need for a valid linguistic domain to be established on linguistic rather than socio-historical grounds. Their positions, however seem to assign little or no significance to socio-historical factors in the development of these Creole languages. Other linguists, such as Ian Hancock and Arends, Muysken and Smith[15] clearly indicate that proper consideration of the socio-historical factors is fundamental to the proper understanding of the nature of Creole languages and of the circumstances that would normally lead to their development.

This chapter attempts to enhance the claims for consideration of socio-historical conditions by investigating another set of contact situations, those between the indigenous Amerindian groups and the Europeans, mainly Dutch, in Guyana. It is argued that there are other contact situations in the Caribbean, Guyana in this instance, which situations are not known to have produced lasting contact languages. Any differences between such situations and those that actually produced Creoles would provide considerable guidance on the matter of the significant socio-historical considerations.

The period of contact between the Europeans and the indigenous Amerindian groups in Essequibo, and Berbice, the original Dutch Colonies in what is now Guyana on the northern sea coast of South America, may conveniently be divided into three phases: the early contact and trading period, the early plantation or settlement period, and the later plantation phase. Although the colony of Demerara was developed out of Essequibo, its origin and development were different and patterns of communication in the earlier colonies would have been well set by the time of its establishment.

The early contact phase, stretching from the earliest contacts in the late nineteenth century, is characterized by brief intermittent and irregularly scheduled visits to the colonies for the purpose of trading with the native Indians. During this phase, the contact between the Europeans, among whom the Dutch were perhaps the more significant for the purposes of this chapter, and the indigenous Amerindians, who were always in the majority, would have been intermittent.

Mary Noel Menezes says, "The mobile Indians defied statistics."[16] Consequently, it is difficult to estimate the number of Amerindians with whom the Dutch and other Europeans came into contact. It is clear, though, that no more than a handful of Dutch traders, certainly less than a hundred, were in touch with hundreds and perhaps thousands of Amerindians during this phase. Tens of thousands of other Amerindians, not directly involved in the trade, were nonetheless *in situ* in these colonies. These Amerindians exercised confident control of the environment.

N.O. Poonai notes that "the Indian's sense of independence and confidence in his control of his (habitat) environment was a source of considerable confidence".[17] Menezes notes further that "the Spaniards unwisely tried to demilitarise them (the Caribs) by setting them in mission areas, thus restricting their prized freedom, and for their pains won the undying hostility of the Caribs. The Dutch, to whom commerce and not religion was the goal, shrewdly summed up the position when they arrived, assured the Caribs of their freedom, and enlisted them for the purposes of trade and later for hunting runaway slaves."[18]

The basic practice appears to have been for the Dutch to arrive in their boats, and to sail up the rivers to the established trading posts. The Amerindian groups brought their produce to these posts. At this point, trading was carried out, either directly with the Dutch sailors and traders or with any traders who might themselves have had a more or less permanent location for the specific purpose of trade. The contacts would have allowed at least two opportunities for the development of a trade language or pidgin; the first would have been with the sailors and the second with the settled traders.

It would be misleading to regard the several Amerindian groups with whom the Dutch came into contact as a homogeneous group on virtually any basis – ethnic, linguistic, habitat, frequency of interaction with Europeans. For the entire Dutch colonial period a distinction has to be made between the contact with the coastal groups on the one hand and that with the more hinterland groups on the other. On the coast, the Dutch encountered four groups: Caribs (Kalinha), Arawaks (Lokono), Akawaios and Warraus.

The Caribs (Kalinha) inhabited in the main the Essequibo coast and the Courentyne areas. They were generally stereotyped by Europeans as hostile even to fellow Amerindians. Indeed, Caribs are reported to have destroyed a number of Berbice plantations as early as 1668. Later, when plantations were fully established, the Caribs served as policemen of the plantation system, being used mainly to capture runaway slaves and, in Essequibo, for the supply of (illegal) Indian slaves mainly from the Orinoco region in neighbouring Venezuela. For these reasons, interaction with them was likely to have been very cautious and would have been attended by a high degree of tolerance or even respect.

The Arawaks were regarded as a gentler people. They occupied the lower river areas and the coastal waterways. This group was perhaps the one with whom contact was most regular, as they inhabited the areas where the early Dutch settlers lived. Indeed, Anna Benjamin noted that they took up residence amid the Amerindian population that was apparently comparatively numerous during the early contact period.[19] An early map of the Berbice area indicates that the Dutch lived in Arawak villages in Berbice. This group of Indians supplied the regular needs of the settlers including, as shall be indicated later, the need for wives.

The Akawaios inhabited, in the main, the Upper Mazaruni River, Berbice, Demerara and parts of the Courentyne rivers. They were perhaps the most nomadic of this set of contact groups and were known to travel long distances for the purposes of carrying out vendettas. Charles Dance records a case of one set of Akawaios traveling from the Roraima region in western Guyana to the Berbice River in the east, a distance of about three hundred miles, to carry out one such act of revenge.[20] They were thought to be feared by the by the "gentler groups" and were considered "natural enemies of the "warlike" Caribs. Unlike the Arawaks, their contact with the Dutch seems to have been restricted to trade at the posts.

The Warraus occupied the more swampy sectors of the low-lying coastland and were the fishermen and boat builders of the territories. They were therefore the chief providers of transportation in what, even today, still is an area criss-crossed by significant canals, creeks, rivers, and swamps.

Relations with each of these groups were essential to the survival of the early Dutch settlers. Benjamin has noted that the Dutch needed the Amerindians too much to destroy them by conquest. Since the Dutch appeared to be so dependent on the indigenous groups for their very survival, their presence could hardly have been significant enough to affect the linguistic self-confidence of the native Indians. Consequently, it was very unlikely that they would have adjusted their language significantly enough to allow for the development of new languages such as Creoles.

The Indians traded in the main in annatto, letterwood and dyes. This early period is characterized by functional and numerical dominance of Amerindians within a geographic environment with which they were totally familiar, and in which the European was totally dependent upon the Amerindian for virtually everything, including food, water, security, transport and health. P.M. Netscher says that initial trade was conducted with considerable hostility and murder once the Indians felt that the deals were unfair.[21]

The picture one gets in this early period is one in which the Dutch dependence upon Amerindians made it more likely that the former would have had to find solutions to their linguistic and communication problems. They were not in a position to dictate choice of medium. Certainly, the settlers, who were few, too powerless, too dependent on the Amerindians, would have had to be the ones to adjust their language. The sailors were no less dependent upon the Amerindians though the contacts would have been more intermittent than those of the settlers. Aggressive and even violent episodes in the trade suggest that the sailors also had to be cautious. It should come as no surprise, therefore, to find that the contemporary sources contain no references to the existence of a pidgin nor do they contain any samples of a linguistic compromise.

One of the first references to the early plantation phase provides some clues to the situation. Adrian van Berkel provides two potential insights to the dominant options. As his vessel approached Berbice, he notes,

> We then perceived some Indians, commonly called Bokyes* (Bucks). Some of the sailor-men who had often been there *asked if they might take the boat ashore to buy Palmyt and were allowed to go.* . . . . Here we were visited by some Indians, with women and small children. Several of our ship's crew who had been there frequently *and knew something of their language, began to talk with them,* and to do business with certain Knick-knacks.[22]

The fact that the sailors asked and were allowed to go suggests a certain level of concern for safe relations with the Amerindians. The passage also makes it clear that it was the sailors who attempted to learn the language of the Amerindians. The "something of the language" that the sailors knew could have been an incipient pidgin but it might just as well have been the European learner's version of the Amerindian's languages. If indeed it were a pidgin then both sides would have been motivated to contribute to it and to tolerate it. If it were a European's learner language then it would have been the European's learner construct of the Amerindian's language. For some creolists there would have been no difference between the two since pidginization, for them, is only the early stage of adult second language learning. The difference lies perhaps in the mechanisms used for pidginization and the extent to which these are the same as those used for second language acquisition. One significant difference would be the extent to which the Amerindian or the European base structures are the ones simplified.

Later in his account, van Berkel recounts an incident that provides considerable evidence of the communication process.

> While I was busy preparing the said merchandise, some Indians came to the fort with their wares which *my interpreter* dispatched. They were simple people where counting is concerned as I have noted on so many different occasions. Because when they come to the trading-post with a parcel of thirty balls of paint called Oriane (Arnato) they do not know to count them in succession. They put five balls together according to the fingers of the hand, and then again five others. When I saw this for the first time I asked *my interpreter* the reason for it: he told me that their number does not extend beyond five.[23]

The observation that the Amerindians used the base five for counting may be regarded as evidence that they did retain their own system for this purpose.

One hundred and fifty years later, William Hilhouse, one of the more outstanding postholders and protectors of the Indians, commented on the relationships between the early Dutch and the Amerindians:

> The secret of attachment of the old Dutch proprietors and the Indians, consisted in the colonists taking the Indian women for their housekeepers; *and of course acquiring some knowledge of their language*, and becoming what may be called "broomstick relations".

The Indian is proud of these connections and though he makes it a point to tease, harass, and defraud the European usurper, who has no connection with him – yet, the moment the family compact is entered into, *and the Indian is addressed in his own language*, nothing can exceed his faith, attachment and honourable conduct to his white relation.[24]

This clearly underscores the linguistic self-confidence of the Indian. The reference to Old Dutch proprietors is to be read as early colonists since this is the context of Hilhouse's writings.

The second phase marked a transition in primary focus from trading to plantation agriculture. During this period, which started in the third quarter of the seventeenth century and ran up to the beginnings of the period of rapid expansion in about 1720, there was a gradual shift particularly in Berbice. According to Benjamin, Berbice continued to trade along traditional lines for a long time.[25] The plantations grew slowly until the third decade of the eighteenth century. At the arrival of van Berkel in 1670, there were a mere five plantations in Berbice. These increased to eight in 1720 and by 1735, G.T. Galbano-Elephantius comments that there were a mere thirty-five planters on the Berbice River but that the numbers were increasing rapidly.[26] Alvin Thompson says there were ninety-three land grants in 1733 and eighty planters by 1735.[27]

This period is described by Thompson as the embryonic plantation phase and is essentially seen as that referred to here as the early settlement or plantation phase. The picture might be altered slightly if consideration were given to the fact that, according to Netscher there was an Amerindian uprising in Berbice, which destroyed estates on which "many were massacred and their estates ruined".[28] This might, in part, account for the apparent slow growth in plantation numbers available to present-day researchers. It might also account for the relative slow growth of these colonies by comparison with the Surinam colony which was established some fifty years after the Guyana ones.

During this time, Essequibo appears to have had a greater commitment to the plantation system. The number of plantations grew no faster than it did in Berbice, however. Though there were only three company plantations there in 1700, there were eighteen planters there from as early as 1687 and there were thirty-five estates in 1735. However, the first sugar mill was set up at Brower-shoek as early as 1656 and the orientation of the colony was more towards the production of sugar than to the traditional trading. Such trade as existed in Essequibo seemed to have concentrated mainly on the Amerindian slave trade in which Amerindians in contact with the colonists provided slaves from the Amazonian groups. This was one means of supplementing the chronic short-age of labour that characterized the plantations during the Dutch colonial period. These slaves were brought from the Orinoco region in Venezuela because there were specific laws in the Guiana territories prohibiting trade in local Amerindians.

There are no specific records on the language situation among these groups of slaves or between them and the Dutch planters. Since they were a minority anyway it would be reasonable to assume that they were assimilated linguisti-cally into the speakers of the Dutch lexicon Creole that is known to have been the primary form of language on the Essequibo plantations.

During the early plantation phase, trade with the Amerindians continued, though on a reduced and, in the case of Essequibo, a more specialized scale. The patterns of trade appear to have become more stable. Traders were employed to interface directly with the Amerindians in the interior of the colonies. These traders were of African descent. They were few in number. Fourteen were documented for 1700 and eleven in 1702. Their primary quali-fication was the ability to speak some of the Indian languages, Carib and Acawaio, according to Benjamin, being the most essential.[29] Carib was valid because it was thought to hold a key to other Cariban languages that were spo-ken in the Guyana interior. The Acawaios, themselves a subgroup of the Carib language family in Guyana, were encountered in some numbers in the interior of the colony. They were also part of the early contact group of traders, as was noted above, and they continued to be involved in trade.

The linguistic situation in the interior did not appear to have changed much during the plantation phase since the contact remained essentially intermittent and the traders continued to use the Amerindian languages.

On the coast, by contrast, the linguistic situation was profoundly affected by the switch to plantation agriculture. For one thing it introduced a third group, speakers of West African languages, in increasing numbers as the demand for cheap free labour rose. This group, though they shared a common cosmology, was considered to be a heterogeneous one linguistically, though less so in the case of Berbice than in the case of Essequibo. The West Africans altered the demographic and social structure of the colonies. The availability of slave labour altered the power structure. There was now a section of the population over which the Europeans had a high level of control especially for the provision of labour. This factor removed some of the absolute dependence of the European on the Amerindians. During the early plantation phase, the African group grew to become numerically the second largest group after the Amerindians in the plantation context. Their numbers increased slowly so that as late as 1712 there were only 895 slaves in Berbice and in Essequibo there were only 690 as late as 1710. The Africans in Essequibo appear to have been less linguistically homogenous than those in Berbice who, by available linguistic evidence, must have been mainly Eastern Ijo, probably Kalabari speaking.[30]

Not only did the presence of the Africans change the demographic structure of the colonies but it also brought about a change in the social relationships between the Dutch and the Arawaks among whom they lived in the earlier period. The situation was slowly reversed to one in which Amerindians, the Arawaks in particular, gravitated to the plantations, supplying provisions and a paid labour force for land clearing and other activities. The Amerindians were clear to distinguish between their status and that of the slaves.

In these circumstances, it was the West Africans, rather than the Amerindians, who had sufficient social upheaval and dislocation, both physical and mental, to allow them, as a group to develop the sense of linguistic inadequacy in the current contexts. This is the kind of linguistic insecurity that underpins any desire to acquire another form of expression. This sense of linguistic inadequacy is also to be considered one of the critical factors in the development of Creole languages.

There is no surviving evidence of the development of a Creole or pidgin language based on any Amerindian language during the period when the circumstances would have led linguists to expect such developments. The Christian church developed high levels of sensitivity to the language situation in the colonies. It is therefore instructive in these contexts to find that the Moravian church established a mission to the Amerindians on the Berbice River in 1738 and maintained a presence there until the slave uprising of 1763 but used the Arawak (Lokono) language rather than any sort of Amerindian contact language. It would be difficult to rule out the possibility of the formation of an Amerindian/Dutch contact language, but it is clear that any such putative contact language did not survive. Had it done so its survival would not have gone unnoticed particularly by the church. Further, if it had survived it would probably have served as a basis for the two Creole languages, Berbice and Skepie Dutch, that developed on the plantations in the respective colonies. However, both these Creole languages have been clearly demonstrated to have been the product of African/Dutch interaction in the colonies with the seminal input being from the West African languages and Dutch.

Several reasons may be adduced for the failure to uncover any evidence of Amerindian/Dutch contact languages. In the first place, any such languages, being oral, would have disappeared once the need for them ceased to exist. In addition, written evidence would have been set down at the whim and fancy of whichever European was interested enough to set it down. But the business of the European was hardly the documentation of contact convenience languages. Such documentation would have been a byproduct of some larger objective. Literacy was not a norm among the Europeans either. Finally, if any Europeans did actually set down the information, their writings have not been yet been uncovered after considerable searching.

By the time the plantation system became firmly established there would have been little chance of an Amerindian/Dutch Creole or contact language developing. By this time trade would have lost its significance to the plantation crops of sugar, cotton and cocoa in the main. None of these required constant contact with the Amerindians. Further, there is some eighteenth-century evidence that any such contact was carried out in the language developed and used by the slaves.

The essential argument of this chapter is that the social and historical factors in the early Guyana colonies do not suggest that there was sufficient cause for the Amerindian groups in Guyana colonies to feel so insecure about their language as to want to adapt it to any new set of circumstances. There was a lack of a common communication medium. There were a large number of Amerindians interacting with a small number of Europeans. The contacts were intermittent. The Dutch shared a common language. Trade was the major reason for the contact.

The absence of any creolization or pidginization in these colonial contact circumstances suggests that the historical and social correlates of these processes must have been different from those that existed in these and similar contact situations. The critical areas of difference appear to be the fact that the contact presented no major physical or social dislocation for the large heterogeneous indigenous group and that, as a consequence, their linguistic self-concept remained a positive one and lacked any sense of insufficiency. In addition, the Amerindians were self-assertive and inflicted harsh punishment on the Europeans who made the mistake of trying to impose their will upon them. These latter were perhaps critical in ensuring that no creolization of language took place out of the meeting of indigenous Amerindian and European, mainly Dutch, contact in these colonies. The technological and other advantages, including the ability to write, brought by the Dutch, simply did not, in the circumstances, outweigh the natural advantages of the indigenous groups.

Notes

1. Jacques Arends, *The Early Stages of Creolization* (Amsterdam: John Benjamins, 1995), 3.

2. Donald Winford, introduction, *Structure and Status of Pidgins and Creoles* (Amsterdam: John Benjamins, 1997). 3. Peter Roberts, "Concepts of Creole: The Legacy of Moreau de S. Mery, J.J. Thomas and others" (paper presented at the Eleventh Biennial Conference of the Society for Caribbean Linguistics, St Maarten, August 1996).

4. John A. Holm and Francis Byrne, eds., *Atlantic Meets Pacific: A Global View of Pidginization and Creolization*, Selected Papers from the Society for Pidgin and Creole Linguistics (Amsterdam: John Benjamins, 1993).

5. Ian Robertson, "Creole and UnCreole: Challenging the Stereotype" (paper presented at the Seventh Biennial Conference of the Society for Caribbean Linguistics, Nassau, Bahamas, 1988).

6. Arends, *Early Stages*.

7. Holm and Byrne, *Atlantic Meets Pacific*.

8. Derek Bickerton, "Creoles and West African Languages: A Case of Mistaken Identity?", *Substratum versus Universals in Creole Genesis: Papers from Amsterdam Creole Workshop April 1985*, ed. P. Muysken and N. Smith (Amsterdam: John Benjamins, 1986).

9. Derek Bickerton, *Roots of Language* (Ann Arbor: Karoma, 1981); Douglas Taylor,

Languages of the West Indies (Baltimore: Johns Hopkins University Press, 1977); Talmy Givon, "Prologomena to Any Sane Creology", in *Readings in Creole Studies*, ed. Ian Hancock (Ghent: Storia Scientia, 1979), 3–35.

10. Mervyn Alleyne, personal communication, 2002.

11. N. Smith, I. Robertson and K. Williamson, "The Ijo Element in Berbice Dutch", *Language in Society* 16, no. 1 (1987): 49–89.

12. Frederick G. Cassidy, *Jamaica Talk: Three Hundred Years of the English Language in Jamaica* (London: Macmillan, 1961); Frederick G. Cassidy and Robert Le Page, *Dictionary of Jamaican English* (Cambridge: Cambridge University Press, 1967).

13. N. Smith, I. Robertson and K. Williamson, "The Ijo Element in Berbice Dutch", *Language in Society* 16, no. 1 (1987): 49–89.

14. Claire Lefebvre, *Creole Genesis and the Acquisition of Grammar: The Case of Haitian Creole* (Cambridge: Cambridge University Press, 1998).

15. J. Arends, Pieter Muysken and Norval Smith eds., *Pidgins and Creoles: An Introduction* (Amsterdam/Philadelphia: John Benjamins, 1994).

16. Mary Noel Menezes, *British Policy towards the Amerindians in British Guiana, 1803–1873* (Oxford: Clarendon Press, 1977), 23.

17. N.O. Poonai, "Extinct Tribes and Threatened Species of the Southern Savannahs", *Timehri*, no. 43 (1967): 78.

18. Menezes, *British Policy*, 23.

19. Anna Benjamin, "A Preliminary Look at the Free Amerindians and the Dutch Plantation System in Guyana during the Seventeenth and Eighteenth Centuries", *Guyana Historical Journal* 4–5 (1992–93): 1–21.

20. Charles Dance, *Chapters from a Guyanese Log-book* (Georgetown, Guyana: Royal Gazette Establishment, 1881), 16–17.

21. P.M. Netscher, *History of the Colonies of Essequibo, Demerary and Berbice: From the Dutch Establishment to the Present Day*, trans. W. Roth (The Hague: Nihoff, 1888), 71.

22. Adrian van Berkel, *Travels in South America between the Berbice and Essequibo Rivers and in Suriname, 1670–1689*, trans. Walter Roth (1695; repr. Georgetown, Guyana: Daily Chronicle, 1941), 9–10; emphasis added.

23. Ibid., 19; emphasis added.

24. William Hilhouse, *Indian Notices: Or Sketches of the Habits, Characters, Languages, Superstitions, Soil, and Climate of the Several Nations*, intro. and notes by M.N. Menezes (1825; repr. Georgetown, Guyana: National Commission of Research Materials on Guyana, 1978), 12; emphasis added.

25. Benjamin, "Preliminary Look".

26. G.T. Galbano-Elephantius, ed., *A Voyage to the New Colony of Berbice in 1735* (Demerara: Jamieson, 1877).

27. Alvin Thompson, *Colonialism and Underdevelopment in Guyana 1580–1803* (Bridgetown, Barbados: Carib Research and Publications, 1987), 35.

28. Netscher, *History*, 71.

29. Benjamin, "Preliminary Look", 5.

30. Smith, Robertson and Williamson, "Ijo Element".

12.

AN ANNOTATED BIBLIOGRAPHY OF THE WORKS OF BARBARA LALLA AND IAN ROBERTSON

Compiled by

[NIALA DWARIKA-BHAGAT, KAREN ECCLES, MICHELLE GILL AND MARSHA WINTER]

INTRODUCTION

THE ANNOTATED BIBLIOGRAPHY PRESENTS the publications of professors Barbara Lalla and Ian Robertson and should serve as a useful resource to researchers of Creole linguistics and Caribbean literature language analysis. It was compiled by selecting a list of published works indicated in the curriculum vitae of each author. These comprise the following:

- authored or co-authored books
- chapters in books
- published articles
- edited books

Extensive efforts were made to ensure the accuracy of the bibliographic information and that the entries conformed to the sixteenth edition of the *Chicago Manual of Style*.

ORGANIZATION OF THE ENTRIES

The annotated entries are arranged into (1) books and (2) published articles, which include chapters in books. They are arranged in chronological order. Because of space constraints, book reviews and conference papers were omitted from the annotations. A few of the works appear in various sources; in cases like these, the annotations are based on the first appearance of the work.

One challenge was acquiring the articles and books, which were not all readily available. It was necessary to consult libraries located on other campuses of the University of the West Indies, use the British Library's interlibrary loan service and in some cases source items from the authors themselves.

The work that follows could not have been accomplished without the assistance of the following persons: Glenroy Taitt, Valerie Youssef, Paula Morgan, Claudia De Four, deputy campus librarian of the Alma Jordan Library, as well as the staff of the West Indian and Special Collections Division of the Alma Jordan Library.

BARBARA LALLA

Books

1. *Voices in Exile: Jamaican Texts of the Eighteenth and Nineteenth Centuries.* With Jean D'Costa. Tuscaloosa: University of Alabama Press, 1989.

This work is one of two volumes by Barbara Lalla and Jean D'Costa, the second being *Language in Exile: Three Hundred Years of Jamaican Creole. Voices in Exile* highlights a collection of songs, poetry, folklore, letters and other writings that represent the birth and evolution of Jamaican Creole language and culture against a background of pre- and post-emancipation Jamaica during the eighteenth and nineteenth centuries. Within the historical accounts, Jamaican Creole is presented as a debased representation of Jamaican culture, only spoken among the unschooled and uncultured and therefore not considered socially acceptable by the plantocracy. The text also argues that African and European settlers were exiled in Jamaica, distanced by geography, language and culture from their place of origin. Alienation is therefore identified as common to both, despite the differences in physical treatment and social stature.

The text is enriched with illustrations, including a map of Jamaica depicting settlements in the late eighteenth century, and historical figures associated with the slave trade whose writings are presented in the volume, as well as artifacts of the slave trade.

2. *Language in Exile: Three Hundred Years of Jamaican Creole.* With Jean D'Costa. Tuscaloosa: University of Alabama Press, 1990.

This is a companion volume to *Voices in Exile. Language in Exile* is based on works written in and about Jamaica in the eighteenth and nineteenth centuries and discusses the development of Jamaican Creole against the background of Jamaica's social history. The emphasis of this volume is interaction with the language, including the sound system and orthographical problems of the Creole languages. It connects varieties of early Jamaican Creole to its modern form. *Language in Exile* differs from its companion text in having a linguistic focus, while *Voices in Exile* captures the historical legacy of the language through sermons, songs, early letters and folklore. *Language in Exile* is divided into two parts. Part 1 explores the historic and demographic background of Jamaican Creole, while part 2 outlines a chronological sequence of events. It is similar to its companion volume in providing a rich set of illustrations of maps, plates, charts and tables.

3. *Defining Jamaican Fiction: Marronage and the Discourse of Survival.* Tuscaloosa: University of Alabama Press, 1996.

In *Defining Jamaican Fiction,* Lalla explores representations of the Maroons in relation to the Jamaican literary canon. She lifts the Maroon from the infamy and notoriety of oral history, sociohistorical records and fictional works, redefining a group typically marginalized for their acts of resistance. Lalla moves beyond conceptualizations of marronage as flight from colonial servitude, escapism, social isolation and violent resistance; instead, she repositions the marooned psyche within the context of British romanticism and the Caribbean canon, offering insights on exile and resistance as dimensions of Caribbean identity. The text is divided into two parts. Part 1 is "Outsides In: External Views of Alienation in Jamaica", and part 2 is "Inside Out: Jamaican Perspectives on Exile and Resistance". The latter shows how postcolonial literature revisits diverse aspects of Jamaican history and experience. *Defining Jamaican Fiction* features references a wide range of Jamaican literary works, from the earliest to the contemporary period.

4. *English for Academic Purposes: A Distance Education Course for Caribbean Students.* With Joanne Blake and Dianne Thurab-Nkhosi. St Augustine,

Trinidad and Tobago: Faculty of Humanities and Education, University of the West Indies, 1997.

This self-instructional text is designed to help students grasp tertiary-level English-language skills. It is divided into two main parts, and each is composed of units, which are further divided into sections. *English for Academic Purposes* encourages self-paced learning facilitated by activities and practice exercises. In part 1 language is defined and its functions identified; a distinction is established between the spoken and written language. Lalla demonstrates the multilingual nature of the Caribbean and instructs on the style required for academic writing. Part 2 provides students with strategies for writing and producing a scholarly essay.

5.   *Arch of Fire: A Jamaican Family Saga.* Kingston: Kingston Publishers, 1998.

Lalla's first novel recounts Jamaica's history through the lived experiences of an interlocking network of families. It depicts the Jamaican nation-family as comprising rich ethnic and cultural diversity. Its earliest inhabitants included the Tainos, enslaved African labourers on sugar plantations owned by white European slave masters and managed by an overseer class, and East Indian indentured labourers. The author explores the interrelationships that evolve among the different ethnic groups and cultures, and the social, ethnic and class consciousness that governed these interactions. Lalla asserts the salient point of connectedness by use of the mnemonic device of a sprawling family tree. The evocation sits at the interface of fiction and history and the private and public domains, as the catalysts that propel characters are also the key events of Jamaican history. The text is replete with references to historical sites and place names as well as persons who have contributed to Jamaica's economic, social and political development.

6.   *Writing about Literature: A Self-Instructional Course.* With Paula Morgan. St Augustine, Trinidad and Tobago: School of Continuing Studies, University of the West Indies, 2005.

Writing About Literature is a self-instructional handbook for tertiary-level students of literature. Morgan and Lalla focus on the central tenets of academic writing and literary analysis. The course, complete with self-access strategies and self-assessment exercises, is divided into ten units that engage the student in critical thinking and analytical skills in a start-to-finish approach. The first six units engage critical thinking and analytical skills applicable to prose, poetry and drama. Significant consideration is given to the fundamentals of academic research as the authors devote four units to topics such as general research techniques, Internet research, note-taking, citation, editing, compiling bibliographies and submission guidelines. Each unit presents an overview, establishes objectives and concludes with a summary. The work also supports the current literary curriculum by drawing examples from Caribbean and non-Caribbean sources.

7. *Postcolonialisms: Caribbean Re-Reading of Medieval English Discourse.* Kingston: University of the West Indies Press, 2008.

Middle English, the spoken and written vernacular of England circa 1100 to 1500 and its (re)-appreciation in a Caribbean context, is the predominant subject of this book. Middle English arose out of several language varieties, including that of Anglo-Saxon, Anglo-Danish, Anglo-Latin and Anglo-Norman tribes. Lalla contends that British literature – medieval to postmodern – has been the frame of reference for the literary minds of the Caribbean, and its instruction continues at secondary and tertiary levels in formally colonized nations. Yet little attention has been paid to Caribbean approaches to the British canon. The enquiry combines historical research, linguistic analysis and literary thought and constitutes a new area of linguistic inquiry. Lalla's re-visioning offers Caribbean insights into Middle English poetry. She postulates that the society that produced Middle English literature – itself a vernacular language of the "ordinary" folk – had its own history of cultural contact, loss, displacement, conquest, fragmentation and re-integration that is not dissimilar to that of the Caribbean. It too developed on the basis of conquest and subjugation out of which emerged new voices seeking survival and a renewal of identity. This discourse, Lalla argues, finds its cross-cultural equivalent in Caribbean postcolonial society. Some major works re-examined include the *Canterbury Tales, Piers Plowman* and *The Pardoner's Prologue.* An extensive ninety-two-page bibliography supports the work.

8. *Beyond Borders: Cross-Culturalism and the Caribbean Canon.* With Jennifer Rahim. Kingston: University of the West Indies Press, 2009.

Lalla is co-editor of this text, which presents a canon of anglophone Caribbean cultural studies perspectives from twelve distinguished Caribbean scholars. The Caribbean as a collective space with myriad frames of experience is a long-standing preoccupation of cultural writers and thinkers, and the work continues this tradition while engaging in latter-day literary discourse. It embraces contemporary cross-cultural Caribbean themes such as postcolonialism, Caribbean collective identity, language and popular culture. The four-part compilation reflects these themes: language and cultural evolution; beyond borders: questioning the canon and negotiating subjectivities, finding ease and the way forward. The collection reads as a lively textual debate on diverse contemporary issues.

9. *Cascade: A Novel.* Kingston: University of the West Indies Press, 2010.

Barbara Lalla's award-winning second novel set in Jamaica and Trinidad deals with the aching vulnerabilities, devastating losses and fragile victories of aging within a tumultuous Caribbean framework. The country house, Cascade, offers regular retreat for the four elderly protagonists, Ellie, Dan, Ivy and Rosemarie, who are related by blood and marriage and plan to retire together. Their former genteel lifestyle and hoped for tranquillity for their later years are assaulted by the violence, anarchy and crime that attends the emergence of modern Jamaica, which is portrayed as traumatized and teetering on the brink of social collapse. After a criminal attack, Ellie and Dan relocate to Trinidad, while Ivy, the guesthouse owner, and Rosemarie, a former nursing matron, remain in Jamaica to their own peril. The development of Cascade as guesthouse and geriatric home and its eventual mismanagement provide a catalyst for exploring changing family values, violence against the person, dislocation and fragmentation. Cascade also becomes a symbol of hope as the characters hold fast to their moral compass, directed by love, commitment, humour and courage. This multi-vocal novel is told from diverse perspectives governed by the author's firm grasp on all of its worlds and on its complex temporal sequences. The power of *Cascade* to draw the reader into its worlds can be attributed largely to its richly evocative sustained images and metaphors. Finally it is a narrative about the role of memory in the construction of the human subject.

10. *Created in the West Indies: Caribbean Perspectives on V.S. Naipaul.* With Jennifer Rahim. Kingston: Ian Randle, 2010.

In 2007 the University of the West Indies, St Augustine, honoured the life and work of Trinidadian Nobel laureate and internationally acclaimed writer, V.S. Naipaul. *Created in the West Indies* is a collection of essays based on these deliberations and covers the major themes of history and representation, home and belonging, self and the creative writing process. The collection is organized into three sections that highlight the multifaceted range of Naipaul's literary pursuits: (1) "Circuits of Self-Refashioning", in which the focus is on identity; (2) "Form Matters", which expresses Naipaul's preoccupation with literary form and (3) "Rethinking Naipaul on the Thresholds of History and New Horizons", which provides a conclusion of sorts by disclosing new perspectives on Naipaul and his work as they relate to what Jennifer Rahim terms his "historical sense". The cadre of distinguished literary authors and scholars in this work include Jean Antoine-Dunne, Edward Baugh, Bridget Brereton, Gordon Rohlehr, Evelyn O Callaghan, Paula Morgan, Rhonda Cobham-Sander, Barbara Lalla, Vijay Maharaj, Jennifer Rahim, Lawrence Scott, Bhoendradatt Tewarie and Sandra Pouchet-Paquet.

ARTICLES

1. "Sources for a History of Jamaican Creole". *Carib* 1 (1979): 50–66.

The evolution of modern Jamaican Creole is the focus of this work, which notes that Jamaican Creole, Standard English and a continuum of intermediary language forms have been of interest for over two hundred years. Lalla states that theories have been advanced about the origin and development of Jamaican Creole, but their veracity must be substantiated by examining the most archaic written Jamaican Creole records. But even here, Lalla writes, there are problems of collection, classification, interpretation and evaluation, consequent on the paucity of records of a language steeped in the oral tradition, with low levels of documentation, error by recorders, and incorrect recording of chronological diachronic phenomena and orthography. Lalla supports her arguments with textual references and phonological examples. Lalla notes that sources for tracing the history and heterogeneity of Jamaican Creole are derived from private collections, old newspapers, published tales, tape recordings, travellers' tales and journal entries. She declares that accurate textual reconstruction of archaic Jamaican Creole is a most rewarding endeavour.

2. "Quaco Sam: A Relic of Archaic Jamaican Speech". *Jamaica Journal* 45 (1981): 20–29.

Lalla acknowledges that the orality of Jamaican Creole makes it impossible to trace its history. Attempts have been made to use written records for this task, but this is at the risk of interference from Standard English, referred to in the article as the "prestige tongue". She notes that the verses of songs that are part of traditional folklore have captured a specific historical context that is particularly valuable in providing a context for Jamaican Creole. Lalla then examines five published texts, noted as A, B, C, D and E, of the old slave song "Quaco Sam" to provide background for Jamaican Creole.

3. "The Consonant System of Early Jamaican Creole". *Carib* 3 (1983): 37–51.

The article attempts to reconstruct the sound system of early Jamaican Creole by examining textual material from the eighteenth and nineteenth centuries. However, Lalla asserts that the "comparative method is unsuited to tracing patterns within the Creole because of the continued influence of the Standard English". She points to the complexity of Creole, which consists of several varieties overlapping with the basilect on one end of the continuum and Standard at the other. Early texts reveal that there was much variability even then and also show the influence of Standard English and West African languages on the Jamaican Creole phonological system. Lalla concludes that the early consonant system is far more similar to West African patterns like Twi than to English.

4. "Tracing Elusive Phonological Elements in Early Jamaican Creole". In *Focus on the Caribbean*, edited by M. Görlach and J.A. Holm, 117–32. Amsterdam: John Benjamins, 1986.

Lalla explores the phonological features associated with Jamaican Creole in its early stages with a view to arriving at a solid description of its sound system. To guide this exploration, the author relies on written documents about early phonology of Jamaican Creole along with foundation material from the comparative work of Mervyn Alleyne[1] and the lexical study of F.G. Cassidy and R.B. Le Page.[2] She admits to the difficulty in this undertaking as there are uncertainties about the particular sound features of the language and their distinctiveness. This is affected by the absence of written records for a language that is significantly oral by nature, the social variation due to inputs from other languages and the time span covered by written records.

5. "Black Laughter: Foundations of Irony in the Earliest Jamaican Literature". *Journal of Black Studies* 20, no. 4 (June 1990): 414–25.

The irony identified in Lalla's essay is that the patrimony of eighteenth- and nineteenth-century Jamaican literature survives not through local oral records but through various European literary conventions authored or documented or both by white colonials. Journals, reports, songs, tales, anecdotes and even some letters by Jamaican blacks account for the documentation of the oral tradition by white writers of the period. This documentation presents flaws and ironies in the literary representations of the black slave/white master relationship. In her discussion of the form and structure of the literary works, Lalla posits that the subterfuges of West African folk hero Anancy derive great structural integrity as they convey the bold wit and moral code of the slave community. Conversely, the commentaries in song and prose are weaker, and ironic and literary representations in satire, parodies and other works do not necessarily match the traumatic reality of and response to slavery. The blatant stereotyping of Jamaican blacks is glaring even while the white writer/documentalist records humour directed at the black self and the "massa". The black slave's spiritual world view presents social and religious conflicts reflecting disquiet with God, the universe, society and self. Lalla alludes to dichotomies within Jamaican society wrought by a value system that was unequal and fractured.

6. "Defining Functional Literacy at Tertiary Level". In *Proceedings of the Symposium*, edited by Olabisi Kuboni, 14–21. St Augustine, Trinidad and Tobago: Faculty of Education, University of the West Indies, 1992.

Lalla discusses here the need for functional literacy at the tertiary level. She expresses the need to clearly define the term given her observations of student performance and elaborating on the skills and competencies required for a

functionally literate student, which include competence in academic communication and negotiation. Additionally, the need for specific skills such as verb
control, awareness of a clear distinction between abstract and general terms
for academic communication, as well as skills in listening, objective comprehension and analysis are highlighted. Lalla argues that, where there is a lack
in functional literacy, there will be shortfalls in performing certain tasks and
suggests corrective measures and strategies.

7. *Studies in Caribbean Language 2.* With Pauline Christie, Velma Pollard and
    Lawrence Carrington. Papers from the Ninth Biennial Conference of the
    Society for Caribbean Linguistics (1992). St Augustine, Trinidad and
    Tobago: Society for Caribbean Linguistics, 1998.

Lalla is one of a quartet of editors of the publication that emerged from the
Ninth Biennial Conference of the Society for Caribbean Linguistics held in
Barbados in 1992), and focused on the theme "Caribbean Linguistics at the
Crossroads". The publication features a compendium of papers from nineteen
distinguished Caribbean linguists on issues related to variation within and
across Caribbean Creole vernaculars, the integration of standard forms into
Creole speech, aspects of Creole discourse that examine Black English vernaculars present in rap and reggae lyrics and dread talk; semantics and lexicogra-
phy. The text covers anglophone, francophone and hispanophone linguistic
issues. The editorial conclusion is that the collection of papers "reflects the
movement in Caribbean linguistics towards re-definition of the terms and concerns of the field", which serve to highlight not only the flexibility of regional
languages but also areas as yet unexplored.

8. "Word Mesh: Dimensions of Change in the Formation of a Creole Lexi-
    con". In *Old English and New: Studies in Language and Linguistics in Honor
    of F.G. Cassidy,* edited by Joan H. Hall, Nick Doane, and Dick Ringler, 127–
    42. New York: Garland, 1992.

In this article on lexical modification of Jamaican Creole, Lalla observes that
development and change in the Creole lexicon are paralleled by the same types
of changes in the Standard English dictionary. She extrapolates from examin-
ing/comparing English/Jamaican Creole synchronic and diachronic complexities, the role of syntax and various data gathered through lexicographical

fieldwork and documented evidence. Lalla notes that the Creole lexicon has inputs, multiple etymologies and reinforcements that result from other language influences, as well as flexibility because of the multi-functionality of the English language. The essay concludes in part that Creole vocabulary has developed by formative processes; it now exists "in a lexical continuum in which different speakers occupy different ranges".

9. "Discourse of Dispossession: Ex-Centric Journeys of the Un- Living in *Wide Sargasso Sea* and the Old English 'The Wife's Lament' ", *Ariel: A Review of International English Literature* 24, no. 3 (July 1993): 55–72.

Literary comparisons of the female protagonists of Jean Rhys's *Wide Sargasso Sea* and Old English "The Wife's Lament" form Lalla's preoccupation in this essay. Referencing diverse periods, cultures and landscapes, she seamlessly explores female psyches that are physically and psychologically exiled from place and self, invoking imagery of dead women walking. Although physically exiled, their anguish is played out in the confined and psychologically unstable spaces of their minds, where the foci are their multi-dimensional dreams, visions, hallucinations and memories. The action of both narratives takes place on the margins of reality where past and present overlap, creating even more dissonance. Lalla alludes to the dis-spiritedness and deep-seated alienation of the female personae as a condition of the woman in a patriarchal colonial society.

10. "Dungeons of the Soul: Frustrated Romanticism in Eighteenth and Nineteenth Century Literature of Jamaica", *Multi-Ethnic Literature of the United States* 21, no. 3 (1996): 3–23.

The literature from and about Jamaica produced by British writers before the abolition of slavery is the focus of Lalla's literary criticism. She suggests that the voice of the poor, untutored black is misrepresented and questions the representations of the Jamaican personae, values and society conveyed using the vehicle of European Romantic expression. She argues that instead of expressing resistance, rebellion, orality and freedom, Jamaican literature is riddled with romantic and exotic themes reflective of an ordered, imaginative European society. She notes that beyond the existence of actual native verse, there is otherwise an overlooking of the development of folk expression and an imposed constraint on the geographically located voice of the Jamaica of the period. There appear to be no parallels between the notions expressed in the nascent oral traditions reflective of blacks' vulnerable human condition and the romantic literature crafted by white writers in the same time period. The body of Lalla's essay is thereafter devoted to a discussion of a core set of novels set in Jamaica in the nineteenth century that support her viewpoint.

11. "Registering Woman: Senior's Zig-Zag Discourse and Code- Switching in Jamaican Narrative". *Ariel: A Review of International English Literature* 29, no.4 (October 1998): 83–98.

Olive Senior's short story "Zig-Zag" presents a literal zig-zag of themes and ideological perspectives that intersect and reflect the fragmented Caribbean psyche. Language is the literary tool and one of the "zig-zag" nuances that drives characterization in the story. The action is played out through a shifting narrative memory and changing perspectives. Lalla cites Senior's use of code-switching, orality, memory and changing perspectives as being pervasive in the development of the child protagonist Sadie, who owns the ambivalence of having to choose between language codes to conform to existing social ideals. Her code-switching is central to social expectations yet is also an important aspect of her development and reflective of a quintessential aspect of Caribbean setting and characterization. Lalla suggests that orality presents complexities and ambivalences for Sadie, as the very utterance of Jamaican Creole is perceived as backward and a hindrance to social progression.

12. "A Socio-Linguistic Approach to Critical Analysis in the Caribbean". In *Studies in Caribbean Language 2: Papers from the Ninth Biennial Conference of the Society of Caribbean Linguistics, 1992*, edited by Pauline Christie, 112–27. St. Augustine, Trinidad and Tobago: Society for Caribbean Linguistics, 1998.

In this paper Lalla focuses mainly on the sociolinguistic setting of Jean Rhys's classic *Wide Sargasso Sea*, which is linked intertextually with Charlotte Brontë's novel *Jane Eyre*. Lalla focuses on Rhys's deployment of intertextuality to shed light on the theme of displacement. The essay examines the nature and status of the mother tongue for the nineteenth century white Creole woman in the Caribbean, who is seeking to define herself within her space. Furthermore, she explores the myriad ways gender, class and ethnicity have an impact on the characters' use of language. Lalla also examines the notion of time and the overall nonlinear structure of the narrative as pivotal to Rhys's evocation of displacement.

13. "Conceptual Perspectives on Time and Timelessness in Martin Carter's 'University of Hunger' ". In *All Are Involved: The Art of Martin Carter*, edited by Stewart Brown, 106–15. Leeds, UK: Peepal Tree Press, 2000.

This paper explores the linguistic and literary style of Carter's 1954 lyrical poem. Lalla identifies "University of Hunger" as a poem of resistance on one level and on another of painful and fragmented processes of individual and collective fashioning of Caribbean people. Lalla examines how time is employed as a literacy device to convey Carter's historical vision: time shifts between past and present; time is history in action, and its passage is reflected in alternative points of view of the narrative voice depending on time. Lalla also comments on the linguistic construction of the poem – Carter's use of Standard Caribbean English and the integrity of his Creole language codes and literary representations. She suggests that Carter rewrites history through "shifting perceptual and conceptual perspectives" such that there is an alternate response to the Caribbean human condition that changes the voice of lament to one of challenge.

14. "Creole and Respec' in the Development of Jamaican Literary Discourse". *Journal of Pidgin and Creole Languages* 20, no. 1 (2005): 53–84.

This article examines the development of Creole linguistics as part of Caribbean literary discourse, with particular reference to Jamaican literature. The author identifies four phases of development of Creole representation in literature: ventriloquist, censorship, alternative and expansion. Lalla notes that up to the nineteenth century, the Creole voice was not a distinctive one, as early writers of Creole were simply documenting discourse rather than presenting a local viewpoint. Much of that early literature comprised travelogues and novels of adventure. In the censorship phase there was a fierce battle between folk and Anglo traditions, but Creole was still not a vehicle of unique expression. The alternative phase was characterized by a greater movement between Creole and Standard English, and writers used Creole for expression and social commentary so that there emerged a clear Caribbean voice and identity. In the current expansion phase, the use of the Creole voice in literature has become more assertive. Although there is still no standardized form of Creole, it has clearly become more respected as a voice of expression in Caribbean literature.

15. *Virtual Realism: Constraints on Validity in Textual Evidence of Caribbean Language History.* Society for Caribbean Linguistics Occasional Paper, no. 32. St Augustine, Trinidad and Tobago: Society for Caribbean Linguistics, 2005.

In this paper, Lalla provides a framework for reconstructing a history of the Creole language from written text. She outlines some of the challenges faced in analysing Creole language given the variation that exists across Caribbean territories. She presents a template for analysing Creole texts and explores what validity entails when evaluating written evidence of change in Creole language. She states that scribal evidence may be meta-discursive or representational. Lalla outlines the linguistic characteristics that should be sought out when examining texts and provides guidelines for identifying discursive and meta-discursive characteristics. The study also suggests parameters for using the biographical background of the author as an analytical aid.

16. "Creole Representation in Literary Discourse: Issues of Linguistic and Discourse Analysis". In *Exploring the Boundaries of Caribbean Creole Languages,* edited by Hazel Simmons-McDonald and Ian Robertson, 173–87. Kingston: University of the West Indies Press, 2006.

The objective of this essay is to define issues raised by the representation of Creole in literary works. Lalla writes of a link between language code choice, setting and identity that highlights ideological perspectives within the Caribbean setting. She postulates that the literature of the anglophone Caribbean is distinguished by use of a Creole language code albeit in varying degrees of the region's vernaculars, forms and author intent. Creole dialectic representations are analysed within a linguistic framework, and examples from the Caribbean literary canon are discussed in the context of writers' use of Standard English and Creole languages.

17. "Healing into Poetry: Metaphor as a Mechanism for Meta-Discourse in the Poetry of Lorna Goodison". In *Caribbean Literature in a Global Context*, edited by Funso Aiyejina and Paula Morgan, 317–29. Port of Spain, Trinidad and Tobago: Lexicon, 2006.

This paper identifies Goodison's narrative perspective as resonating with anguish born out the African slave heritage, yet warrior-like in the recognition of the innate capacity of the poet-healer. Lalla cites the line as the primary metaphor underscoring Goodison's meta-discourse of wounds inflicted by race, class, gender and history. The line as metaphor dominates Goodison's imageries of things linear – rivers, bloodlines, stripes, subways birth canals, tightropes to name a few. Lalla concludes that lines constrain the artist to create in a process of anguish but also mark the identity of the woman warrior/poet as a survivor and healer.

18. "Signifying Nothing: Writing about Not Writing in *The Mystic Masseur*". *Anthurium: A Caribbean Studies Journal* 5, no. 2 (Fall 2007). http://anthurium.miami.edu/volume_5/issue_2/lalla-signifying.html (accessed 13 January 2013).
   Also appeared in *Created in the West Indies: Caribbean Perspectives on V.S. Naipaul*, edited by Barbara Lalla and Jennifer Rahim, 99–110. Kingston: Ian Randle, 2011.

This essay explores concepts of "nothingness" interwoven throughout V.S. Naipaul's *The Mystic Masseur*. Lalla explains that while on one level the narrator alludes to the protagonist's notions and actions of grandeur, on the other level all things of potential significance are undermined and ultimately undefined by Ganesh's own fictive sense of importance and Naipaul's clever manipulation of the narrative perspective. Lalla indicates that concepts of "nothingness" are manifested by gaps in information, curious and meaningless speech, rituals that have no significance, fake accolades and a narrative discourse that promises potential but is unapologetically otherwise. Lalla cites Naipaul's "false-document" technique and his engagement with history, which ultimately pitch the protagonist into obscurity as commanding greater attention to a sense and spate of "nothingness" that is reflective of Naipaul's own view of the fragmented nature of pre-independence Trinidad and Tobago.

IAN ROBERTSON

BOOKS

1.   *Choices: Teachers' Guide 1–3.* With Neville Grant, Doris Mayne and Sally Siriram. Essex, UK: Longman, 1995.

This is the *Teacher's Guide* to the student textbooks 1 through 3 in the *Choices* series, which are designed for years 1 to 3 of the secondary school programme. The first chapter lays the foundation for the *Choices* programmes as it outlines the rationale for the approach taken and encourages teachers to be adventurous in their teaching methods. It also discusses the type of English to be taught (Standard English versus Creole), and it offers an overview of some language-teaching strategies and underscores the role of the teacher. The second chapter offers additional guidance on the methods and approaches to teaching reading, listening comprehension, writing and grammar. The guide also looks at the components of each unit of the student textbook, with chapters 3 through 5 providing detailed notes of *Student Workbooks* 1, 2 and 3. These chapters are capped off with two appendices. The first gives points on how to stage a play, and the second provides a clear overview of the programme by outlining the different components of the teaching units and requisite activities over the five-year period.

2.   *Choices: Teachers' Guide 4.* With Neville Grant, Doris Mayne, Sally Siriram. Essex, UK: Longman, 1995.

This book is structured similarly to the *Teacher's Guide Books* 1 through 3. It is the companion to the *Student Workbook* and builds on the knowledge acquired from *Choices* 1 through 3 but may also be used independently. This final install-ment in the English-language programme is meant to prepare students for the Caribbean Examination Council (CXC) English examinations or similar exam-inations. The first chapter introduces the teacher to the learning objectives of *Choices*, the organization and components of each unit. A section discusses Creole and Standard English. While the book offers guidelines, it encourages teachers to use their own professional skills and judgement, demonstrating that teachers have the flexibility to LARA: leave out, amend, replace or add.

The second chapter provides suggestions on how the listening-comprehension exercises should be managed given that the aim of the course is to encourage students to speak a language that is internationally intelligible. The book comes with a glossary of literary terms, and an overview of the *Choices* programme from year 1 to 5.

33. *Communication Studies for Self-Study and Distance Learning.* With Veronica Simon. Bridgetown, Barbados: Caribbean Examination Council, 2004.

This is a textbook designed for students preparing for the Caribbean Advanced Proficiency Examination (CAPE) communication studies syllabus. The guide is designed for persons pursuing the subject part-time as well as those enrolled full-time in an educational institution. The introduction outlines the purpose of the course, its aim, structure and the resources needed. The book is arranged in thirteen modules that address the skills and content of a specific module of the communication studies syllabus. The guide includes such topics as language in society, writing, study skills, elements of research and the process of communication and summary skills. Each study guide is arranged in eight sections: introduction, content, objectives, activities, feedback, examples, end test and key points. Course assignments are included so that persons using the book can check their progress during the course.

4. *Exploring the Boundaries of Caribbean Creole Languages.* With H. Simmons-McDonald. Kingston: University of the West Indies Press, 2006.

Robertson and Simmons-McDonald are editors of this volume of essays written in honour of linguist Pauline Christie, and the book is structured to promote the exploration of specific themes in Caribbean language. The essays are divided into three main themes: definition and description, language and education and language in the Caribbean society. The first section features contributions by Robertson, who writes about Berbice Dutch; this is followed by two chapters written by Donald Winford, which discuss the tense aspect of Belize Creole and the phonological patterns in Tobagonian speech, respectively; the final chapter in this section is by Hubert Devonish, who discusses phonological variations present in Jamaican Creole. The second section looks at various aspects of language in the context of West Indian education; it includes contributions by Dennis Craig, Valerie Youssef and Hazel Simmons-McDonald.

The final section examines the use of Creoles in various settings: Kathryn Shields-Brodber discusses code-switching by callers of a radio programme in Jamaica; Martha Isaac focuses on language attitudes in St Lucia and Velma Pollard writes about the linguistic code Jamaican Rastafarianism.

ARTICLES

1.   "Dutch Creole in Guyana: Some Missing Links". *Society for Caribbean Linguistics Occasional Paper*, no. 2. Kingston: Society for Caribbean Linguistics, 1974.

The author suggests that accounts written by linguists working in Guyana understate the Dutch influence on Guyana's linguistic legacy and by extension the vibrancy and widespread use of Creole Dutch in Guyana. He counters this by providing proof of the usage of Creole Dutch among the inhabitants during the late eighteenth and early nineteenth centuries. Robertson further acknowledges the demise of Creole Dutch among the descendants of African slaves in modern Guyana, especially those living along the coastal areas. He attributes this to a process of secondary relexification to English, occurring in the early nineteenth century through the development of the Guyanese education system, coupled with the imposition of that new target language.

2.   "Dutch Creole Speakers and their Locations in Guyana in the Nineteenth and Early Twentieth Centuries". *Society for Caribbean Linguistics Occasional Paper*, no. 4. Kingston: Society for Caribbean Linguistics, 1976.

The author highlights Creole Dutch as the dominant form of communication in Guyanese territories during the eighteenth and nineteenth centuries continuing to the early twentieth century and evolving from interactions between Dutch settlers and native Indian tribes. Robertson regrets the sparse reference to Dutch and Amerindian influence on Guyana's linguistic history and attributes this to historical accounts focusing only on coastlands while Dutch and Amerindian settlements were concentrated in the lower middle reaches of rivers. He also notes African influence on the language due to the presence of slaves working on sugar plantations owned by Dutch planters. Robertson includes quotations from reports that indicate the widespread use and vibrancy of Creole Dutch as a lingua franca and notes that interactions between runaway slaves and the Amerindian population also supported this development.

3.   "A Preliminary Word List of Berbice Dutch". *Society for Caribbean Linguistics Occasional Paper*, no. 5. Kingston: Society for Caribbean Linguistics, 1976.

The author provides a preliminary list of 416 words in English along with corresponding words in Berbice, Essequibo and Standard Dutch. The list is primarily based on Berbice Dutch; however, the author has also included the Essequibo (Skepi) Dutch dialect. The list is presented with an indication of several limitations, such as the presentation of words taken only from dialects in the twentieth century while excluding possible sources from the seventeenth and eighteenth centuries, the unavailability of relevant Africanisim source documents, uncertainty in presenting non-Dutch sources, as well as concerns with adequacy and relevance in Dutch source materials used.

4.   "Dutch Creole Languages in Guyana", *Boletin de Estudios Latinoamericanos y del Caribe* 23 (1977): 61–68.

The author identifies areas of Dutch settlements in Guyana with the intent of establishing regions in which Creole Dutch languages emerge. He provides a historical context for the origin and development of Creole Dutch and supplies information about its speakers, who were primarily African slaves on sugar plantations and the Amerindian population. The article offers an argument for the spread of Creole Dutch to the Amerindians as being the result of three main factors: contact with runaway slaves, maroon settlements and trade.

5.   "Redefining the Post-Creole Continuum: Evidence from Berbice Dutch". *Society for Caribbean Linguistics Occasional Paper*, no. 14. St Augustine, Trinidad and Tobago: Society for Caribbean Linguistics, 1982.

Robertson examines the thoughts and arguments of linguistic scholars on the course of development of a post-Creole continuum in the Caribbean. He highlights Berbice Dutch as providing strong evidence for the capacity of the decreolization process to continue apace even when the Creole and the Standard in contact do not continue to share the same lexical base, an original requisite feature cited by De Camp. Robertson supports his argument by citing specific features in Berbice Dutch in which the lexical base of the Standard changed from Dutch to English but where a smooth transition to a new target was accomplished and the decreolization process proceeded apace.

6.   "The Dutch Linguistic Legacy and the Guyana/Venezuela Border Question". *Boletin de Estudios Latinoamericanos y del Caribe* 34 (1983): 75–97.

Robertson describes the Guyana-Venezuela border conflict that originated between Dutch and Spanish colonizers who occupied territory in Guyana and Venezuela, respectively. He presents the conflict as continuing after Britain gained Dutch territory in Guyana and even after Venezuela gained independence from Spain. In 1895, Britain was forced by the United States to agree to an arbitration to settle this conflict under the principles of the Monroe doctrine. In 1899 linguistic arguments were presented in the arbitration agreement that allowed Britain to validate its claim to the lands involved in the conflict. The author presents the range of linguistic arguments that emanated from the arbitration proceedings.

7.   "The Dutch Linguistic Legacy in Guyana: Berbice and Skepi Dutch". *Carib* 3 (1983): 11–23.

This paper briefly reviews the history of the Dutch presence in Guyana, which dates back to at least the early seventeenth century. Robertson argues that previous studies on the linguistic legacy of the Dutch in Guyana tended to examine it superficially, overlooking perhaps the significance of the Dutch lexical items, the place names and phonetic details. These studies have also ignored the lexical items that were part of the Amerindian languages: Carib and Arawak, in particular. Moreover, they have also missed the most significant Dutch linguistic legacy, the existence of two mutually non-intelligible Creoles, Berbice Dutch and Essequibo Dutch (Skepi), the latter bearing some similarity to Negerhollands of the Danish West Indian islands. He accounts for these Dutch-based Creoles, which have their roots in African-Dutch contact, having been retained by people of Amerindian or mixed African and Amerindian stock and concludes by stating that Guyana is unique in the Caribbean because its Creoles are the only ones developed in a Dutch colony. He cites the shift in the location of Dutch settlements to up-river locations on the arrival of the British around the late eighteenth century, which minimized the competition between English and Dutch as allowing the Dutch-based Creoles to flourish. Included at the end of the article are some Dutch lexical items in use, place names, Dutch lexical items found in Arawak and examples of Skepi and Berbice Dutch.

8. "The Significance of Berbice Dutch Suffixes". In *Studies in Caribbean Language*, edited by Lawrence Carrington, Dennis Craig and Ramon Todd Dandare, 211–16. St. Augustine, Trinidad and Tobago: Society for Caribbean Linguistics, 1983.

Robertson first provides a context for the significance of Berbice Dutch suffixes by presenting and discussing views of the characteristics of pidgin and Creole languages. He quotes from linguistic scholars such as Hymes, Hall, Le Page, Samarin, De Camp and Sankoff. While some scholars identify pidgins as static and lacking in development in lexicon and grammar, others oppose this view and find similarity in dynamism with Creoles. Robertson seeks to highlight Berbice Dutch as providing evidence for this dynamism through identifying various suffixes within it. The form and source of some of these suffixes are presented in the article.

9. "The Marking of Tense, Mood and Aspect in the Berbice Dutch Creole Language". With Silvia Kouwenberg. In *Beiträge zum 4. Essener Kolloquium über Sprachkontakt, Sprachwandel, Sprachwechsel, Sprachtod*, edited by Norbert Boretzky, Werner Enninger and Thomas Stolz, 49–87. Essen, Germany: University of Essen, 1987.

This paper discusses the tense/mood/aspect (TMA) system of contemporary Berbice Dutch. Robertson and Kouwenberg examine the features that characterize TMA, such as the use of temporal particles; modal auxiliary verbs; general verbs that carry aspectual, modal or time-related meaning and the context of the discourse, which may also indicate modal or aspectual features or location in time. The chapter also looks at the use of stative and nonstative verbs in Berbice Dutch. The authors highlight instances in which Eastern Ijo, specifically the Kalabari dialect, has influenced TMA, as well as the instances in which Guyanese English has had an impact on the language. They also explore whether the Berbice Dutch TMA bears similarity to all other Creoles, concluding that Muysken's (1981) universalist model accounts for the tense and modal-ity markers and some of the features that distinguish this variety from other Creoles as both universal and substrate influence are said to shape it.

10. "The Ijo Element in Berbice Dutch". With S.H Norval Smith and Kay Williamson. *Language in Society* 16, no. 1 (1987): 49–89.

This discussion attempts to account for the origin of Berbice Dutch. Robertson presents four hypotheses in an attempt to explore the origin of this Creole. The first hypothesis speculates that Berbice Dutch may have arisen out of slave traders' contact with the Kalabari dialect of Africa. The second hypothesis suggests that it may have arisen from overseers'/planters' attempts to impose lexicon on Eastern Ijo. The third speculates that it originated from Eastern Ijo and the final hypothesis claims that it replaced Eastern Ijo, precipitated by the influence of Dutch Creole. Robertson is of the view that the fourth hypothesis is the most plausible. The author analyses the phonology, morphology and lexical system of the language, and, by a process of deduction, concludes that Eastern Ijo had extensive influence on it.

11. "Berbice and Skepi Dutch: a Lexical Comparison". *Tijdschrift voor Nederlandse Taal en Letterkunde* 105, no. 1 (1989): 3–21.

Robertson identifies Berbice Dutch, Skepi Dutch and Negerhollands as cases of Creoles with a Dutch-based lexicon. Berbice Dutch and Skepi Dutch are noted as not mutually intelligible, and he presents an analysis of two hundred lexical items based on Swadesh's word list to corroborate this. Robertson further notes that Skepi Dutch is more related to Negerhollands, while Berbice Dutch consists of Eastern Ijo lexical items, thus making it the oldest of the three Dutch-based Creoles.

12. "Some Patterns of Language Use in the Period of Transition from Dutch to British Rule in the Guiana Colonies". *International Journal of the Sociology of Language* 85, nos. 1–2 (1990): 51–60.

The paper argues that the transition from Dutch to British colonialism in nineteenth-century Guyana was a protracted one, so much so that it complicated the linguistic situation in Guyana. In 1814, the Dutch ceded the Guyana colonies of Essequibo, Demerara and Berbice to the British. Up to that period

Dutch control of the territories, which dated back to the early seventeenth century, was literally unbroken. Robertson examines the social interaction and the
linguistic competencies of the various ethnic groups. During the period of
Dutch rule, there were interactions between the Europeans and Amerindians,
Europeans and slaves, and the Amerindian and Africans. The Europeans, however, were not a homogeneous group, as they included French as well. During
the period of transition from Dutch to British rule, both the Dutch and English
languages existed side by side, such that official proclamations of the government were issued in both languages, and the courts, religious ceremonies and
the newspapers of the day adopted a bilingual approach. Europeans were forced
to become bilingual as well. The Amerindians were least affected by the bilingual situation, since they only used the Dutch-lexicon Creole to communicate
outside their group. Robertson concludes that the language policy during transition from Dutch to British rule led to a state of national bilingualism, in
which slaves used both English and Dutch-lexicon Creole. Some persons were
genuinely bilingual, and there is evidence of this in Berbice-Dutch lexical items
left over from the English-Dutch interlingual Creole used by the slaves.

13. "The Tense-Mood-Aspect System of Berbice Dutch". In *Pidgin and Creoles
     Tense/Mood/Aspect Systems*, edited by John Singler, 169–84. Amsterdam:
     John Benjamins, 1990.

Based on fieldwork conducted by Robertson between 1975 and 1980, this paper
examines the features of the tense/mood/aspect (TMA) system of Berbice
Dutch. It illustrates the use of preverbal particles and suffixes, which help to
differentiate Berbice Dutch from other basilectal Creoles in the Caribbean.
Robertson asserts that there are two characteristics of Creole in the Caribbean
that ought to be considered when describing a TMA system: First is the temporal zero point, which is determined by the speakers and may have little to
do with time. Second is that time is determined by the context of the discourse.
To conduct a proper analysis the author argues that an entire examination of
the predicate system is needed. Robertson describes the TMA of Berbice Dutch,
the predicators and the markers with which they occur, the suffixes added to
the base to indicate durative and iterative aspects, suffixes used to indicate past
tense, and verbs formations for past and future tense. He also discusses the
combination of markers available in Berbice Dutch to indicate irrealis. He
notes that the modal auxiliary present in the TMA system and the mixing of

preverbal particles with suffixes illustrate the growing inroads Guyanese Creole has made into the system.

14. "A Realistic Appraisal of Literacy in an Oral Culture". In *Literacy in the Modern World: Proceedings from the Symposium*, edited by Olabisi Kuboni, 45–49. St Augustine, Trinidad and Tobago: Faculty of Education, University of the West Indies, 1992.

This is an exploratory essay that looks at the high value placed on writing over speech and oracy. Robertson asserts that literacy has become vital to development in modern society. He notes that illiteracy global statistics indicate that the rate is highest in developing countries, among the world's female population and on the Asian continent and argues that there seems to be a close link between literacy levels and economic development. However, he emphasizes that the relationship between literacy and development is not a simple one, since there are countries that are achieving significant levels of development despite low levels of literacy. Literacy is an important aspect of education but oracy plays a much greater role. Highlighting the differences between speech and writing, he asserts that any society that is steeped in oral tradition places great value on human relationships. Oral societies are those that possess different ways of preserving aspects of their culture and history, have no long tradition of writing and have developed a range of oral practices for dealing with different types of materials and levels of complexity. Robertson notes it would be unacceptable if such societies were to lose the wealth of information that is handed down in that mode.

15. "The Ijo Element in Berbice Dutch and the Pidginization/Creolization Process". In *Africanisms in Afro-American Language Varieties*, edited by Salikoko Mufwene, 296–316. Athens: University of Georgia Press, 1993.

According to Robertson, Berbice Dutch is the only Caribbean Creole for which an African source language has been identified. There is sociohistorical evidence to account for Eastern Ijo's influence on Berbice Dutch. Both univeralist and substratist theories regarding Creole genesis are used as platforms to identify and discuss the substratum influence on Berbice Dutch, a Creole spoken by fewer than one hundred speakers on the Berbice River in Guyana. Robertson undertakes to examine specific features that may indicate the Eastern Ijo influence on the grammar of Berbice Dutch in order to gain greater insight into the pidginization and creolization process. To this end suffixes, negation, and third-person pronouns and demonstratives are examined. Robertson discovers significant retentions, transfers, reductions and expansion in the grammar. He concludes by saying that his findings do not make a satisfactory case for substratum theory as fully explanatory of the process of creolization and pidginization and offer the opportunity to do further investigation into the roles of universal and substrate influences in the creolization process.

16. "Berbicaanse Woorden [Berbice Dutch Words]". *Amsterdam Creole Studies* II (1994): 67–74.

Robertson asserts that the primary goal of his paper is to analyse and establish the significance of a list of forty-four items collected by Pieter Constantijn Groen on Berbice Dutch. Robertson suggests that the list is potentially helpful in determining demographic patterns at a critical period in the colony's history. Additionally, the list acts as a guide to the processes used by Creole languages to expand their lexicon.

17. "Language Education Policy: Towards a Rational Approach". In *Caribbean Language Issues: Old and New*, edited by Pauline Christie, 112–19. Kingston: University of the West Indies Press, 1995.

In this article, Robertson starts a discussion that will help to reshape attitudes towards Caribbean Creole language and subsequently effect the development of a sound Caribbean language-education policy. He presents the fundamental position that any language-education policy must be premised on its potential to contribute to the wider goals of education and functioning in society. Robertson proposes that in order for one to determine how language education can do this it is important to understand the nature of language and its social impact within the Caribbean context.

18. "Language, Calypso and the Classroom". In *Music in the Caribbean*, edited by Beverly J. Anderson, 133–56. New York: McGraw Hill, 1996.

The author argues that, given the challenges faced by teachers of Standard English in anglophone Caribbean contexts, every effort should be made to use indigenous resources in English-language teaching. One such resource is calypso, which has its strongest presence in Trinidad and Tobago. Robertson maintains that the calypsonian has always been concerned with education and proficiency of language use and that some of the better calypsonians had considerable education and commanded that language. To illustrate calypsonian commentary on the sociolinguistic and psycholinguistic traditions of Trinidadian society, he refers to the Mighty Cypher's humorous "Fresh Water Yankee", which focuses on Trinidadian con man Joe who pretends to be a Yankee to outsmart another man. He also notes that there are many calypsos that are composed in Standard English, such as "Black or White", written in the 1940s by Lord Kitchener. The author laments that the educational policy geared towards the use of calypso in the classroom has not been more widely focused, since attempts to use it have been restricted to the teaching of social studies and history but not English. Robertson asserts that calypsos provide a good opportunity to develop students' awareness of the need for appropriateness of language use and creative writing skills; however, like any teaching tool, they should be carefully considered, monitored and evaluated by educators.

19. "The Nineteenth Century in Berbice, Essequibo and Demerara: A Rich Linguistic Legacy". *Kyk-over-al*, no. 48 (1998): 85–96.

Using evidence from historical sources, Robertson discusses the ethnic groups that influenced the linguistic complexity of nineteenth-century Berbice, Essequibo and Demerara, the territories that make up modern-day Guyana. He attempts to correct the impression that the society was linguistically homogeneous. The discussion begins with a look at the Amerindian languages but due to the absence of concrete historical evidence, the author concludes that it is difficult to determine if these languages are the same as those existing in contemporary Guyana. The European colonizers, particularly the Dutch and English, left an indelible mark on the spoken language, as by 1803, the territories were under British control. However evidence suggests that during the period of transition from Dutch to British rule, a bilingual policy was adopted with respect to the Dutch and English languages, until eventually the latter dominated. On the other hand, the French controlled the territories for less than two years, yet their influence is seen in the names of places, particularly in Demerara. The African slaves arrived in two waves, and according to Robertson the Eastern Ijo were particularly dominant in the first wave, as at least 40 per cent of the Creole spoken as late as 1992 derived from this language group. Within the indentureship period, Robertson notes that the Chinese and Portuguese immigrants remained linguistically isolated but that nonetheless Portuguese words did influence the word stock of the Creoles. The Indic languages also had a considerable influence on the Creole English spoken, especially in the areas of phonology and lexicon.

20. "Educational Linguistics for the Caribbean: Some Considerations". *Caribbean Journal of Education* 21, nos. 1–2 (April–September 1999): 75–85.

Although education and linguistics share a strong link, they are not afforded the respect they both deserve. The merger of these two disciplines is referred to as educational linguistics and is meant to identify the linguistics skills needed by society, the linguistics awareness needed for functioning effectively at all levels of society and the nature and roles of the specific linguistic knowledge that are relevant to the decision-making processes in the education system. A macro approach to education that involves an understanding of the nature and processes critical to the function of educational linguistics is needed. The Van Lier model illustrates the context of educational language use and outlines the interplay between classroom, community and society, as well as the various stakeholders involved. In Robertson's view, there is a greater need to focus on the goals of education, especially in the Caribbean. However this cannot be accomplished without a strong cadre of professionals acquainted with the discipline, political will and abandonment of the notion that language education is just about developing skills in the manipulation of language. Coupled with this, there should be increased public awareness about the principles of educational linguistics through public education programmes.

21. "Challenging the Definition of Creole". In *Exploring the Boundaries of Caribbean Creoles*, edited by H. Simmons-McDonald and Ian Robertson, 3–20. Kingston: University of the West Indies Press, 2006.

The author is concerned with the lingering controversy in clearly characterizing and defining languages labelled as "Creole" and distinguishing them from other languages such as pidgins. He suggests that prior characterization and definitions of Creole need to be examined as currently inadequacies exist. He offers the Berbice Dutch language as providing evidence for these inadequacies given its features and historical development within Dutch colonies in Guyana.

22. "Guyana's Dutch-Lexicon Creoles: The Demerara (Disconnection)". *Arts Journal* 5, nos. 1–2 (March 2009): 81–91.

This paper explores the possible existence of a Dutch-lexicon Creole in Demerara, one of the former British Guiana colonies. According to Robertson there is historical data to support the use of a Dutch-lexicon Creole in the colony but no actual sample of this language that has been found. This research represents a continuation of the work carried out on Berbice Dutch and Essequibo Dutch (Skepi), which survived well into the twentieth century, more than seventy years after the Dutch withdrew from the Guiana colonies.

The paper seeks to determine whether a Dutch Creole existed in Demerara, whether it was linguistically similar to Berbice Dutch and Skepi and questions what became of the language if it actually existed. Robertson provides a plausible explanation for the absence of a sample of this Creole. He uses historical data to argue for the possible existence of a Demerara Creole. He determines that there is political evidence to suggest that Skepi may have been the Creole spoken in Demerara but argues also that there is geographical evidence to suggest that Berbice Dutch could have been the Creole spoken. He also claims that there is a possibility there was a mixed Creole spoken in these territories. Robertson concludes that a Dutch Creole did exist in Demerara but that it may not have survived with the influx of English-speaking planters because of the insecurity of the Dutch speakers in Demerara.

NOTES

1. Mervyn Alleyne, *Comparative Afro-American: An Historical-Comparative Study of English-based Afro-American Dialects of the New World* (Ann Arbor, MI: Karoma, 1980)
2. Frederic G. Cassidy and Robert B. Le Page, *Dictionary of Jamaican English*, 2nd ed. (Cambridge: Cambridge University Press, 1980).

CONTRIBUTORS

PAULA MORGAN is Senior Lecturer, Department of Literary, Cultural and Communications Studies, University of the West Indies, St Augustine, Trinidad and Tobago. Her publications include *Language Proficiency for Tertiary Level: Writing about Literature* (co-authored with Barbara Lalla); *Writing Rage: Unmasking Violence in Caribbean Discourse* (co-authored with Valerie Youssef); and *The Culture of Violence: A Trinidad and Tobago Case Study* (co-edited with Valerie Youssef).

VALERIE YOUSSEF is Professor of Linguistics, Department of Modern Languages and Linguistics, University of the West Indies, St Augustine, Trinidad and Tobago. Her publications include *The Languages of Tobago: Genesis and Perspectives* (co-authored with Winford James); *Writing Rage: Unmasking Violence in Caribbean Discourse* (co-authored with Paula Morgan); and *The Culture of Violence: A Trinidad and Tobago Case Study* (co-edited with Paula Morgan).

MARÍA LANDA BUIL is Lecturer, Centre for Language Learning, University of the West Indies, St Augustine, Trinidad and Tobago, and coordinator of the Spanish programme.

NIALA DWARIKA-BHAGAT is a reference librarian, Medical Sciences Library, University of the West Indies, St Augustine, Trinidad and Tobago.

KAREN ECCLES is a librarian, West Indiana and Special Collections, Alma Jordan Library, University of the West Indies, St Augustine, Trinidad and Tobago.

MICHELLE GILL is a librarian, Multimedia and Information Technology Unit, University of the West Indies, St Augustine, Trinidad and Tobago.

BARBARA LALLA is Professor Emerita, Language and Literature, University of the West Indies, St Augustine, Trinidad and Tobago. Her publications include *Postcolonialisms: Caribbean Re-reading of Medieval English Discourse*; *Defining Jamaican Fiction: Marronage and the Discourse of Survival*; and, with Jean D'Costa, *Language in Exile: Three Hundred Years of Jamaican Creole* and *Voices in Exile*. She is also author of the novels *Cascade* and *Arch of Fire*.

NIVEDITA MISRA is a doctoral candidate in Literatures in English, Department of Literary, Cultural and Communication Studies, University of the West Indies, St Augustine, Trinidad and Tobago. She was formerly Assistant Professor, Satyawati College (E), University of Delhi, India.

VELMA POLLARD is retired Senior Lecturer in Language Education, University of the West Indies, Mona, Jamaica. She is the author of *Dread Talk: The Language of Rastafari* and *From Jamaican Creole to Standard English*. Her poetry and fiction publications include *Leaving Traces, The Best Philosophers I Know Can't Read or Write, Homestretch* and *Karl.*

JENNIFER RAHIM is Senior Lecturer in Literatures in English, University of the West Indies, St Augustine, Trinidad and Tobago. Her publications include *Beyond Borders: Cross-culturalism and the Caribbean Canon* and *Created in the West Indies: Caribbean Perspectives on V.S. Naipaul* (both co-edited with Barbara Lalla). Her poetry and fiction publications include *Between the Fence and the Forest, Approaching Sabbaths* and *Songster and Other Stories.*

IAN ROBERTSON is Academic Director, Evening University, University of the West Indies, St Augustine, Trinidad and Tobago. His publications include the Longman Caribbean English series *Choices* (books 1–5 and the teachers' guides; co-authored with Neville Grant, Doris Mayne and Sally Siriramand) and *Exploring the Boundaries of Caribbean Creole Languages* (co-authored with Hazel Simmons-McDonald).

LISE WINER is Professor in the Second Language Education Program, Department of Integrated Studies in Education, McGill University, Montreal, Canada. Her publications include the *Dictionary of the English/Creole of Trinidad and Tobago*, and, as editor, the annotated editions the Trinidadian historical novels *Adolphus, a Tale, & The Slave Son; Warner Arundell*; and *Rupert Gray: A Tale in Black and White.*

DONALD WINFORD is Professor of Linguistics, Ohio State University. His publications include *Predication in Caribbean English Creoles* and *An Introduction to Contact Linguistics*, and he is editor of the *Journal of Pidgin and Creole Languages.*

MARSHA WINTER is a librarian with the Digital Library Services Centre, Alma Jordan Library, University of the West Indies, St Augustine, Trinidad and Tobago. She is co-author (with Portia Bowen-Chang) of *Samuel Selvon under Scrutiny: An Annotated Bibliography of Selected Criticism of Selvon's Novels.*

CPSIA information can be obtained at www.ICGtesting.com
Printed in the USA
BVOW04s1904230813

329287BV00004B/25/P

9 789766 404109